SISTER MARY

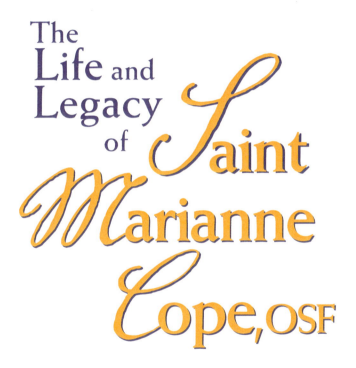

The Life and Legacy of Saint Marianne Cope, OSF

The Life and Legacy of Saint Marianne Cope, OSF
Sister Mary Francis Gangloff, OSF

with:
Sister Alicia Damien Lau, OSF
Sister Anne Marie Saphara, OSF
Sister Barbara Jean Wajda, OSF

Copyright ©2012, Sister Mary Francis Gangloff, OSF All rights reserved

Cover images: Provided by Sr. Fran Gangloff, used with permission
Cover and book design: Tau Publishing Design Department

No part of this book may be reproduced, stored in a retrieval system or transmitted in any form or by any means - electronic, mechanical, photocopying, recording, or otherwise - without written permission of the publisher.

For information regarding permission, write to:
Tau Publishing, LLC
Attention: Permissions Dept.
4727 North 12th Street
Phoenix, AZ 85014

ISBN 978-1-61956-082-6

First Edition November 2012
10 9 8 7 6 5 4 3 2 1

Published and printed in the United States of America by Tau Publishing, LLC
For additional inspirational books visit us at TauPublishing.com

TauPublishing.com

Words of Inspiration

Dedication

This book is dedicated
To all those who read it –
With wishes for –
God's Blessings of States of Grace
In all the Places they find themselves

"Hawai'i is not a state of mind, but a state of grace."

- Paul Theroux

"... From a State of Grace"
... in reference to St. Marianne Cope as one of two new saints from New York State ... headline in *The New York Times*, October 14, 2012, Sunday Observer column

Table of Contents

Introduction   11

Part One
We have a Saint
For New York, for Hawai'i, for the World

Chapter 1
Canonization, Beatification, Exhumation   17
Sisters Blanche Marie, Barbara Jean, Alicia Damien   22

Chapter 2
21st Century - The Old and the New   33
Sisters Cheryl, Anne Marie, Mary Laurence, Wilma   33

Chapter 3
A Sense of History and Geography   59
History - of New York State, of Hawai'i   59

Chapter 4
History of Hansen's Disease   71
The L-word and also early treatments   71

Part Two
Life of Mother Marianne

Chapter 5
Barbara Koop – The Child, The Teen, The Adult   **83**
Heppenheim, Germany and Utica, New York   84

Chapter 6
Sister Mary Anna / Mother Marianne   **91**
Sisters of St. Francis   92
St. Anthony Convent, Syracuse   94
Schools and Hospitals   95

Chapter 7
Missionary to Honolulu, Hawai'i   **101**
The Letter, the Trip   102
A Moment in Buffalo, N.Y.   106
Kaka'ako, Kapi'olani, Kalihi, Maui   108

Chapter 8
Kalaupapa, Hawai'i   **125**
Kalawao and Kalaupapa   126
Edward Clifford Visits   128
Marianne at Age 50   129
Death of Father Damien   132
Robert Louis Stevenson Visits   134
Baldwin Home   135
Convivencia   138
Interfaith Sharing   143
Father Pamphile, Father Juliotte   146
Visitors – Jack London and Katherine Gerould   149
Death of Mother Marianne   156

Part Three
In the Footsteps of Mother Marianne
The Sisters who followed her at Kalaupapa

Chapter 9
Deceased Sisters and Graves — 161
A Mid-20th Century Visitor – Ernie Pyle — 179

Chapter 10
Na Kokua - The Helpers — 183
Living Sisters - Interviews and Stories — 184

Chapter 11
Music and Musical Instruments — 229
Hymns honoring St. Marianne — 232

Chapter 12
Voices of the Patients of Kalaupapa — 241
Henry, Margaret, Olivia — 245

Part Four
The St. Marianne Photo Album

Mother Marianne - 1887 - elected Mother Superior   255

Birthplace and Childhood Home
Heppenheim, Germany - 1838   256
Utica, NY - Hometown   257

A Sister of St. Francis
Sisters of St. Francis and St. John Neumann -1855   258
St. Elizabeth Hospital, Utica;
St. Joseph Hospital, Syracuse   259
Oswego - Convent of 1870s   260

A Moment in Buffalo, NY - Train Station - 1883   261

Missionary to Hawaiʻi
Chapels at Kakaʻako, Kapiʻolani   262
Maui, Hawaiʻi - Malulani Hospital   263
Mother Marianne in blue gingham work apron - 1899   263
Our Lady of Peace Cathedral, Honolulu - 1843   264
Land Map of Molokaʻi - 1897   264

Kalaupapa on Molokaʻi, Hawaii
Mary and Rose   265
St. Francis Wooden Church - early 1900s   266
Women and Girls 1   267
Women and Girls 2   268
Women and Girls 3   269
Girls and Women with Sisters   270
Gravesite of Mother Marianne
and Death of Father Damien -1889   271

Legacy of Mother Marianne - those who followed
Sisters' graves and cemeteries   272
St. Francis of Assisi Church, St Elizabeth Chapel
Kalaupapa 21st Century   273

Rome, Italy - The Canonization - 2012
Scarves worn by pilgrims   274
Sisters at Special Services   275

States of Grace - New York and Hawaii
Paintings of St. Marianne   276
Stained glass windows honoring St. Marianne   277
Kalaupapa today   278
St. Marianne Garden and Sunset in Kalaupapa   279

Afterword
Franciscans and Lepers   281

Acknowledgements
Thank You to…   285

Appendix
Permissions   289
Sources and Resources   291
About the Collaborators   299

Index   **301**

At Bishop Home, Kalaupapa, Sister Elizabeth Gomes stands on the porch with a group of young girls in pretty blue dresses (c. 1901 – 1907)

Photo: Courtesy of the Congregation of the Sacred Hearts of Jesus and Mary

Introduction

As the time approached for the canonization of St. Marianne Cope, the Sisters of St. Francis, especially those who have special connections to Mother Marianne, wanted to share their memories of assignments and volunteer times and visits to Hawai'i and Kalaupapa as well as to the key places of her life in central New York.

Thus the title –
The Life and Legacy of Saint Marianne Cope
with an underlying theme of States of Grace in New York and Hawai'i

Hawai'i was not one of the United States in the 1880s when Mother Marianne led a group of sisters to Honolulu and then to Maui and to Kalaupapa on Moloka'i. She and her companions and later missionaries lived through the changing times - of annexation as a territory - and even later missionaries through the time of statehood.

Those of us working on this book have tried to share both text and photos that illustrate aspects of Mother Marianne's life not already shown in previous works. While we have included the basic stories of her life and missionary labors, we have also included some stories of the more than 60 sisters, who down through the years have filled assignments in Kalaupapa as well as many na kokua (helpers) who have volunteered there.

We have provided stories of visitors to the Hawaiian Islands over the years as well as the voices of the patients and residents.

Also, we have linked aspects of Mother Marianne's life to the history of New York State, the history of Hawai'i, and the history of Hansen's disease (leprosy) and its treatments to gain insights into the lives of the missionary sisters and those people they cared for and lived among from the 1880s onwards to the present day. We have taken special note of the changes that resulted from the 1969 lifting of the isolation of persons with Hansen's disease and the continuation of some patients and residents who made Kalaupapa their home place.

Some photos taken at Kalaupapa in the first decade of the 20t^h century have come to light. Father Paul Juliotte, assigned there from 1901 to 1907 took portraits for the patients to send home to their families. Other priests and brothers of the Congregation of the Sacred Hearts (SSCC) also took photos at that time. The photography of those days used glass plates and just recently the Congregation of the Sacred Hearts, the community of Father Damien de Veuster, has transferred these images to digital formats. Thus, we have passed by some of the photos more often used in favor of these glass slide / lantern photos of more than 100 years ago. We also tried to locate some interesting photos of Mother Marianne's presence in central New York State.

We have collaborated with each other and with many other sisters to develop 12 chapters that offer our slant on Mother Marianne's life and legacy. Two of us live in New York State and two of us in the State of Hawai'i. We hope that this mosaic of memories about Mother Marianne, this quilt of questions with some answers, this tapestry of truths from many perspectives offers our readers a window into the life of St. Marianne that inspires – States of Grace – all the spiritual places they find themselves.

Introduction

Sister Alicia Damien Lau
Sister Barbara Jean Wajda
Sister Anne Marie Saphara
Sister Fran Gangloff

August 9, 2012

Part One

We Have a Saint
for New York, for Hawai'i, for the World

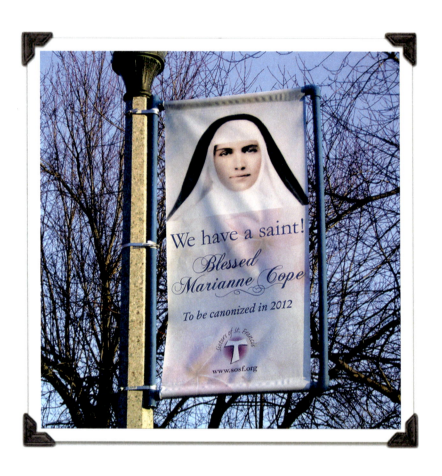

Photo: Sister Fran Gangloff

Chapter 1

Canonization, Beatification, Exhumation

"How many graces did He not shower down upon me," she assured Paul Cope, *"from my birth till now—Should I live a thousand years I could not in ever so small a degree thank Him for His gifts and blessings.—I do not expect a high place in heaven—I shall be thankful for a little corner where I may love God for all eternity."*
-*MM – P&E*

In this chapter

People of the State of Hawai'i and of New York State rejoiced and celebrated as Pope Benedict XVI canonized St. Marianne Cope on World Mission Sunday October 21, 2012. People around the world felt deep joy for this new saint of the Catholic Church.

The Sisters of St. Francis of the Neumann Communities, a union of several groups of Franciscan Sisters, honored one of their own early members.

Patients of Hansen's disease, some still in residence at Kalaupapa, Moloka'i, wept with emotion as the second saint from their tiny settlement received the highest honor of the Catholic Church.

The Cause for the Canonization of Mother Marianne Cope, with its steps of venerable and blessed as well as the required miracles and exhumation of remains, came to its fulfillment in the October 2012 ceremony.

We have a Saint!

"And in Mother Marianne she met the only other woman in all Hawai'i who possessed so fully the powers of the spirit. The queen felt, without need for words, how in this holy woman from America she, too, could find strength and comfort in her times of need."
-Hanley, O.S.F. Sister Mary Laurence; O. A. Bushnell (2009-11-01). *Pilgrimage and Exile*: Mother Marianne of Moloka'i (Kindle Locations 2363-2365). Mutual Publishing, LLC. Kindle Edition.

Prelude to the Canonization / and Postlude

Always in My Heart

In New York State – in Buffalo, to be exact – the world premiere of the play – *Always in My Heart*, authored by Joan Albarella and performed by Jackie Albarella, took place on September 18, 2012, at SS. Peter and Paul Church in Williamsville, N.Y. an early mission of St. John Neumann. This presentation offered those in attendance a dramatized view of the life and legacy of St. Marianne Cope in preparation for the canonization of this saint of New York State.

The Albarella sisters also provided a repeat performance on Sunday, October 21, the day of the canonization, at St. Mary of the Angels in Williamsville for the stay-at-home sisters. The play will also travel to parishes in Buffalo and the surrounding area as well as to and Utica, both in central New York. Plans also included performances of *Always in my Heart* for some time after the canonization in various places – of grace.

Chapter 1: **Canonization, Beatification, Exhumation**

November Song

In Hawai'i, the play entitled - *November Song* - authored by George Herman and updated by Sister Mary Laurence prior to 2011, entertained audiences in Honolulu and elsewhere as high school students put on their performance during the 2012 -2013 season. The text of the play focuses on the several times that significant events in the life of Mother Marianne took place in the month of November of various years.

Summer War / the Touch

Kumu Kahua Theater produced a third play about Mother Marianne in October 1985. Brian Burgess titled his play – *Summer War*. Later, with the title changed to – *The Touch* – the play took to the stage in the 1992 – 1994 season and in the 1999 – 2000 season in Hawai'i.

Canonization of St. Marianne Cope
Beatification and Exhumation

On Mission Sunday, October 21, 2012, Pope Benedict XVI canonized St. Marianne Cope (1838 – 1918), a Franciscan sister who spent half her life in the Hawaiian Islands among those afflicted with leprosy.

Patients of Kalaupapa, the former settlement for people affected by leprosy, along with their na kokua (helpers) as well as many Sisters of St. Francis of the Neumann Communities and other pilgrims attended the canonization ceremonies in Rome, Italy.

Bishop Larry Silva of Honolulu, Hawai'i, led the group of pilgrims from there. The website noted that the canonization "will be exuberantly celebrated around the world."

Bishop Robert Cunningham led the pilgrims from Syracuse. This group also visited Assisi, Italy, the birthplace of Franciscanism.

For the Franciscan sisters, Mother Marianne is one of their very own members. "We have a saint!"

For Germany, she is a native daughter, born in Heppenheim, and baptized at the church of St. Peter.

For central New York, she is remembered for her faith and good works. Her companion saint at the canonization – Kateri Tekakwitha – is also a daughter of New York. Both women lived in the Mohawk River Valley of New York.

For Hawai'i, and especially for Kalaupapa, Moloka'i, Mother Marianne is "one of their own," a "Beloved Mother of Outcasts" and the second saint for the tiny peninsula. St. Damien is the first canonized saint of Kalaupapa.

The day of canonization brought to fruition the years of a labor of love on the part of the sisters and many others.

The Beatification and Canonization Process

The official cause for the beatification and canonization of Mother Marianne Cope began on May 14, 1983. The decree of her virtues came on April 19, 2004, and with it the title of Venerable. The affirmation of a first miracle came on December 20, 2004, when Pope John Paul II declared her Blessed.

The required exhumation of her remains and transferal of them to St. Anthony Convent in Syracuse, N.Y. took place early in 2005.

On May 14, 2005, the beatification ceremony took place in Rome, Italy, and Blessed Marianne's feast day was set as January 23, the day of her birth, because St. Edith Stein, a victim of the Holocaust, had August 9th (the day of Marianne's death) as a feast day. In a spirit of ecumenism, the USA Episcopal Church celebrates the feast of both St. Damien and St. Marianne on April 15, the death date and Catholic feast of St. Damien.

On December 6, 2011, the Vatican Congregation for the Causes of Saints accepted the second miracle and forwarded their approval to Pope Benedict XVI who in turn signed and promulgated the decree for

Chapter 1: **Canonization, Beatification, Exhumation**

the canonization of St. Marianne Cope.

In February 2012, the Vatican set the date for the canonization as October 21, 2012, for Marianne and also for Kateri Tekakwitha, a Native American of the mid 17th century and a native of New York.

The sisters and others put in place plans for the pilgrimage to Rome and other events before and after the canonization ceremony.

Events – Fall 2012

http://www.stmariannecope.org/events.html

First Miracle – Kate Mahoney

http://www.stmariannecope.org/miracle_case.html

Second Miracle – Sharon Smith

http://www.stmariannecope.org/miracle_case2.html

Cause for beatification and canonization

http://www.stmariannecope.org/history_cause.html
http://www.stmariannecope.org/sainthood_process.html

Exhumation of Mother Marianne's Remains

The author of the play about Mother Marianne – *Always in My Heart* – and the author of - *A Graced Life* – a talk about Mother Marianne – both began their works with the story of the exhumation of the remains of Mother Marianne and the transfer of the remains to the Shrine in Syracuse, N.Y. Both authors presented the valid reasons for doing so as well as the emotions of the longtime patients of Kalaupapa and of the Franciscan sisters involved in the events surrounding the exhumation.

Sister Blanche Marie with Sister Mary Laurence

Sister Blanche Marie Messier

Sister Blanche Marie Messier shared her thoughts in August 2012 about her years working with Sister Mary Laurence Hanley on the Cause of Mother Marianne

Sister Blanche Marie Messier, a long time associate with Sister Mary Laurence Hanley, both members of the Sisters of St. Francis of the Neumann Communities, typed many of the documents needed for the beatification and canonization process. Sister Blanche Marie now resides at Jolenta Convent in Syracuse, and has written many of her memories.

In her own Words

Reliving the Process

"I have been reliving the parts of the process over and over again. This began in 2011 when Pope Benedict XVI declared that the Blessed Marianne Cause reached the time for canonization. Sister Mary Laurence, such a determined worker, had just passed into her eternal reward after declaring that her work was done.

Chapter 1: **Canonization, Beatification, Exhumation**

"Sister Grace Anne (Dillenschneider) came into our Jolenta Convent dining room to tell us that a miracle case towards Mother's canonization had passed the Vatican Medical Team's scrutiny as an extraordinary happening with no other explanation except God's own work.

"The Vatican's theologians, working at the Congregation for the Causes of Saints, declared that this cure was due to Blessed Marianne's intercession. When I heard about this miracle cure, the excitement of the pre-beatification events came back to me full force.

Sister Blanche recalls earlier events

"On April 19, 2004, the late John Paul II declared the Servant of God, Mother Marianne Cope, had practiced heroic virtue and was worthy of the title of Venerable.

"Meanwhile, Father Peter Gumpel, SJ, Cause Relator at the Vatican, continued his guidance along with Sister Mary Laurence to explain the necessity of exhuming Venerable Marianne's remains with enough time before the beatification process could begin. One of the reasons to not wait until after Mother Marianne would be beatified is the fact that many misguided persons might try to claim a portion of the remains. It would be much safer for the exhumation to take place before the beatification, plus there would be more time to plan for a suitable place and other decisions in regards to this happening.

"All the sisters were invited to share their thoughts and ideas. Many wished for Mother Marianne to stay in Hawai'i but her grave on an island peninsula in the Pacific Ocean proved very unfavorable. The ecological situations of the water and moisture seeping into the ground, and thus her grave, meant that action must take place soon. Considerations of Hawaiian interests and the central New York interests received due consideration in the decision to exhume and then move the remains to St. Anthony Convent in Syracuse, N.Y."

The 2004 - 2005 events.

"In December 2004, Pope John Paul gave the go ahead for Mother

Marianne's beatification. Later it was decided that this event would take place on Pentecost Sunday, May 15, 2005, along with the beatification of some other European venerables. Many sisters planned to go on the Franciscan Pilgrimage to Rome for the day preceding and the day following the beatification.

"During the last week of January 2005, a special Sunday Mass, with the forensic expert, his helpers, and the sisters in attendance, took place at St. Francis Church on Kalaupapa, Moloka'i. The exhumation process began the next day with the team using shovels and special types of sifters for this type of job. Some of the sisters who were present could help out. Reporters and photographer from the Syracuse Post Standard sent daily, well-written articles along with photographs of the findings and this kept all of us in this area (Syracuse) well informed.

"At the Bishop Home campus in Kalaupapa, St. Elizabeth Convent served as a place to store and clean and examine the relics from the grave. Mother's remains were placed in a special container to be brought to Honolulu for the container to be permanently sealed by a specialist. Sister Davilyn Ah Chick took photos of the preparation of the special container being uncovered, opened and the soldering process by an expert in this field. Soil was collected for both Hawai'i and the Mainland. Relics needed special preparation for preservation here at the St. Anthony Convent campus.

"Special Masses in Honolulu, at both the Cathedral of Our Lady of Peace and at St. Francis Convent chapel, sent the remains of Mother Marianne on their way. Because a plane carrying someone's remains would not be allowed to make a stop for a change to another plane, Mother Marianne's remains flew by a nonstop plane to Washington D.C. Photos of the sisters from the nearby residences of Virginia and the Capitol show the rear of the hearse carrying Mother's remains to a nearby funeral home. Sister Patricia Burkard, general minister of our congregation at that time, accompanied the remains from Kalaupapa all the way to the Capitol and on to Syracuse.

"Excitement and anticipation ran sky high as we waited after supper for the hearse to stop at the St. Anthony Campus. Finally in the dark of the night the hearse arrived.

Chapter 1: **Canonization, Beatification, Exhumation**

"Mother Marianne had returned home!"

"We piled out of St. Anthony and Jolenta with high anticipation. Walkers and wheelchairs came to the hearse where the back was opened for the handicapped to approach and touch or kiss the coffin. Then the hearse proceeded through the driveway towards the side of the convent where the rest of us crowded around the back of the hearse as it was opened a second time. All kissed the coffin holding Mother's remains.

"The hearse then proceeded to the Cathedral of the Immaculate Conception in the city of Syracuse, where many of the faithful had gathered and waited. Many sisters piled into cars and proceeded to the same cathedral.

"Bishop James M. Moynihan offered a special welcome ceremony and all us present including the faithful from different parts of the Diocese of Syracuse took part. Afterwards, the undertakers brought the coffin to the funeral home. The rest of us returned home with a tremendously happy, tired feeling and you can guess the rest.

"The next day many places held special Masses to observe the arrival of the remains of Mother Marianne. At the cathedral, the coffin received many, many kisses from the crowds, including some of our sisters from Utica and other nearby convents. The Knights of Columbus attended Mass at both the cathedral and at St. Anthony Convent. The Knights of Malta also came to the Mass at St. Anthony chapel. They may have been at the Cathedral as well. My memory escapes me here.

"After the second welcome home Mass, the undertakers moved the coffin behind the altar at St. Anthony Convent chapel, which has since been renovated. After the beatification ceremony, the remains of Mother Marianne came to rest in a special reliquary.

"I had planned to conduct tours of the Mother Marianne Museum but this had had to wait because of the crowds. Instead, I sat and welcomed everyone and answered questions.

"One exclamation repeated joyfully so often was,
'We have a saint right next door!'"

Sister Barbara Jean Wajda, OSF

Sister Barbara Jean Wajda, OSF, of Honolulu, Hawai'i, shared these thoughts in January 2012 that she gathered from others about the 2005 exhumation

In her Own Words

"At the moment when they brushed the dirt away and they saw her face (remains), they felt very close to Blessed Mother Marianne. It was very inspiring, an emotional experience.

"The sisters were humbled; they felt privileged to be there. I asked Sister Patricia Burkard about the feelings of the patients and residents at Kalaupapa. Sister Patricia indicated that there were mixed feelings. On the one hand, it was difficult for them to see the remains of Blessed Mother Marianne being removed from their resting place. However, there were factors that softened the impact on the patients and residents.

"As the delicate sifting occurred, it became clear that all the fragments

Chapter 1: **Canonization, Beatification, Exhumation**

could not be removed. The fact that some of the fragments remained in the ground was consoling to patients and residents.

"It was explained at meetings with the patients and residents that, for the process of canonization, the remains needed to be at a location accessible to the universal church. The restricted accessibility of Kalaupapa did not meet this requirement, whereas the shrine in Syracuse did.

"I attended a meeting with the residents and patients and the National Park Service about two years ago. There are very strong feelings on the part of patients and their families about memorializing those who have died and are buried on the peninsula and about the land use. Park service administration and those connected with the process listened carefully to the input of those in attendance, answering questions and accepting all ideas presented as legitimate concerns."

Sister Alicia Damien Lau, OSF

Sister Alicia Damien Lau, OSF, of Honolulu, Hawai'i, on January 23, 2012, feast of St. Marianne Cope, wrote about the exhumation of 2005.

In her Own Words

"The process of exhumation of Mother Marianne from her gravesite was primarily for the "body identification" during the inquiry stage of the process of Mother becoming Venerable.

"In Sister Mary Laurence's letter to some sisters in March 2004, she stated: 'Before the end of the inquiry stage an official verification of the remains of the person takes place to certify that the one in the grave is the same as the one proposed as the candidate for sainthood. The body may have to be brought up for identification and "treated" and lowered again. However, because there should be an exhumation near beatification time, those working on causes for sainthood avoid doing this procedure twice.'

"Our congregation struggled with the decision of where her permanent resting place should be. Our advisor from Rome asked this question - where should she be in 100 years?

"The Sisters of St. Francis never had 'control' over Bishop Home nor her gravesite. The land is owned by the Hawaiian Home Lands. Some buildings were managed by the Department of Health, and currently, the National Park Service is managing most of the buildings. This includes Bishop Home, the land surrounding the Home and Mother's gravesite.

"I was there for the week of the exhumation process. I agree with many of the comments; it was an awesome sight. Perhaps the most memorable event came when all of her remains were removed and laid out in Bishop Home, everyone except Sister Frances Cabrini (Morishige) and I were up, watching over her and praying.

"The next morning, before Mother's remains were placed in the zinc box and sealed, we were privileged to hold her skull in our hands. We prayerfully and gently passed it to the next sister. When it was my turn, I took it, and a chill went though my body. The emotions that I felt - leaves me speechless - even to this day. It is very hard to describe the moment - a most precious moment in my life."

Chapter 1: **Canonization, Beatification, Exhumation**

http://www.blessedmariannecope.org/Archives/2007/archive_feb2007.html

Kalaupapa in Poetry

In a lovely book with photos, Takayuki Harada composed his *Kalaupapa in Poetry* (2010) with sensitivity to the living and deceased persons with Hansen's disease who made this place their home. One of these persons was Taka's brother Paul who lived there since the 1960s and died in 2008. Taka was a mere one year old when Paul moved to Kalaupapa. Taka and his wife visited Kalaupapa many times to see Paul and his wife Winnie.

Two of the special moments for Taka included the return of the relic hand of Father Damien in 1995 and the exhuming of the remains of Mother Marianne in 2005. Taka's presence at both events as well as visits to each of their grave sites moved his spirit to write poetry about these two saints who so graced that tiny peninsula and its settlements of Kalawao and Kalaupapa.

Past, Present, and Future – of the Sorrowful Settlement

Elbow bump

After the lifting of the ban in 1969, and when patients of Kalaupapa attended church outside the settlement, they used the "elbow bump" as a sign of good faith without touching other people's hands. This greeting and sign of good faith became popular throughout Hawai'i in the 1970s. (In 2006 and 2009 with the scare of avian flu and swine flu, interest in the elbow bump increased as a way to avoid the spread of germs."

In 1969, Hawai'i lifted the isolation policy for patients of Kalaupapa. Although remedies for Hansen's disease (leprosy) found their ways into medical treatments in the 1940s and 1950s, the fear of contagion of the disease delayed lifting the ban. It took another 20 years for the isolation policies to come to an end.

Mother Marianne and about 40 sisters who followed her footsteps to Kalaupapa lived and worked under this quarantine policy through 1969. A few sisters lived and worked at Kalaupapa during the transition and several sisters on assignment or as volunteers lived and worked there after the ban had been lifted.

1969 – the Year that Changed the World

Some have called 1969 the year that changed the world. Men walked on the moon. Woodstock music attracted thousands. Protestors marched to seek peace and to oppose the Vietnam War. Some say that the Internet began in 1969 with the IMP – interface message processor.

1969 – feast of St. Elizabeth of Hungary

Another significant change came in 1969 as a follow up to Vatican II. In Mysterii Paschalis, Pope Paul VI updated the liturgical calendar for the universal Roman Catholic Church. More emphasis was given to the feasts of Christ. The dates for feasts of many saints changed and this included the feast of St. Elizabeth of Hungary, a favored saint of Mother Marianne. When she received her religious name in 1862 and pronounced her vows in 1863, she did so on November 19, then the feast of St. Elizabeth. She also observed her jubilees on November 19 in 1888 and 1913.

With the 1969 revision of the calendar, the feast of St. Elizabeth of Hungary now falls on November 17. Several sources give November 17, 1231 as the death date of St. Elizabeth.

1969 – End of isolation

For those affected by Hansen's disease and those na kokua who ministered to them, the 1969 end to isolation and banishment marked a turning point in their personal and collective lives at Kalaupapa.

This lei-crowned woman lived at Kalaupapa in the early 20th century

Photo: Courtesy of the Congregation of the Sacred Hearts of Jesus and Mary

Chapter 2

21st Century
The old and the new

Had not the seraphic saint himself said: "More than all grace and all the gifts of the Holy Ghost, which Christ vouchsafed to his friends, is the conquering of yourself and the willing endurance of suffering, injustice, contempt, and harshness."
-P&E

In this Chapter

Sisters of St. Francis in the 21st century find inspiration in Mother Marianne and carry on compassionate concern for outcasts as she did. Sister Cheryl Wint listens to visitors at the Damien and Marianne Heritage Center in Honolulu. Sister Anne Marie Saphara, through her ministry in the Communications Office of the Sisters of St. Francis of the Neumann Communities, spreads the word about St. Marianne.

Sister Mary Laurence Hanley, who died in 2011, spent many years of research and writing about the life and legacy of Marianne, and authored - *Pilgrimage and Exile*.

Sister Blanche Marie Messier, now in residence at Jolenta Convent in

Syracuse, worked with Sister Mary Laurence in the Mother Marianne Museum in Syracuse and had many stories to tell.

Sister Wilma Halmasy lived and worked for many years in Kalaupapa. Her writings appear in a book titled – *Letters from the Land of Long Farewells*.

Sister Mary Laurence Hanley (1918 – 2011)
Author of the official biography of Mother Marianne – *Pilgrimage and Exile: Mother Marianne of Moloka'i*

"My work is done," she told the sisters in the Fall 2011. Sister Mary Laurence felt sure that the Vatican would soon announce the canonization of Mother Marianne Cope.

For 35 years, Sister Mary Laurence worked on the cause, the biography, and the museum dedicated to Mother Marianne. Sister Mary Laurence steeped herself in everything Marianne and came to a deep understanding of the saint's life story and lived virtues.

Chapter 2: **21st Century**

Sister Mary Laurence died on December 2, 2011. And the Vatican made its announcement on December 20, 2011.

Back in 1974, Mother Viola asked Sister Mary Laurence to work part time on the cause of Mother Marianne. That summer task continued for 35 years during which she dedicated her life to promoting Mother Marianne as an equal in her own right to Father Damien, and not merely holy by association with him.

By 1977, Sister Mary Laurence took on full time work in research and writing about Mother Marianne, especially her years at Kalaupapa at the settlement for leprosy patients. In 1980, Sister Mary Laurence co-authored with O.A. Bushnell, a historian in Hawai'i, the definitive biography of Mother Marianne – *Pilgrimage and Exile*.

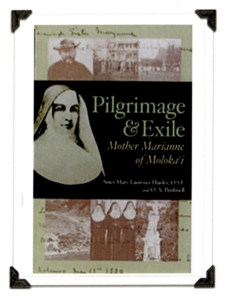

(Bushnell also authored the book – *Moloka'i* – telling of the patients of the settlement and the priest who came to offfer service to them.)

In *Pilgrimage and Exile*, Bushnell came to know Mother Marianne and the Franciscan sisters who came to the settlement to be of service to the patients.

Sister Blanche Marie Messier

In her own words

How did I get involved in the first place?

"Sister Mary Laurence received an assignment to do part-time work on the possibility of our widely-known, saintly member called "Mother Marianne of Molokaʻi".

"Sister Mary Laurence began to gather information about the life of Mother Marianne Cope, who had passed into eternity at the age of 80 at Kalaupapa, Molokaʻi, on August 9, 1918. Sister began by writing letters and visiting many places, including Hawaiʻi across the Pacific Ocean and across the Atlantic Ocean to Rome, Italy, on several occasions.

"I happened to be at Alverna Heights in Fayetteville, N.Y. to rest for a little while. Some sisters had helped for a very short time, usually with typing, and had to leave for their usual work or new assignment. I did like to type and I was sort of looking for a job like this to help

Chapter 2: **21st Century**

anywhere, or really more so where I would be really needed.

"Mother Viola already had plans for me for more library work elsewhere. I did have such jobs in the past but usually in libraries where real joys abounded. I had to stop teaching because of totally unexpected and complete loss of hearing. After about a week of typing some of Sister Leopoldina's stories from those early days in Kalaupapa, Sister Mary Laurence approached me. She suggested that I ask Mother Viola if I could stay on to help her with the work.

"I left a note on Mother Viola's desk. I explained that Sister Mary Laurence was unable to do this job alone and I would be happy to help her. "Is this ok or not?" I asked.

"A few days later I asked, 'Did you find my note?' She invited me in asked me to repeat my question. 'Do you really want to help sister?' I answered, 'Yes and I do like to type and sister states that she is really in need.'

"'OK' came the reply, 'but only for six months.'

"Well somehow these six months turned into 35 years plus a little over a month more."

How we got started

"I received materials to study, especially about our community's beginnings in Philadelphia and our sudden painful separation when the Syracuse sisters became a separate foundation in the Diocese of Albany, N.Y. As I studied, I could not help but notice Sister Mary Laurence's marvelous enthusiasm and her desire to share her thoughts.

"I just loved to listen to stories about the work in progress and the places of interest. Also, the letters I typed from her handwritten letters began to be as adventurous as her trips and the information, which she accumulated.

"Two large boxes of letters written by Brother Joseph Dutton came from the Wisconsin Historical Society Archives. Father Damien had asked and begged for helpers. When Joseph Dutton arrived, Father Damien was so overjoyed he decided to call him Brother and the title stuck. Joseph Dutton had also written many letters from Kalaupapa to the University of Notre Dame. Work began to multiply to enormous proportions and therefore Mother Viola gave Sister Mary Laurence full charge and relieved her from other part time office work.

"One of the stories Sister Mary Laurence told me was the fact that original letters had been sent to the Vatican officials but these were returned. The work must be in typed form. The Vatican sent this directive to Mother Viola. In those days the older way of debating back and forth between lawyers and a judge called the relator was the very time consuming ways to determine and prove the sanctity of individuals. Sister did express some discouragement at times as loads and loads of information poured in.

"I do hope I will be able to see some kind of progress and will I ever see Mother Marianne beatified?" She expressed this on quite a few occasions.

"I must confess, even though not out loud to anyone before typing this, that I myself had the very same feeling.

"Sister Mary Laurence traveled to Hawai'i and visited the Congregation of the Sacred Hearts Archives there. At the same time, she learned that the main archives for the Sacred Hearts Fathers and Brothers was now located in Rome, Italy. Thus letters in French and on microfilm had to be sorted and translated. These letters came from Bishop Herman Koeckemann, Father Leonore Fouesnel, Bishop Gulstan Ropert, and other priests working in the Hawaiian Islands. Communications between Bishop Koeckemann, Father Leonore, and Father Damien also took place.

"Sister also gathered so very much information from census records, and directories from the period of time when Mother Marianne's family arrived in Utica. Her youngest brother John somehow became lost. Sister was unable to find any information except for when Barbara Koob, their mother, passed into her eternal reward. Sister found some information on the inheritance left by the mother and her wishes for the children who stayed at home to help when their father Peter became ill.

"We put together copies of records both typed and sometimes copies of originals, plus newspaper articles, the total came to 27 volumes in the end. These were acquired from all the letter writings, travels all over Utica to various archives, record keeping parts of court houses, and often asking questions on Schuyler Street houses and the factory and all.

"Sister Mary Laurence also traveled to Heppenheim, Germany, to locate some records from St. Peter Church where Mother Marianne's parents were married, along with birth and baptismal records, plus the number of children from both families."

Sister Wilma – (1921 – 2006)
At Kalaupapa from 1946 to 1955, 1962 to 1969, 1974 to 1990

Author of – *Letters from the Land of Long Farewells*

Sister Wilma Halmasy lived and worked as a nurse in Kalaupapa for 30 years beginning in the 1940s. She gave testimony about Mother

Marianne in the 1980s and attended the beatification of Blessed Marianne in 2005.

In her book, *Letters from the Land of Long Farewells*, she writes the story of the Sisters of St. Francis at Kalaupapa. She says that over the years 61 sisters worked there under the Department of Health of Hawai'i.

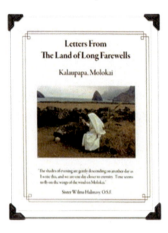

By narrating stories of stressful times and amusing times as well as the day-to-day kinds of events, the reader comes to know of the courage of Sister Wilma and the other sisters. The photos give the reader an idea of how the sisters live and work with the current patients of Kalaupapa Peninsula with all its beauty and history.

One of the most delightful chapters tells about Christmas plans and happenings. Sister Wilma possessed a love of beauty, music, and nature - all qualities that Mother Marianne also cherished.

In 1988, on her 50th anniversary as a religious she wrote, "the most important thing which I continue to value is being able to follow in the footsteps of Mother Marianne and Father Damien for more than half of my religious life."

In her retirement, Sister Wilma resided at Jolenta Convent in Syracuse, so named for Mother Jolenta who also worked at Kalaupapa.

Sister Wilma died on June 27, 2006.

To those who would follow in her footsteps, she offered this advice: "If you take the step, then give your all."

Sister Cheryl Wint
Helper at the Damien Marianne Heritage Center, Honolulu

A story of a Sister of St. Francis working in Hawai'i

Early in 2012, Sister Cheryl Wint as a novice in the Sisters of St. Francis, travelled to Hawai'i to be of service to the poor. Sister Cheryl, who was born in Jamaica, entered the congregations in 2009 to listen to God's call to her to serve others.

"I think it is a wonderful time to be in religious life," Sister Cheryl said. "There is a sense of despair and I think that God is saying to us as religious, it is time to work in the vineyard."

She is very much attracted to social justice causes.
"I am called to public service," she said. "My jobs prior were also with people."

While in Hawai'i, Sister Cheryl gave tours at the Damien and Marianne of Moloka'i Heritage Center at St. Augustine by-the-Sea Parish in Honolulu.

"From my perspective," Sister Cheryl said, "Mother Marianne must have been a very down-to-earth person as she integrated a lot of her personal life into her ministries."

"For me, since I entered the convent, I have found it to be one joyful journey," she said.

In her own words

After Sister Cheryl returned from her five-month stay in Hawai'i, she reflected on all it meant to her.

The Damien and Marianne Heritage Center

"Upon my arrival at the Damien and Marianne Heritage Center, I was blown over by the photos and the various storylines about the pictures. The layout of the center shows great attention to detail in a very tasteful way and shows great thoughtfulness with seating throughout the museum. All of this adds to the serenity of the center. As visitors reflect on what they see and read, they often feel overwhelmed with emotion.

"I heard many stories during my time at the center. The Hawaiian people like to say 'I'd love to come and talk story with you folks.'

"My first experience of talking story happened with the daughter and granddaughter of one of the patients of Kalaupapa. This story gave the family and me a moment of very mixed emotions: pride, fascination, sadness, discovery, and humility all rolled into one.

"As the family started to share their story of the daughter, they did not know the true identity of her parents until she turned 21. I felt a great sense of sacredness as they told me this story of how she learned of her birth at Kalaupapa and then of her journey to one of her aunts on a neighboring island where she grew up. To this day, I still feel the impact of this Kalaupapa elder's story.

"I also realize that the daughter felt strong emotions. I cannot imagine what it feels like to have not known, and still to not have known about or seen a picture of one's parents, and then to see the photo at the Heritage Center. I knew I was on hallowed ground as this family talked story with me."

Pilgrimage to Kalaupapa

"On my first pilgrimage to Kalaupapa, I wasn't sure what to expect. From the moment I boarded the bus for the Honolulu Airport, another passenger began to talk story with me about how she wants to learn more about her grandmother whom she never met. The passenger's mother had told stories about cousins who grew up knowing the grandmother.

"For this trip, this passenger brought along another woman and her daughter whom she had met in the hotel during her stay at Honolulu. They felt some intrigue to go to Kalaupapa, not only because of their new friend, but also because they wanted to do something different than the usual tourist things.

"Anyway, we head out on a nine-seat plane and this particular passenger tells me that she is not Catholic and so she is not sure how to navigate her search once she gets there. She asks me to assist her.

"I assure her that it is not a requirement to be Catholic and the patients of Kalaupapa both back in the time of Damien and Marianne – and now – held various religions. I also tell her the stories I know about Marianne and Damien and about life in the settlement in the 1800s.

"We arrive and I am immediately struck by the landscape and the weather. I feel a certain serenity and a strong presence of the Other. I sense a sacredness about the place from the very beginning and it only intensifies as I move along on this journey.

"I also sensed that the others on the tour felt the sacredness as there were moments of deep silence and a realization that talking would have been out of place.

"As our guide meets us and explains things on the tour, we hang on every word. Based on my Heritage Center training and readings, I could validate whether the guide told facts or myths. The sisters who reside at Kalaupapa met me at the major stops along the route and filled in other details about Mother Marianne for me.

"The more I saw and learned that day, the more I knew that I had to go back for several days of retreat. I wanted to make a self directed retreat based on the ideas I got from Murray Bodo's book, *A Retreat with Francis and Clare*."

"The passenger I met on the bus looked for information in the only bookstore on the island. One of the Kalaupapa patients, a man who works behind the desk at the bookstore, took one look at her and said to her: 'You are related to Mrs. So and So, aren't you?' Those of us who knew her take one look at this passenger and watch her go from a stunned look to the color draining from her face. We see her nod Yes and finally find her voice again. Though we all felt eager to hear the story, we moved away so she could speak with him privately.

"The bookstore man not only knew her grandmother but knew where she lived and gives instruction to the tour guide to point it out to her once we get there. We feel stunned at her luck, but also know that the Divine is in charge. She can no longer hold back the tears and we all experience her excitement.

Mother Marianne

"To do what she did, Mother Marianne had to have great courage, faith, strength, and resolve. It took all these virtues and more to totally relocate, to implement the processes and procedures of caring for patients with leprosy, to restore the dignity of dying souls, to set standards for the patients, to establish the institutions of health care and orphan care, and to serve the other sisters as superior. Mother Marianne also navigated the politics of the times and practiced

Franciscan values at their best, all imbued with a deep love of God. "For me, the Prayer before the Crucifix of St. Francis of Assisi becomes more real and tangible in my life.

St. Francis' Prayer
Before the San Damiano Crucifix
Most High, Glorious God,
enlighten the darkness
of my heart.

Give me
right faith,
sure hope
and perfect charity.

Fill me with insight and wisdom
that I may fulfill
your will.

"Indeed, Mother Marianne is a saint. Our congregation celebrates the blessing of her sainthood during our lifetime."

Absolute Faith

During the spring of 2012, a special display, titled Absolute Faith: St. Damien and Bl. Marianne and the People of Kalaupapa, gave visitors a chance to see photos from the very early 20th century.

From glass plate negatives of photos taken by Father Joseph Juliotte who worked at Kalaupapa from 1901 to 1907, amazing portraits showed several of the patients of those years when Mother Marianne was in her later years. She would have known these people whose eyes look out from the century old photographs. Brother Louis Leissen also took photos during his years at Kalaupapa and processed his photos in his own darkroom.

Stories have come down through the years that these photos were taken so that the patients could send pictures to their loved ones.

More and more, authors are taking into account the people of Kalaupapa – their voices, their experiences, their memories, their writings, their music. It is good that this display title included the people of Kalaupapa.

The Manoa Journal, a magazine of the Pacific cultures, published 15 of these images in the Winter 2011 issue titled Almost Heaven.

The Absolute Faith Display received the 2012 Preservation Award Medal at the 37th annual Historic Hawai'i Foundation Preservation Awards ceremony on May 11, 2012

Sister Anne Marie Saphara

Childhood Scrapbooks and Lifelong Love of Mother Marianne

A story of a central New York follower of St. Marianne

Chapter 2: **21st Century**

A native of Auburn, N.Y. Sister Anne Marie's interest in "nuns" began at age 9, when she started a scrapbook of clippings from magazines and newspapers about sisters. In her teens, she launched a second scrapbook, which includes a 1976 article on Mother Marianne in the magazine entitled Empire, of central New York.

Fond of Mother Marianne since Childhood

Childhood Scrapbooks

Mother Marianne entered the convent in central New York – at Utica and then Syracuse in the early 1860s. Just about a hundred years later, a 10-year-old girl in central New York – at Auburn - took a liking to the story of Mother Marianne and to collecting all things about nuns. Anne Marie's scrapbooking over several years gives evidence of her great interest.

Though yellowed and fragile, the pages of the scrapbook reveal many aspects of women religious in the 1960s and 1970s. Anne Marie's clippings from magazines and newspapers show the movies of the era – *The Nun's Story*, *Heaven Knows, Mr. Allison*, *The Singing Nun*, and others, as well as television shows such as Hallmark's *The Cradle Song*.

Clippings of many, many communities show sisters who served as firefighters, missionaries, teachers, doctors, nurses, and graphic designers. Saints like St. Elizabeth Ann Seton and St. Edith Stein show up on the pages.

The inside of the back cover of one of the scrapbooks reveals a collage of maybe 200 or more faces of "nuns" – the common noun for women religious. While many of the sisters in the scrapbooks show the sisters of the Diocese of Rochester, to which Auburn belongs, Anne Marie also pasted in the Sisters of St. Francis of the Diocese of Syracuse.

1976 - Could she be a saint?

Of special interest in Anne Marie's collection, the April 18, 1976, article from Empire (Sunday Magazine of central New York - of the local

Auburn newspaper) asks the question "Could she be the next American Saint?" as the subtitle of the cover story, Utica Nun's Courage and Inspiration by J. Michael Kelly.

In 1976, the United States had only one saint – Mother Seton. In 2012, with the canonization of Mother Marianne Cope and Kateri Tekakwitha, the United States has 12 Catholic saints.

Kelly, as author, points out that the Sisters of St. Francis, the congregation that Mother Marianne belonged to, began examining her life in 1974 with "intensive research" and much praying.

The sisters doing the research were soon "swamped with correspondence, anecdotes, and faded photographs."

Arlene LaRue, columnist, writes about the "matron of Molokaʻi"

Sister Anne Marie also saved two newspaper columns by Arlene LaRue, a writer in the 1930s through 1970s. Upon her retirement in 1977, Ms. LaRue continued to write columns until 1993, the year of her death.

The two columns that Sister Anne Marie saved probably date to 1980, the time of the publication of the first edition of *Pilgrimage and Exile*, the official biography.

Ms. LaRue thinks that *Pilgrimage and Exile* "would make a good movie" – as "a saga of adventure and high drama." This columnist points out that the book is "a warts and all 'type of biography' ".

Thinking back to a talk she heard in 1944 by Dr. T. Wood Clark of Utica, Ms. LaRue tells how she first learned of "lepers" (the word used then for patients with Hansen's disease) and how the emissaries of the king and queen of Hawaiʻi came looking for helpers to care for the persons who had contracted Hansen's disease. Ms. LaRue writes of Mother Marianne as "the matron at Molokaʻi" and tells how Mother Marianne was selected as one of six historical subjects for the bicentennial edition of Catholics in America (1976).

The columnist also tells how the Oneida Hall of Fame included Mother Marianne in 1938 and how Mother Aileen Griffin of the Franciscan Sisters in Syracuse, in the 1980s, nominated Mother Marianne for the Women's Rights Hall of Fame in Seneca Falls.

So, Anne Marie kept her teenage scrapbooks and pondered her call to religious life.

After a career in graphic design and a role as wife and mother, Sister Anne Marie entered the community of Mother Marianne in 2007. She now works as a graphic designer in the congregational communications office of the sisters. She looks forward to her final vows in 2013.

In her own words – Second Chances
Sister Anne Marie Saphara

"I learned that Mother Marianne was a no-nonsense woman who was practical, spiritual, and truly a 'woman of vision.'

"I wished I could have known her when she was alive. "

"The Syracuse Franciscan sisters founded Mercy Hospital in my hometown of Auburn, N.Y. and it was at Mercy that I had my first encounter with one of the sisters. Typical of the 1950s, having a tonsillectomy was quite a common procedure for young children and I was one of them. An orderly wheeled me into the operating room; on one side of me were my parents, their eyes full of concern. On my other side was a sister nurse. I was convinced she was an angel. All dressed in white, her veil, stiffly starched, framed her face, and made her look so different from anyone else in the room. I thought she HAD to be an angel, like those on the holy cards.

"Auburn is close to Syracuse and the Syracuse newspapers and television stations were our source for local and world news. In the early 1980s a feature called "All our Yesteryears" in the Syracuse paper told the story of Mother Marianne Cope and how the community initiated her cause for sainthood. I cut out and saved every article about Mother Marianne and to the surprise of many people, I still have them, all yellowed and practically falling apart.

"I also saw that a book was being written by one of the sisters. Since these were the days before online ordering and large bookstores, I did not know how to purchase that book. Then life got in the way and I put the book on my "back burner."

"In 1983 I moved to the Washington, D.C. area. In the early 1990s my sister asked me what I wanted for Christmas. Remembering the book, I told her that if she could locate *"Pilgrimage and Exile"* by Sister Mary Laurence Hanley that could be my gift. She called the sisters in Syracuse and the book was mailed to me. I got my Christmas wish.

" *'Pilgrimage and Exile'* is a wonderful book and by the time I got to the part of Mother Marianne's death, I was in tears. I had to put the book down repeatedly to dry my eyes so I could continue my reading. I learned that Mother Marianne was a no-nonsense woman who was practical, spiritual, and truly a "woman of vision." I wished I could have known her when she was alive.

("I probably would have been another Sister Leopoldina Burns, who was her loyal 'Franciscan daughter.' ")

"Later on, as Mother Marianne's cause for canonization was becoming a reality, I thought that she, who preferred the background and avoided publicity, would be very uncomfortable with all the attention she was now receiving. Her desire for anonymity could be one of the reasons why there are so few photos of her.

Second Chances

"They say there are no second chances in life, but sometimes I think I am an exception. From my elementary school days I always wanted to be a sister. Just when I was about to fulfill my dream after being accepted by a diocesan community in my senior year of high school, the post Vatican II era with its upheavals and changes within religious communities changed my mind about entering.

"My intention of waiting for a while was intercepted once again by life getting in the way. Marriage, motherhood, divorce and annulment, and career ambitions filled the next 40 years of my life. I had everything I wanted but the nagging thought that I should be a sister kept popping into my head; first occasionally and then relentlessly.

"Finally, I said to Lord, "OK. I'll follow through on this, but when they turn me down, leave me alone because no community wants me!" I was surprised to find out that many communities do accept older vocations, even women who are mothers.

"On a visit home, my sister and I drove to Syracuse to visit the Mother Marianne Museum. Sister Mary Laurence was our guide and the moment I stepped into St. Anthony chapel, I felt this is where I belonged. Later, I kept in contact with Sister Mary Laurence and visited her whenever I was in the area.

"Finally I drew up the courage to see if the community would accept me as a candidate. After the lengthy process of interviews, psychological assessments, and other paperwork, in 2007 I was accepted as a candidate.

"I know that is through my interest, admiration and love of Mother Marianne that I am now a member of her Franciscan community. She guided me throughout and continues to be my inspiration as I proceed in the steps to making my final profession."

Greater Love – Syracuse - 100

In 1860, seven Sisters of St. Francis left Philadelphia, PA; four went to Assumption School in Syracuse, N.Y. and three went to St. Joseph School in Utica, N.Y. These pioneer sisters worked with great courage in what was then the Diocese of Albany, N.Y. in the years just before and during the Civil War.

Mother Bernardina came to Utica as the superior of the group and it was here that Barbara Koop came in contact with the Franciscan sisters and developed a desire to join them.

With Mother Bernardina as friend and mentor, Barbara did join the convent in 1862 and became known as Sister Mary Anna.

Over time her name evolved into Sister Marianne. She worked at schools and hospitals in central New York State.

In 1877, the sisters elected Mother Marianne as the second superior general and re-elected her in 1881. During her years as mother superior, she oversaw the construction of a larger chapel at the St. Anthony convent and its dedication on October 30, 1879.

This document explains that this chapel lasted for 71 years and was replaced in 1950 with the chapel currently in use.

The anniversary book dedicates a section to Hawai'i, and in turn to schools and hospitals on the islands. The text lauds the great sacrifice of the pioneer sisters, led by Mother Marianne, as they took up ministry in that faraway place.

The sisters ran Kapi'olani Home for healthy children of parents who had the disease of leprosy for 53 years in the home's several locations. In all those years, only two children in the sisters' care contracted Hansen's disease.

Five years into their work on the islands of O'ahu and Maui, three of the sisters, again led by Mother Marianne, moved to the Island of Moloka'i and to the Kalaupapa settlement on the north shore peninsula.

The 100 year anniversary book points out that Bishop Home at Kalaupapa consisted of several buildings: cottages, infirmary, dining hall and kitchen, laundry, social hall, and the sisters' cottage known as St. Elizabeth as well as St. Elizabeth Chapel.

Over the late 19th and early 20th century years, the patient population living in the cottages averaged about 100 and sometimes rose to 150 persons afflicted with the disease for which they were exiled.

In 1938, at the request of the government, the sisters took on the supervision of the hospital, an outgrowth of the infirmary. The sisters also taught school, including religious education over all those years.

Chapter 2: **21st Century**

In 1958, a celebration at Our Lady of Peace Cathedral in Honolulu honored the 75th anniversary of the sisters going to Kalaupapa, Moloka'i. Mother Jolenta and Sister Remigia, both from Syracuse, as well as the sisters who lived in Hawai'i, attended this celebration.

A celebration also took place at Kalaupapa with a procession to the grave of Mother Marianne. Father Charles A. Kekumano, in attendance, spoke at the gravesite, saying: " … she brought relief, comfort, and sunshine."

The anniversary book explains how the sisters pioneered in the field of nursing care for patients afflicted with Hansen's disease as well as exemplifying the centuries-long traditions and culture of their Franciscan heritage.

Greater Love, August 15, 1960, Syracuse, N.Y. Sisters of the Third Order of St. Francis, The Province of St. Anthony of Padua, One Hundred Years of Dedicated Service 1860 – 1960.

Update on recent Ministries in Hawai'i

St. Francis Healthcare System, Honolulu, Hawai'i

"Let us make the very best use of the precious moments and do all in our power for His dear sake and for His greater honor and glory."
Saint Marianne Cope / http://www.stmariannecope.org/

In her Own Words

Sister Agnelle Ching, with Jerry J. Correa, Jr. – on website - http://www.stfrancisHawai'i.org/mission/our-patron-saint

"St. Francis Healthcare System of Hawai'i has the distinct privilege of being associated with Saint Marianne Cope, who was canonized a saint by Pope Benedict XVI in 2012. Our legacy of caring in the islands can be directly traced to Saint Marianne, who came to Hawai'i with six Sisters of St. Francis from Syracuse, N.Y. in response to a special call of God to care for those afflicted with Hansen's disease.

"Moved by compassion, Saint Marianne and the sisters headed for Hawai'i aboard the Mariposa in 1883. Knowing that God was with them, they came fearlessly and unreservedly, determined to make a positive difference in the lives of all those whom they touched.

"We are intensely aware that St. Francis Healthcare System exists today because Saint Marianne and the Franciscan sisters said "yes" and never looked back. Nearly 129 years later, that same spirit of caring continues today. Through various programs and services, St. Francis Healthcare System cares for the most vulnerable in our community, including Hawai'i's rapidly growing older adult population, and we continually explore new ways to expand our service to others.

"As we proudly celebrate the canonization of Hawai'i's second saint, the St. Francis Healthcare System 'ohana (family) renews our commitment to our mission of creating healthy communities in the spirit of Christ's healing ministry. As in the words aptly spoken by Saint Marianne, we too will continue to do everything in our power to bring glory to the name of our Lord Jesus Christ through the transforming power of the Holy Spirit."

Malulani Hospital, Maui and Malulani Health Systems

At Wailuku on the island of Maui, Malulani Health Systems traces its origin to the time in 1884 when Mother Marianne Cope came to the area to set up a hospital. At the request of Queen Kapi'olani, Mother Marianne and two other sisters came to St. Anthony Church and set up the hospital and also a school.

Malulani means – "under the shelter of protection of heaven" – a name given by Queen Kapi'olani at Mother Marianne's invitation.

The sisters kept the hospital going into the 20th century, until 1929, until lay people began serving in administration. The hospital served the general population. It was not a leprosarium.

Over time, plantation hospitals at Lahaina, Pu'unene, and Paia closed and Malulani served as the community hospital for all the people of Maui.

The contemporary mission of Malulani Health and Medical Center remained true to the original mission: "serving the people of Maui with the best possible healthcare available and with a true spirit of caring for the community." – as stated on its website. The service area included Lanai and Molokaʻi islands as well as Maui – and visitors as well as residents.

http://www.malulani.org/vision.htm#legacy

In 2007, Maui Memorial Hospital took over the care of Maui residents and Malulani became non-operational.

St. Francis School, Manoa, Oʻahu

As a legacy to St. Marianne Cope, St Francis School in Honolulu sits away from the city of Honolulu in Manoa Valley, a favorite place of Mother Marianne. The school states its mission as "quality education in a spirit of joy."

The Sisters of St. Francis established the school in 1924 as a way to honor Mother Marianne whose very reason for entering the convent had been to teach children and work in the field of education.

In its early years, the sisters ran St. Francis as a girls' high school. Today, it offers a setting of Catholic education for toddlers through 12th grade students, both girls and boys. The Sisters of St. Francis of the Neumann Communities continue to sponsor the school and welcome students from Hawaiʻi and from several other Asian countries.

http://www.stfrancis-Oʻahu.org/mission_philosophy.php

http://www.facebook.com/pages/Saint-Francis-School-Manoa/119927468048817

Lasting Legacy in Central New York

St. Elizabeth Hospital – established in 1866

When Mother Bernardina lived in Utica, N.Y. and taught school at St. Joseph Parish, she noticed the needs of the poor and visited the sick in the west side of the city. When St. Joseph Parish donated a house on Columbia Street, Mother Bernardina, assisted by Sister Marianne, opened a small hospital. The first patient arrived on December 12, 1866.

Over the years, the sisters administered this hospital and added buildings and advanced treatments and technology. Mother Marianne's basic beliefs about health care continue in the deep respect for each person and the whole person towards spiritual, physical, and emotional wellness.

As of 2012, St. Elizabeth Medical Center at 2209 Genesee Street, Utica, sits on a 25-acre campus with 201 beds and almost 2,000 employees. Quality health care is extended to 14 other locations including the new St. Elizabeth Medical Arts facility in new Hartford, N.Y.

The Sisters of St. Francis continue to sponsor St. Elizabeth Medical Center. The hospital's web page offers a section on Mother Marianne.

http://www.stemc.org/

St. Joseph Hospital – Established in 1869

Five Sisters of St. Francis took a bar and dance hall building and transformed it into a 15-bed hospital on top of Prospect Hill, Syracuse, N.Y. in 1869. Sister Marianne Cope served as administrator of the hospital and superior of the convent from 1870 through 1877, a period of great growth of both hospital and the city. In 1877, elected as provincial superior, she became known as Mother Marianne.

St. Joseph Hospital, the first general hospital in the city, now has a medical staff of more than 800 physicians and dentists along with

Chapter 2: 21st Century

almost 4,000 other health care professionals and support staff. In addition, more than 1,000 volunteers devote their time to patient care programs.

The Sisters of St. Francis continue to sponsor St. Joseph Hospital, which honors the memory of the role that Mother Marianne played in its foundation.

http://www.sjhsyr.org/

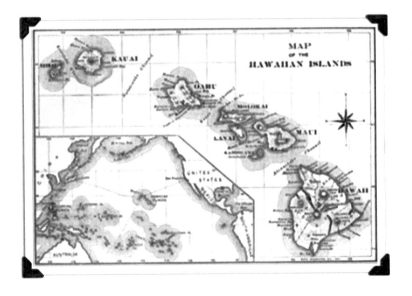

Photos: Public Domain

Chapter 3

A Sense of History and Geography
Places and Times of Mother Marianne's Life

"Almighty God has chosen to define my religious life by two places: Syracuse, New York where I trained and prepared; and the Hawaiian Islands where my heart and mission led me closer to my Lord. My body may lie in state at our Motherhouse in Syracuse, but part of me will always be in Molokai."
-Joan Albarella, opening lines of play – Always in My heart

She had a fine command of English: it is clear, direct, uncomplicated, and yet not without the graces of a woman perfectly at ease in both the language and the social situations in which she is employing it.
-P&E

In this Chapter

Both New York State and the Islands that became the State of Hawai'i have a long history.

Hawai'i traces its origins to volcanic eruptions some 70 million years ago. As the volcanic eruptions accumulation, some of the islands rose above sea level.

Polynesian peoples began to live on the islands thousands of years ago. Native Hawaiians today trace their ancestry back 2,000 years to these early settlers of the Pacific archipelago.

The history of Hawai'i falls into four general periods: antiquity, monarchy, territorial, and statehood.

New York State traces its history back to the Ice Age and melting glaciers that shaped the landscape, to a period of woodlands and first peoples, to explorations by Europeans, along with settlements and colonization, to statehood at the time of the American Revolution.

Sister Alicia Damien traced the story of Hawai'i while Sister Fran traced the story of New York.

Brief history of New York State

A sense of the places and times of Mother Marianne's early life took place in the geography and history of New York State, especially Central New York and the Mohawk Valley, once her parents moved the family from Germany to the new world.

Glaciers, woodlands, and First Peoples make up the prehistory and early history of the area now known as New York State. In the 1600s and 1700s, French missionaries and explorers came in contact with the Five Nations of the Iroquois League, also know as the Haudenosaunee – People of the Longhouse. From east to west, these peoples included the Mohawk and Cayuga of the East, the Onondaga and Oneida of Central New York, and the Seneca as the Keepers of the Western Door. Later, the Tuscarora, also of Western New York, joined the Iroquois Confederacy as a sixth nation.

Franciscan, Jesuit, and Sulpician missionaries came with the early explorers and brought Christianity to the area. In the mid 1600s, some of the Jesuits met martyrs deaths and are remembered as the North

Chapter 3: A Sense of History and Geography

American martyrs. Three of the eight saints – Isaac Jogues, Rene Goupil, and Jean de LaLande - came to die in the Auriesville area, of New York State. The others died in Midland, Ontario, Canada.

Kateri Tekakwitha, a convert to Catholicism, lived from 1656 to 1680 in the Mohawk Valley. Kateri is one of six companions to Mother Marianne at the 2012 canonization ceremony.

By the late 1600s, following French and Indian Wars, the area became a British colony with suppression of Catholicism and harboring priests became a crime. What had been New Amsterdam on the Atlantic coast became New York under British rule.

With the Revolutionary War, beginning in 1776, New York colony became New York State. Religious freedom allowed Catholics to practice their faith more openly and Christians settled in various places. In the early years, all of the United States formed one diocese with its bishop in Baltimore. In 1808, four dioceses emerged as Baltimore, New York, Philadelphia, and St. Louis. All of New York State belonged to the New York Diocese.

The Irish came to dig the Erie Canal (later named the New York Barge Canal in 1918, a hundred years after its completion) and by 1825 canal traffic brought people and cargo to Buffalo, N.Y. and on to the Great Lakes.

Immigrants moved westward through the Hudson and Mohawk Valleys and the Canal into ethnic settlements of Irish, Germans, Poles, Italians, and other mostly European groupings. By the 1830s and 1840s, parishes with resident or visiting priests sprang up.

Father John Neumann (now Saint) came via the Erie Canal to Buffalo in 1836 and visited the rural parishes through 1840. So, when Barbara Koop was born in 1838, St. John Neumann worked in the 20 western counties of New York State. By the time Barbara came to Central New York, namely Utica, John Neumann had joined the Redemptorists and worked largely in Pennsylvania.

In 1847, New York State became three dioceses – New York, Albany, and Buffalo.

In 1859, the Order of Friars Minor Conventuals (Franciscan priests) came to Syracuse and established themselves at Assumption Parish and in parishes in other cities and towns of the region.

In 1860, the Sisters of St. Francis, headquartered in Philadelphia, came to Utica and Syracuse and worked with the OFM Conv. Fathers. In 1861, other Sisters of the Philadelphia foundation came to Buffalo, N.Y..

The Civil War raged on from 1861, just before Barbara Cope entered the convent through her first years as Sister Mary Anna. New York State's people participated in this war.

Also, in the 1860s, railroads became the popular form of travel and transportation. The New York Central line came from New York City to Buffalo, N.Y. and connected with other lines from there. In 1883, the West Shore line came from the Mohawk Valley to Depew, N.Y. and Buffalo, N.Y..

Many of the early missions of the Sisters of St. Francis relied on trains that had terminals in the towns where Catholic parishes were located. Mother Marianne and her six companion sisters travelled on trains across the country to San Francisco to get their boat to Hawai'i

In 1868, 12 counties of Western New York became the Rochester Diocese, leaving 8 for the Buffalo Diocese. In 1886, Syracuse became a diocese, separate from Albany.

Mother Marianne had already gone to Hawai'i before Syracuse became a diocese. Once in Hawai'i, she worked in the Honolulu Diocese.

In 1892, Mother Frances Cabrini (now Saint), crossed New York State and spent time in Buffalo. Another New York State saint, Elizabeth Ann Seton, was born in New York City in 1774.

Other events such as World War I and World War II and Vatican II affected New York State as well as the rest of the world. Mother

Chapter 3: **A Sense of History and Geography**

Marianne reached 80 in 1918 and must have known of the war that began in 1914. She died shortly before the end of that war.

New York State motto:
Excelsior – Ever Higher

A Saint for Central New York

As the time for the canonization of St. Marianne Cope drew near, CNY Central's Matt Mulcahy and WCNY's Liz Ayers, both of whom travelled to Rome for the ceremony, produced a series of vignettes called Mother Marianne Minutes for their respective television stations. The two also produced a St. Marianne documentary that aired on Thanksgiving 2012 evening in the central New York area. The Minutes were available at YouTube.

Another New York person connected with Hawaii is Charles Reed Bishop. His memory lives on at Kalaupapa in the Bishop Home campus.

Charles Reed Bishop
Prime benefactor of Bishop Home at Kalaupapa

Born in 1822 in New York State at Glens Falls near Lake George, Charles Reed Bishop grew up in the Methodist tradition at a tollhouse in the Hudson River where his father served as toll collector. He was two when his mother died and an aunt and later a grandfather helped raise him. He attended Glen Falls Academy for grades 7 and 8 and then became a clerk at a local business.

At age 24, he set out with a friend for the Oregon Territory. They travelled by boat around South America and arrived in Honolulu and decided to stay there.

Mr. Reed involved himself as a businessman and in 1849, and became a naturalized citizen of the Kingdom of Hawaiʻi. He invested in the sugar industry on Kauaʻi and served as commissioner of customs for Hawaiʻi. Also, in 1849, he began to court Bernice Pauahi Paki, a direct descendent of Hawaiʻi's Royal House of King Kamehameha. The couple married in May 1850.

In 1853, Bishop was elected to the legislature of the Kingdom of Hawaiʻi. He served in other government positions and founded a bank. In time, he founded the Bernice Pauahi Bishop Museum in Honolulu and funded the Kamehameha Schools.

At the time of Mother Marianne and her companion sisters going to Kalaupapa, Bishop gave substantial funds for the buildings, which became the Bishop Home complex. During Mother Marianne's time and under her supervision 12 buildings were added to the original five.

Once Hawaiʻi changed from kingdom to territory of the United States, Bishop moved to San Francisco where he worked in banking.

In 1905, the Charles R. Bishop Trust Fund sent money to Kalaupapa for repairs and improvements to the Bishop Home buildings.

Bishop died in June 1915, three years before the death of Mother Marianne.

As a fellow New Yorker with Mother Marianne, his name has come down through the years at the Bishop Home campus and services at Kalaupapa.

A Bit of Hawaiian History

It is believed that the first settlers in the islands had migrated from the Marquesas Islands as early as 600-700 CE which is approximately 800 miles north of Tahiti. The Polynesians arrived in Hawaiʻi by outrigger canoes from Tahiti. Lacking instruments of navigation or charts of any kind, the Polynesians sailed into the vast oceans. They used their knowledge of the sky, the stars, the sea and its currents, the flight of birds and many other natural signs.

When Captain Cook arrived in 1778, he knew that the Original Polynesians discoverers had come from the South Pacific hundreds of years before his time. There were approximately 300,000 Hawaiians

Chapter 3: **A Sense of History and Geography**

living on the islands. Captain Cook renamed the Islands the "Sandwich Islands" after the Fourth Earl of Sandwich. However, King Kamehameha protested and said that each Island should be called by its own name, and the entire group of Islands should be referred to as "Islands of the Kingdom of Hawai'i". The period of Kamehameha's rule was also known as one of decline. The Europeans and the American traders exploited the natural resources such as sandalwood, and brought devastating infectious diseases, which over the years, greatly reduced the native population.

The first missionaries came to Hawai'i in 1820 with evangelical zeal. As Calvinists they shaped the religious, political, intellectual, and culture future of Hawai'i. The alien sailors, whalers, traders, and wanderers breathed lawlessness by bringing in firearms and liquor. Christianity also destroyed the ancient deities of their native cultural traditions and customs.

In 1827, priests and brothers from the French Congregation of the Sacred Hearts of Jesus and Mary came as Catholic missionaries to the Sandwich Islands. Founded in 1800 in Paris, France, the religious congregation based its charism around the contemplation of the Sacred Heart of Jesus echoed in the heart of Mary, mother of Jesus. Four years later, in 1831, the Hawaiian chiefs under the influence of the Calvinists expelled the Catholics. However, in 1837, the Catholics missionaries returned but still suffered persecution.

Young King Kamehameha III, who ruled from 1825 until his death in 1854, relied on the missionaries for advice and allowed them to preach Christianity. In 1839, King Kamehameha III granted freedom of worship and by 1883, the Calvinists and Catholics tolerated and sometimes even accommodated each other. Meanwhile, the Mormons arrived in 1852 and Episcopalians in 1862.

In 1848, the islands' feudal land system was abolished, thus making private ownership possible and encouraging capital investments in land. As the sons, grandsons, and sons-in-law of missionaries came of age, they acquired huge sugar cane plantations and managed much of the business. These descendants held more interest in management of commerce, which they used to exert powerful influence over the economy and government of the islands.

Change came at a rapid pace - both in education and commerce. Because the Native Hawaiians were not used to the tedious labor of a plantation worker, the importation of labor from Asia (China and Japan) and the Philippines became necessary. This varied population gave rise to the immense variety of Hawai'i's present diversity of ethnic groups.

With the importation of labor from foreign countries, brought in diseases. In 1853, the Smallpox epidemic killed over 5,000 native Polynesians. It is believed that the Chinese brought leprosy to Hawai'i, and thus calling the disease, the "Ma'i Pake" disease – the Chinese disease.

With the Sacred Hearts of Jesus and Mary's fathers and brothers in Hawai'i for 37 years, they recruited more priests to come to Hawai'i. The Sisters of the Sacred Hearts of Jesus and Mary came to Hawai'i in 1859 to support the fathers and brothers in the field of education. In 1864, Father Damien De Veuster arrived in Honolulu and the bishop ordained him a priest at Our Lady of Peace Cathedral in Honolulu. At the same time, in the 1860s the spread of leprosy had caused alarm and panic and fear. In order to stop the spread of leprosy, the Government Act was instituted in 1865. Those who were suspected of having leprosy were exiled to the island of Moloka'i in the peninsula of Kalawao and Kalaupapa. On January 6, 1866, the first 16 leprosy victims arrived at Kalawao for isolation.

It was not until May 10, 1873, that Father Damien De Veuster arrived at Kalawao/Kalaupapa to care for those with leprosy. He spent 16 years caring for the physical, spiritual, and emotional needs of those with leprosy under a government - sanctioned medical quarantine on an isolated peninsula of Moloka'i.

It was at this same time, European nations were eager to add Hawai'i to their empire. The sugar planters and the American businessmen began to seek annexation by the United States. In 1843, the islands were officially granted their independence from Great Britain and remained a sovereign kingdom until 1893.

Chapter 3: A Sense of History and Geography

King Kalakaua and his wife, Queen Kapiʻolani, ruled the sovereign nation from 1874 to 1891. During this time, King Kalakaua was known to enhance the Hawaiian culture with its hula and chants and had a passion for music, parties, and the finest food and drinks. He was also a leader of a political organization called Young Hawaiians; the group's motto was "Hawaiʻi for the Hawaiians."

It was in 1883 that a request went out to 50 religious communities, asking for "sisters of mercy' to care for the women and children of leprosy which was spreading very rapidly. Mother Marianne Cope, a sister of St. Francis from Syracuse, New York, answered the call and came to the Sandwich Islands.

In July 1897, an organization called the Hawaiian League forcibly took control of the government and presented the King with a new constitution called the "Bayonet Constitution". King Kalakaua had little choice, but to sign it. This new constitution severely restricted his powers and signaled the end of the monarchy. In 1891, the ill King traveled to San Francisco to seek medical treatment. He died in a hotel on January 20, 1891.

Queen Liliuokalani succeeded to the throne when her brother, King Kalakaua, left. Queen Liliuokalani sought to amend the constitution to restore some of the power lost during the reign of her brother. She was on the throne in 1893 when the monarchy was overthrown by a group of American businessmen. The local sugar planters and businessmen feared a loss of revenue and influence and instigated an overthrow. Americans formed a Committee of Safety and declared the monarchy ended. After being imprisoned for eight months in Iʻolani Palace, the queen yielded her throne to avoid bloodshed. In 1884, the Republic of Hawaiʻi was established. On August 12, 1898, the government of the Republic transferred sovereignty to the United States. In 1900, Hawaiʻi became a territory of the United States.

The Territory of Hawaiʻi growth had accelerated in the pineapple industry as well at other crops such as sugar cane, cattle ranching, and tourism. Statehood was proposed in 1937 but the United States Congress refused the concept. They gave the reason as the territory's mixed population and the distance from the US mainland.

The US Navy set up its giant headquarters at Pearl Harbor and the Army built a large garrison at Scofield Barracks. On December 7, 1941, Japanese aircrafts made a surprise attach on Pearl Harbor, plunging the United States into World War II. The post war years brought in importance economic and social developments. A dramatic expansion of labor unions developed and was marked by major strikes in 1946, 1949, and 1958. The unions organized the waterfront workers as well as sugar and pineapple workers. Tourism grew to major proportions in the 1930s due to the advancements of air travel and further advancements in investment and developments.

After seeking statehood for many decades, Hawai'i was finally admitted to the union on August 21, 1959.

Mother Marianne and the sisters worked at the Branch Hospital and established a Home (named after Queen Kapi'olani) for the girls who were born from parents who had leprosy from 1883 to 1885; Mother Marianne then opened a home for the women and children who had leprosy in Kalaupapa.

From 1866 to 1969, about 8,000 patients were exiled and lived at Kalaupapa settlement. In 1946, Sulfonamide drugs came in to use to treat the disease of leprosy. Mr. Hansen had earlier identified the cause of leprosy as a bacteria band infection. Now, the drugs put leprosy in remission and make the disease non-contagious.

However, it was not until 1969, that the Board of Health in Hawai'i ended the isolation laws for the patients in Kalaupapa. The patients were free to leave; however, many chose to stay because this was their home.

In a later chapter, Mother Marianne's work in Hawai'i will be described in depth.

For 53 years, Hawai'i has been part of the United States. As with any young state, it has had its growing pains. However, the sugar cane and pineapple fields are no longer in existence. Tourism and healthcare are the largest industries in the State of Hawai'i.

Chapter 3: **A Sense of History and Geography**

Motto of the State of Hawai'i

Ua mau ke ea o ka aina l ka pono
The life of the land is perpetuated in righteousness.

Four women at Kalaupapa in the early 20th century

Photo: Courtesy of the Congregation of the Sacred Hearts of Jesus and Mary

Chapter 4

History of Hansen's Disease
The L word – and also early treatments

Had not the seraphic saint himself said: "More than all grace and all the gifts of the Holy Ghost, which Christ vouchsafed to his friends, is the conquering of yourself and the willing endurance of suffering, injustice, contempt, and harshness.
-P&E

In this Chapter

Leprosy as a dreaded disease dates back thousands of years to pre-Christian times. Egyptians first knew the disease and at the time of the Roman world, the disease spread to the Mediterranean countries and from Italy into the rest of Europe. The Crusades of the 11th, 12th, and 13th centuries also transmitted the disease and by the 12th and 13th centuries, at much as one fourth of Europe's population may have suffered with the disfiguring and non-curable signs of the disease.

The disease of leprosy

People thought of the disease in those days as a punishment from God and generally banished those who had it to live outside the cities and towns. Treated as outlaws, those afflicted with leprosy had to ring bells or shout out – "Unclean!" to announce their presence. St. Clare of Assisi, St. Francis of Assisi, St. Elizabeth of Hungary and other saints made it their mission to reach out and take care of those who had the disease of leprosy.

People with compassion did make special hospitals called Leprosaria where the sick received food, shelter, and care. The 15th century bubonic plague brought death to many already weakened by the disease of leprosy. For centuries, not much happened.

And then Damien came to Moloka'i and the world took notice.

And Dr. Hansen, and Gandhi, and Dr. Goto, and Alice Bell … and Mother Marianne and the sisters.

In late January, people around the world celebrate the feast day of Saint Marianne Cope on January 23.

A week later, on January 30 / 31, people celebrate World Leprosy Day on a date selected to honor Mohandas Gandhi (1869 – 1948) who died on January 30, 1948 – 30 years after the death of Mother Marianne.

Saint Marianne and Saint Damien, as well as Gandhi expressed throughout their lives and throughout their ministries, a clear compassion and tenderness towards patients with the disease of leprosy.

Jan 30 / 31 World Leprosy Day Connects with the martyrdom of Gandhi

Gerhard Hansen

Gerhard Henrik Hansen (1841 – 1912), a contemporary of Mother Marianne, studied leprosy as a doctor in Norway. In 1873, he isolated the mycobacterium leprae and began to set up medical offices for the treatment of the disease. People often refer to the Medical Museum in Bergen, Norway, birthplace of Gerhard Hansen, as the Leprosy Museum.

Chapter 4: **History of Hansens's Disease**

Raoul Fellereau

Raoul Fellereau created World Leprosy Day in 1954 to raise awareness and concern for those afflicted with Hansen's disease worldwide. The year 2013 will mark 60 years of this effort.

Mohandas Gandhi

A generation after Mother Marianne and Father Damien, Mohandas Gandhi of India took a special interest in the medical and social aspects of leprosy as a disease with no known cure.

Even while he lived in South Africa, Gandhi showed compassion to persons with leprosy. When a beggar knocked at his door, Gandhi brought him in and saw that the beggar was in an advanced state of leprosy. Gandhi prepared food for the beggar, dressed the beggar's sores, and kept him as a guest.

Gandhi also faced quite a dilemma when a leprosy patient he befriended and corresponded with wanted to join the ashram. Fearing that this could well put in jeopardy the health of the children, women, and men already residing at the ashram, Gandhi made the decision to place the friend in a separate cottage near Gandhi's home. There, Gandhi in person provided food and nursed the man's wounded body and soul.

Gandhi's compassion for those with leprosy dates back to his childhood. At age 13, Ladha Maharaja came to the home to recite verses from the Ramayana to Gandhi's sick father. It was said that Ladha had suffered from leprosy but cured himself by praying Ramayana verses and by applying Bilwa leaves to his sores. This helped Gandhi to not have the usual fear of lepers and their disease.

There is a well-known picture of Gandhi tending to Parshure Shastri in Yeravada Jail in 1932. Both men lived in the same prison, but the guards denied Gandhi permission to visit the leprosy ward. Gandhi began a long string of correspondence with Parshure. This same Parshure is the man who later asked Gandhi about coming to the ashram.

Another photo shows Gandhi studying leprosy under a microscope in 1940.

Hawaiian response to the disease of leprosy
by Anwei Skinsnes Law

"Hawaiian response to leprosy:

"First of all, I think it's really important to note that although there was the attempt to exclude people from society from the side of the foreigners, this was not the thinking of the Hawaiian people. In fact, the whole separation of families was far worse for them than the disease itself.

"I think that one reason that Mother Marianne and Father Damien were so beloved by people is that they understood this separation – each of them being separated from their families and Mother Marianne from her religious community in Syracuse. Even though their separation was initially by choice and the separation of the Hawaiian families was not, Mother Marianne and Father Damien also had separation from their community forced on them at different times. They well understood the losses brought about by separation and each did what they could to support those who had been separated from their families and communities.

"At any rate, I think it is very important to make a distinction between the foreigners' response to leprosy and the Hawaiian response. While the foreigners sought to exclude people from society – the Hawaiians sought to keep people included in their families and their communities. They would keep people at home as long as possible and, when permitted, accompany them to Kalaupapa.

"There were five family members with the first group of 12 people sent there and the archive collection has so many letters written in Hawaiian, asking for a family member to go along as a kokua (helper)."

Chapter 4: **History of Hansens's Disease**

Something to Ponder:

"Do not call them lepers anymore, no please remove that word, they are leprosy patients", says Father Joseph Raja Roa, a Montfort Missionary from Bangalore, who for years has worked among people suffering from Hansen's disease, more commonly known as leprosy.

"To Mary, Mother of Mercy and Health of the Sick, we entrust our brothers and sisters who are afflicted by leprosy so that her maternal compassion and nearness may accompany them always, in the daily events of life as well."

Also, it's most appropriate to entrust Hansen's patients to the care of St. Marianne Cope of Kalaupapa, Moloka'i.

http://www.news.va/en/news/world-leprosy-day-when-good-will-bears-fruit

Use of the term "leper"
by Anwei Skinsnes Law

"While this appears frequently in historic references – it did not have the same connotation as it has today. So when Sister Leopoldina and Mother Marianne used it, it was not with the terrible meanings it has today.

"In addition, letters translated from Hawaiian will so often say "we the people who are sick with leprosy" or "we the people overtaken with the leprosy disease". The "people" always come first – as they did with Mother Marianne and the sisters.

"So, I think it's important to really think about use of this term as it is very hurtful and offensive to individuals who have leprosy today. I am sure you know this already, but I just think it is so important to have history be accurate and also sensitive.

"The St. Marianne Museum in Syracuse as well as literature being compiled by the sisters in recent years reflects this. I was interested to see that the booklet for the pilgrimage to Rome for Mother Marianne's canonization had the first section (about St. Francis which I imagine was put together by the Franciscan pilgrimage representatives) filled with the word "leper" while the biographical timeline (which I imagine was put together by the sisters) did not use this word."

-From personal correspondence between Anwei Law and Sister Fran Gangloff

Masanao Goto

"I have not the slightest confidence in our American and European doctors to stay my leprosy. I wish to be treated by Dr. Masano Goto."
- Father Damien, 1886 / http://www.stmariannecope.org/

"We have now a Doctor from Japan here – who makes the treatment of Leprosy a speciality (sic) – he comes daily to the hospital and treats 70 patients … "
- Saint Marianne, 1886 / http://www.stmariannecope.org/

Born in Japan on March 6, 1857, Masanao Goto devoted his life to patients with leprosy both in Japan and in Hawai'i. Known as a leprologist, Dr. Goto brought his treatment to Honolulu in 1885.

Dr. Goto combined moderate exercise with nourishing food, plus special ointments (chaulmoogra oil) and medical baths, along with a type of friction to any areas of numbness. Hawaiian patients found relief of their symptoms and sought the treatment.

Father Damien trusted Dr. Goto's treatment methods and Father Damien sought the Goto treatment for himself as well as bringing what he could of the treatments to Moloka'i.

One of the hardships, among many, for Damien's later years, came in the way his superiors forbade him to come to Honolulu for more treatments after his 1886 visit.

Chapter 4: **History of Hansens's Disease**

Chaulmoogra oil

The use of chaulmoogra oil from the seeds of certain trees, especially the chaulmoogra tree, shows up in writings about the early 19th century in India. Burmese folk tales speak of it even centuries earlier as a treatment for the relief of the symptoms of the disease of leprosy.

In the latter decades of the 19th century, the oil found its way to Hawai'i as a treatment for Hansen's disease, with some relief for the patients, but no cure.

Alice A. Ball – the "Ball Method"

Graduate student Alice Augusta Ball (MS '15) was the first chemist to find an extract to treat Hansen's disease.

A native of Seattle, Alice moved with her family to Hawai'i, and later back to Seattle.

She graduated from the University of Washington with two degrees – in pharmaceutical chemistry and in pharmacy – in 1912 and 1914, respectively.

In 1914, she began studies at the College of Hawai'i (later the University of Hawai'i) and as a graduate student pursued a research study on the effects of chaulmoogra oil in the treatment of patients with Hansen's disease. With her groundbreaking work, she developed a process of injection of chaulmoogra oil, but became ill and died at the age of 24. The chairperson of the chemistry department continued and refined her work – known as the Ball Method – and took it with limited success to Kalaupapa Hospital.

The Ball Method continued as the best treatment until the 1940s when sulfonamide drugs came to the forefront.

1969 – Turning Point

Not only is Kalawao the smallest county in all the States of the United

States, it is also a place where the population continues to decrease. For census purposes, Kalawao County is a county. As for residence and visiting, the Hawaiian Department of Health has jurisdiction over the area.

Under Hawaiian law – monarchy, territorial, and statehood, this tiny peninsula on the north shore of the Island of Moloka'i – persons with Hansen's disease (leprosy) found themselves quarantined and banished from 1865 until 1969.

The year 1969 marked a turning point for those affected by leprosy. The government lifted the ban and the people gained freedom to leave or stay. Some chose to stay in residence in the tiny settlements of Kalaupapa or Kalawao. They had the freedom to travel and return home here. Others chose to move away.

The Sisters of St. Francis chose to continue to stay and minister to those in residence. The sisters no longer had to take excessive means of precaution, only normal ones.

Evidence of these changes show up in the sisters' stories about clothing, food, visiting, and more. The sisters could more freely visit the patients in their cottages and buildings.

About 40 sisters came on assignment over the years from 1888 to 1970 and about another 20 since then. Some stayed many years while others stayed a short time. Also, dozens and dozens of sisters came as na kokua (helpers) to help out during school breaks and other times so those assigned could go for home visits, doctor appointments, vacations, and retreats.

When the Hawaiian government discussed the situation in 1969, some wanted to entirely close down the settlement. Don Ho and Don Picken intervened on behalf of the patients, because many of them wanted to remain there for life. While no new patients needed isolation as outpatient care took care of them, some of the longtime resident patients with physical and emotional scars knew Kalaupapa as their only home for decades.

Chapter 4: **History of Hansens's Disease**

And so, the Sisters of St. Francis continued to come and serve as nurses and helpers.

Both Mother Marianne and Gandhi expressed throughout their lives and throughout their ministries a clear compassion and tenderness towards patients with the disease of leprosy.

Part Two

The Life of Mother Marianne

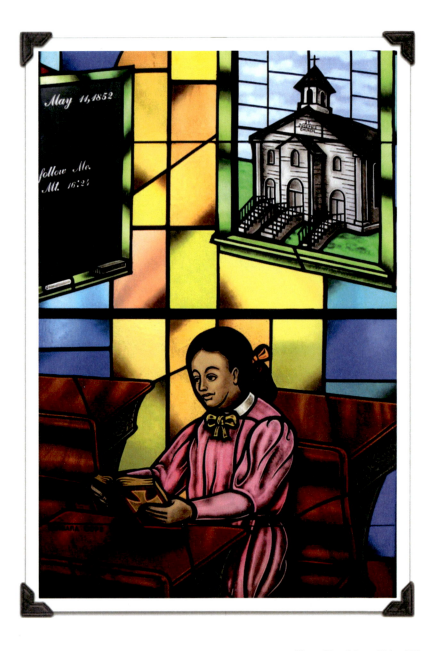

Photo: Tom Mayer, Utica, NY

Chapter 5

Barbara Koop
the Child, the Teen, the Young Adult

If she had not done so in Utica and Syracuse, in Hawaii she discovered the pleasures of gardening. She liked to grow potted ferns and parlor plants. In Honolulu Mr. Gibson noticed this interest and built—"as a present to the Sisters"—a small-glassed conservatory beside the convent at Kakaʻako.
-P&E

In this chapter

The parents of Barbara Koop, born on January 23, 1838, in Heppenheim, Germany, took her the very next day to St. Peter Church for her Baptism.

As a small child, Barbara moved with her parents and siblings to Utica, N.Y. where they registered at St. Joseph German Church. Barbara attended school through grade 8, received the Sacraments of Confirmation and First Communion, and lived as a good parishioner.

When her father took ill, Barbara took a job at the nearby woolen steam factory and helped support her family throughout her teenage years.

Mary Ann Barbara's Birth Date and Ancestry
Birth date and Feast date – January 23

"How many graces did He not shower down upon me," she assured Paul Cope, "from my birth till now - Should I live a thousand years I could not in ever so small a degree thank Him for His gifts and blessings. I do not expect a high place in heaven - I shall be thankful for a little corner where I may love God for all eternity."

- Hanley, O.S.F. Sister Mary Laurence; O. A. Bushnell (2009-11-01). *Pilgrimage and Exile: Mother Marianne of Moloka'i* (Kindle Locations 7674-7676). Mutual Publishing, LLC. Kindle Edition.

When the Vatican set a feast date for Mother Marianne (Barbara Koop), they chose her birthdate of January 23 because St. Edith Stein's feast day falls on the date of Mother Marianne's death – August 9. Some others, including Anne Frank who told her family to observe her birthday after her death, rather than her death date, find remembrances of them observed on their birth dates.

Heppenheim, Germany

In this lovely Rhine Valley, ancient remnants of Roman times linger in towers and walls and bridges. Market crosses stand in town squares. Hildegard of Bingen and other saintly persons came from this land.

Born at Heppenheim, Hessen-Darmstadt, West Germany, on January 23, 1838, Barbara's parents Peter (1787 – 1862) and Barbara (Witzenbacher) (1803 – 1872) took her to church for her Baptism the very next day.

Birthplace and farmhouse of Barbara Koop, 1838

The Koop's ancestral family had lived in the Heppenheim District (then the Grand Duchy of Hesse) for at least two generations. Peter, as a third son, would not have inherited his family's land. That would go

Chapter 5: **Barbara Koop - Childhood, Factory Work**

to the eldest and the others could work for the eldest. This condition of poverty encouraged him to look for alternatives and he settled on immigration.

Peter's first marriage brought into the world nine children, only two of whom reached adulthood. Peter married his second wife on February 14, 1830. Barbara was the fifth child of this marriage. Later, after the family moved to the United States, five more children were born.

Baptized as Maria Anna Barbara, she used the name Barbara during her childhood and young adulthood.

Barbara's godmother was Barbara Koob, daughter of Peter and his first wife.

St. Peter church in Heppenheim lies in the shadow and valley of Starkenberg castle on the hill. Its tall steeple could be seen for miles around the wall-enclosed town with a moat. The windows told Biblical stories.

The baptismal font made as an octagon of gilded copper holds a cover structured like a mirror image of the font. The handle on the font represents the whole world topped by a cross.

Photos of the baptismal church and home parish of Barbara may be found at
http://ourlordand.powweb.com/SAINTS/MotherMarianne.html

Cope Family in Utica

The family moved to the United States and settled in Utica, N.Y. a city near the banks of the Mohawk River and the Erie Canal (later called New York State Barge Canal).

The family joined the Catholic parish of St. Joseph, with about 40 German-speaking families in a city of 10,000 people. This proved to be quite different from the close-knit and walled village of their homeland. Utica offered not trees but the chimneys of factories. At first, the family lived on Varick Street close to the "German church". Peter did not take up farming but found work in the city.

By 1840, the Koob family was one of 65 families attending this parish. St. Joseph was one of the very few German Catholic churches between Albany and Buffalo. At that time, all of New York State comprised one diocese of New York.

In 1841, Peter was able to buy a piece of land and then mortgaged that to buy land on Schuyler Street, at 706, where he built the family home. The address of 706 now sits as a vacant lot, but the Koob / Cope family lived there for 30 years. Peter and his wife kept the name Koob, but the children changed the family name from Koob to Cope. Other spellings in the city of Utica included Koop, Kob, Kap, and Kopp. The Koob Family lived about a half mile from their parish church.

In 1847, the Dioceses of Albany and Buffalo were created. Buffalo consisted of 20 counties, 12 of which are now the Rochester Diocese. The middle of New York State belonged to the Albany Diocese.

About the same time, the Utica Steam Woolen Mill sprang up right across the street from the Cope household.

Barbara attended public school the first few years. As soon as the parish school opened, she went there. In 1848, Barbara received her First Holy Communion. Also, the bishop from Albany came to St. John's, a larger church and the principal Catholic Church in Utica, for Confirmation for Barbara and others.

By the time Barbara finished grade 8, her father was ill and became an invalid. Barbara, as the oldest child at home, went to work in the Woolen Mill to support the family.

Already, at age 15, Barbara had the desire to enter the convent but postponed that wish while helping her family.

By 1855, Peter became a naturalized citizen and all the children automatically became United States citizens. The 1855 and 1860 census indicates that Barbara was at work in a factory, most likely the

Chapter 5: **Barbara Koop - Childhood, Factory Work**

nearby Steam Woolen Mill where the workers made sheets, pillowcases, towels, and underwear.

Steam Woolen Mills of Utica

The Utica Globe Mill (1847 – 1855) and the Utica Woolen Mill (1855 – 1859) and Globe Woolen Mills Company (1859 until 1971 fire) and Globe Woolen Mills Company rebuilt after the fire – all seem to apply to the same company.

Nicholas Devereux, of Ireland, came to Utica, N.Y. when it was just a small village and helped turn it into a city by 1832. Mr. Devereux helped establish the Utica Steam Woolen Mill and served as director, stockholder, and vice president. He also helped establish railroads and water works in Utica.

Nicholas Devereux also helped the Franciscan Fathers come to Allegany County in Western New York where they worked together to establish St. Bonaventure University.

The Cope children were bilingual, speaking English in school and German at home. In 1865, Mrs. Koob could read and write German but not English. The youngest child Catherina by age 21 used English only.

The late Sister Mary Laurence Hanley (d. 2011) in her research and writings shows that Barbara's formative years in Utica give evidence of a happy child and cheerful giver. In a somewhat frugal and austere household, she learned the domestic skills of cooking and sewing, typical of the times. She seemed to have humor and grace and tact as well as intelligence.

There are no childhood photos of Barbara.

In a letter to her nephew in 1898, Mother Marianne tells him that when she was his age and younger, she was obliged to struggle and wait nine long years to accomplish her dream to enter the convent. She encouraged the nephew to practice "duty towards your poor Papa."

By age 15, Barbara went to work in the factory. Her father's aging and illness made it impossible for him to work. For nine years she did this to provide for the family.

Barbara Cope – teen, young adult

"Probably her enjoyment of studies made her want to be a teacher. She had a fine command of English: it is clear, direct, uncomplicated, and yet not without the graces of a woman perfectly at ease in both the language and the social situations in which she is employing it. Spelling, diction, syntax, style are correct without being stiff. Like most Americans, now as then, she did not pay much attention to the rules of punctuation. When circumstances warranted, she used the German and American colloquialisms of her era."

- Hanley, O.S.F. Sister Mary Laurence; O. A. Bushnell (2009-11-01). *Pilgrimage and Exile: Mother Marianne of Moloka'i* (Kindle Locations 478-482). Mutual Publishing, LLC. Kindle Edition.

Like most girls of her time, Barbara left school after grade 8. She had mastered English language skills as shown in her later writings. She also maintained her knowledge of German and was able to speak and write well in both languages.

In a similar manner, Barbara went to work after grade 8 (c. 1852) – as a factory worker in the mill across the street. With her father's illness, her income supported the family.

Mother Marianne Cope

Photo: Courtesy of St. Marianne Cope Shrine
and Museum of the Sisters of St. Francis of the Neumann Community

Chapter 6

Sister Mary Anna/Mother Marianne
A Sister of St. Francis

"I never travelled very far during my early journeys as a sister, but I traveled often.
"The words of St. Francis became my compass and my strength. 'True progress quietly and persistently moves along without notice.' "
-Joan Albarella, Always in My Heart

She did not command: she led cheerfully, with tact and humor and grace, by example at all times, and with a most marvelous understanding of the feelings of her associates.
-P&E

In this chapter

Some Sisters of St. Francis, founded in 1855 in Philadelphia under Bishop John Neumann, came to Utica's St. Joseph Parish and Barbara made their acquaintance.

Wishing to join the Sisters, Barbara did wait and continue working until the death of her father. She entered the convent in 1862 and received the name of Sister Mary Anna Cope, with the change of surname along with her family.

Sister Mary Ann received several teaching and principal assignments in area towns – Syracuse, Rome, N.Y. Oswego, and her hometown of Utica. Mother Mary Bernardina and Mary Anna founded St. Elizabeth Hospital in Utica.

Later, the two leaders of the Sisters established St. Joseph Hospital in Syracuse.

In time, the Sisters elected Mary Anna to be their general superior and she became known as Mother Marianne. She used her leadership skills and compassionate care for everyone she met for the welfare of all.

Then, one day a letter came asking for missionaries who would serve as sister – nurses for the Islands in the Pacific Ocean.

Foundation of the Sisters of St. Francis of the Third Order Regular

St. John Neumann, bishop of Philadelphia, assisted three young women, Anna (Boll) Bachmann, Johanna Boll, and Anna Dorn in forming the Sisters of St. Francis of the Third Order Regular in April of 1855. A year later, the three women professed their vows as Sister Mary Francis, Sister Mary Margaret, and Sister Mary Bernardina in Bishop Neumann's private chapel. The sisters began a school at St. Alphonsus in Philadelphia.

John Neumann died on January 5, 1860, and Bishop Wood became bishop of Philadelphia

While Barbara finished formal schooling and took up work at the factory, the Sisters of St. Francis began new missions from Philadelphia to Syracuse in what was then the Diocese of Albany in 1860 and to Buffalo in 1861. Bishop Wood required both groups in New York State to separate from the Philadelphia Diocese and to belong to the dioceses in which they lived and worked.

Chapter 6: **Sister Mary Anna/Mother Marianne**

Mother Bernardina became superior in Syracuse and Mother Margaret in Buffalo.

Mother Mary Francis, who remained superior in Philadelphia, traveled to Syracuse and Buffalo to assist the fledgling communities and bringing with her additional sisters from Philadelphia.. While in Buffalo in the winter of 1862 – 1863, Mother Francis caught a cold. After returning to Philadelphia, her illness grew worse and she died on June 30, 1863.

Mother Francis left her daughters – Johanna who became Sister Mary Robertine and Kunigunda who became Sister Mary Francis – with the Buffalo Sisters.

In 1860, the Sisters of St. Francis led by Mother Bernardina came to Syracuse and Utica. Barbara held an interest in entering the convent and spoke of this with Mother Bernardina. Barbara continued to work in the factory for nine years, seeing it as the Will of God for her at the time,

In the previous year, the new bishop of Albany had sent Franciscan Friars, OFM Conventual to St. Joseph Parish in Utica.

When the Sisters of St. Francis came in 1860, they settled into a convent named St. Clare and taught in the school. By this time, Barbara was 22 and she came to know the superior, Mother Bernardina, who probably encouraged her to be patient in the delay of entering the convent. She probably told her that duties to parents take precedence.

Peter died in July 1862 at the age of 75. With her mother's blessings, Barbara entered the convent on August 26, 1862, as a postulant at St. Clare Convent in Utica.

A Sister of St. Francis
Barbara's Novitiate at Syracuse

In the late fall of 1862, Barbara travelled, probably by buggy or train, to Syracuse, 70 miles west of Utica, to St. Francis Convent.

On November 19, 1862, at Assumption Parish Church, Barbara and some other young women received the habit of the Sisters and began their novitiate training. Barbara received the name of Sister Mary Anna.

Professed Sister

A year later, five novices were ready to make profession of the vows of religion - poverty, chastity, and obedience - according to the Rule of the Third Order Regular of St. Francis. The newly professed sisters received the black veil and the cross that they would wear. They also signed their last will and testament. This newly professed sister signed hers at the time as Sister Mary Ann Cope.

Sister Mary Anna teaches at Assumption school

In the 1864 Chapter of Elections and Affairs (special meetings of the Sisters), the sisters elected Sister Antonia as general superior (mother superior) and Sister Marianne as vicaria or deputy. She continued her work in the school at Assumption Parish with some of the sisters.

Other sisters moved to a new location of about 20 acres at the north end of the city. The old farmhouse became the convent known as St. Anthony Convent. The sisters turned the living room into the chapel.

Today, St. Anthony Convent at this location houses the Shrine of St. Marianne. Other buildings in and around the block provide offices and residences for the many sisters who live and work there. Also, the central leadership of the united group knows as the Sisters of St. Francis of the Neumann Communities have their offices at this site.

Sister Marianne's name morphed through Mary Anna to Maryanna to Marianne. She served as vicaria at both Syracuse convents while continuing to teach at Assumption School. In those days children were quite docile and sisters were very obedient.

The sisters prayed together the Little Office of the Blessed Virgin

Mary in Latin. This community prayer lasted well into the middle 20th century.

The sisters attended Mass and received Communion in the parish church. Mass was in Latin then and remained so until the mid 20th century.

Sister Marianne had a wonderful ability to lead and direct the sisters without rousing resentment, a quality that kept her in positions of trust.

Schools and Hospitals

Beginning in January 1866 at age 28 and continuing for 17 years, Sister Marianne moved about as local convent superior and school principal. She went to Rome, N.Y. as superior, and then to St. Peter in Oswego on the Lake Ontario shoreline as principal of the school and superior of the convent.

St. Marianne Cope Hall in the former convent – school building on Albany Street in Oswego, N.Y. holds the honor as the only existing building in which Mother Marianne lived. Assigned in 1866 to St. Peter School of St. Peter German Catholic Parish, Sister Marianna (her name at the time) served there as superior of the convent and as teacher and principal of the school until 1869.

The convent - school building of the 1860s, a square structure painted white, still stands next to St. Peter Church. In 1987, the parish re-dedicated the building, which serves as a parish hall, as Mother Marianne Hall. Recently, a new sign honors – Saint Mother Marianne Cope. The interior staircase and bannister of the original building remain in place. St. Marianne would have walked these stairs every day.

When Mother Marianne lived there, the school was downstairs and the convent upstairs. Now the upstairs holds offices while the downstairs provides a hall for parish events.

At the Syracuse convent of the Sisters of St. Francis, the 1860s Record Book of Perpetual Profession reveals, "Sister Marianna has the intention of doing school work in the Order."

As Sister Marianna, she also taught at schools in Utica, Rome, and Syracuse – all in New York State.

In August 1868, she went to her home parish of St. Joseph in Utica and also St. Patrick's. This brought her near to her mother and also her brother John Peter, age 19, still living at home and working in the woolen mill. Other family members lived nearby. And in 1869, Sister Marianne went back to Oswego. All of these assignments came and changed as the needs arose.

In 1866, Mother Bernardina and Sister Marianne started a small hospital – St. Elizabeth in Utica.

St. Joseph Hospital, Syracuse

In 1869, the sisters opened St. Joseph Hospital in Syracuse to treat patients with typhoid and malaria. In June 1870, the sisters appointed Sister Marianne as hospital nurse and administrator, a role she learned on the job. She replaced Sister Dominica, a stormy, abrasive, and harsh person, whose temper often flared. Sister Dominica seems to be the one and only declared antagonist of Mother Marianne.

Sister Marianne made it her philosophy and her practice to make no distinction of color, nationality, or theological belief as to the treatment of patients. All found welcome and care. Sister Marianne always safeguarded the dignity of each and every individual.

The two hospitals were among the first 50 general hospitals in the entire United States. Both St. Elizabeth and St. Joseph continue to this day as hospitals of compassionate care.

During her administration, Sister Marianne arranged for the Central New York Medical College at Geneva, N.Y. to move to Syracuse University and for the medical students to work at St. Joseph Hospital.

"I am happy to inform you that the Sisters of St. Joseph Hospital

Chapter 6: **Sister Mary Anna/Mother Marianne**

cheerfully grant the Medical Students of the Syracuse University the privilege of having admission to the Hospital for clinical instruction."
- Mother Marianne, October 23, 1872 / Unpublished Letters of Mother Marianne

More demanding role

Sister Marianne had a childhood of 15 years, a factory worker job for 9 years, and 17 years as a woman religious, a Catholic sister. In those years she served as teacher and principal of schools and local superior of convents, as founder and administrator of hospitals, as general secretary of the province, and as director of novices.

Hospital ministry brought the most demands of all these roles as it required fund raising, accounting and reporting, supervision of all departments, and relating with people at every level.

The day after Thanksgiving, known as Donation Day, brought in the generosity of the donors. For Sister Marianne, it meant thank you letters to them and she did write the letters while she breathed many a prayer to the Giver of all good things.

On July 9, 1872, Sister Marianne's mother Barbara died at the age of 69. About this time, Sister Marianne learned that she had pulmonary tuberculosis, an ailment that bothered her time and again during her long life.

Also in 1872, Sister Marianne worked for the cooperative arrangements of transferring the medical college in Geneva to Syracuse University.

As general secretary, she handled the business of the whole congregation of the Sisters of St. Francis spread out over central New York State and served as advisor and confidante of her friend, Mother Bernardina.

In 1874, at the General Chapter, the sisters re-elected Mother Bernardina and Sister Marianne as general superior and assistant superior of the congregation.

Elected as Mother Marianne – 1877

At the next Chapter in 1877, the sisters elected Sister Marianne as the general superior, as Mother Marianne. Now she was in charge of 62 professed sisters, nine school missions, and the two hospitals.

In 1881, Mother Marianne was re-elected to a second term of office. Two additional schools had been added to the care of the sisters; one in Albany, N.Y. and one in Trenton, N.J. Expansion was underway at St. Elizabeth Hospital and construction had started on a new chapel at St. Anthony Convent.

The Letter

In June of 1883, Mother Marianne received and read the letter from a priest, Father Leonor Fouesnal, who searched the United States for sisters to come to Hawai'i to serve as nurses. Mother Marianne sat down to write a response to this letter.

"I was not at home when your letter came, hence this late reply.
"I hardly know what to say in reply to it. Shall I regard your kind invitation to join you in missionary labors, as coming from God?
…
"My interest is awakened, and I feel an irrestable (sic) force drawing me to follow this call."
- Mother Marianne, June 5, 1983 / Unpublished Letters of Mother Marianne

Heritage Communities

Mother Bernardina as a good friend of Mother Mary Francis Bachmann, and along with Mother Mary Margaret Boll, blood sister of Mother Mary Francis, formed a small community in 1855.

Bishop Neumann helped these three women establish the Sisters of St. Francis in Philadelphia in April 1855.

The sisters who went to Syracuse were separated from Philadelphia by

Chapter 6: **Sister Mary Anna/Mother Marianne**

the authority of the bishop in 1860. The sisters in Buffalo met their separation in 1863, the same year that Mother Mary Francis died. Over time, other sisters went to missions outside their home diocese and met with bishop-imposed separations. A group in Hastings on the Hudson, N.Y. and a group in Millvale, near Pittsburg, Pa, met this fate. The separations along diocesan boundaries created painful memories for the sisters who had once been in one and the same congregation.

Other groups made their novitiate training with one of the groups and had some affinity for the Franciscan sisters who knew Bishop Neumann.

Heritage Days

In the early 1980s, some sisters from the various branches began brainstorming and meeting. This led to annual Heritage Days at the various regional convents where the sisters learned more about each other. They thought of each other's communities as cousins.

The founding members in 1855 included Mother Mary Francis Bachman, Mother Mary Margaret Boll, who came to Buffalo, and Mother Bernardina Dorn, who came to Syracuse. Mother Marianne belonged to the Syracuse branch, but all the Sisters happily claim her as their Saint.

In 2004, the branches of Buffalo, Syracuse, and Hastings formed a Union named the Sisters of St. Francis of the Neumann Communities. The Franciscan Missionaries of the Divine Child had merged with the Buffalo group in 2003.

In 2007, the Millvale sisters merged with the Sisters of St. Francis of the Neumann Communities. Later, several of the Whitehall sisters merged with the Sisters of St. Francis of the Neumann Communities.

Photo: Sister Barbara Jean Wajda

Chapter 7

Missionary to Honolulu, Hawai'i

Before she assigned the newcomers to duty, Mother Marianne granted them a period of eight days in which to recover from the fatigue of the journey and to adjust to the heat and humidity of Honolulu. Those days of grace also helped them to recover from the shock of seeing their first lepers, in the compound beyond the fence.
-P&E

In this chapter

Mother Marianne led the band of six sisters across the United States by train and from San Francisco to Honolulu by boat. The sisters began their work at Kaka'ako Hospital, a leprosarium. At the same time they settled into a convent in Honolulu.

The sisters had many things to get used to. Once Mother Marianne realized the need for a home for healthy girls of parents with leprosy, she founded Kapi'olani Home in Honolulu.

Mother Marianne also travelled to Maui to set up a hospital and school at Wailuku.

The Letter and the Trip
Marianne and the sisters go to Hawai'i

"The charity of the good knows no creed and is confined to no one place."
- Mother Marianne, 1870s / http://www.stmariannecope.org/

"I hope the Fr. Provincial's good heart will approve my wish to accept the work with leprosy patients in Hawai'i in the name of the great Saint Francis."
- Mother Marianne, 1883 / http://www.stmariannecope.org/

"Seldom has the opportunity come to a woman to devote every hour of thirty years [at Moloka'i] to the mothering of people isolated by law from the rest of the world as have been these people. She risked her own life in all that time, faced everything with unflinching courage and smiled sweetly through it all. She came to Honolulu ready to do whatever was required of her. Without blare of trumpets, Mother Marianne entered upon her duties and through thirty long, wearisome years living apart from the world and its comforts, she labored in the cause of a stricken people. She was a heroine in life; she is a martyr in death."
- Mrs. John Bowler, society woman who met Mother Marianne in 1882 upon her arrival.
Honolulu Advertiser, August 11, 1918
http://www.stmariannecope.org/

Of almost 50 request letters sent to the various congregations of women religious in 1883, Mother Marianne's response was the only positive one. Father Leonor Fouesnel, a priest from Hawai'i travelled the mainland from west to east in search of sisters who would come to serve as nurses. Marianne's answer gave him the one and only ray of hope. The priest did not mention at first that the sister nurses would work with patients with leprosy. He painted quite a pretty picture of the paradise islands and said that he sought nurses for the hospital.

Mother Marianne responded that her interest was awakened and she wanted to join him in missionary labors in the islands. Though some

Chapter 7: **Missionary to Honolulu, Hawai'i**

used the term – Sandwich Islands – the native peoples preferred the term – Hawaiian Islands.

In the 1880s, the Kingdom of Hawai'i with a king and queen made its headquarters in the capital city of Honolulu.

In the early 1880s, a Protestant flavor pretty much ruled the Islands, though liberalist and materialist trends eroded even their sway.

Walter Murray Gibson, a former Mormon, served as prime minister under the king and had the idea to invite "Sisters of Charity" to take care of people with the disease of leprosy. He did care for the needs of the native people and sought proper care for those who were sick, especially those exiled to the Island of Moloka'i.

Walter Gibson

Walter Gibson served as an advocate of value to Mother Marianne and the sisters. He had some faults. The Catholic bishop Hermann saw him as a fox.

When Mr. Gibson had appealed for a "noble Christian priest, preacher or sister" Father Damien said yes to a three-month period at Moloka'i and then almost immediately decided to stay on permanently.

"I am willing to devote my life to the leprosy victims," Father Damien said. He had come to Hawai'i in the place of his brother who had taken ill in Belgium.

(After Father Damien's death, Father Pamphile, this brother of Damien's came out to Kalaupapa for about two years. He found the climate / weather very challenging.
(See a later chapter for more on Father Pamphile.)

In the late 1870s and early 1880s, Mr. Gibson served alternately as legislator and as prime minister. He had secured the approval of the king and queen for better care of anyone who had contracted the disease of leprosy.

The Disease of Leprosy

While today the preferred term is Hansen's disease, in the 1800s leprosy and leper were the terms of use.

The first case of leprosy in a native Hawaiian dates to 1840, coming perhaps from China. By 1882, thousands had it, both natives and immigrants. Bishop Hermann Koeckemann of Honolulu and Mr. Gibson had many discussions about it and hoped that Catholic sisters would be willing to help where Protestants feared to tread.

By 1883, Mr. Gibson served as president of the Board of Health in Hawai'i. He dearly wanted sisters "to come to the help of the sick in this country" and he began his search for hospital sisters.

Many women religious had risen to the need for nurses during the Civil War in the States. And many had nursed in fledgling hospitals.

To some degree, Father Leonor's trip to the U.S. in April 1883 set in motion a kind of struggle between the Catholics and Protestants to secure sister nurses. He sent out the 50 letters (perhaps 47) to various Catholic convents throughout the country.

Mother Marianne's response to him cheered him and he came to Syracuse in July 1883 to talk with her. During the visit, the priest did tell Mother Marianne that the sick people had the disease of leprosy. Sister Leopoldina Burns, a novice at the time, later wrote about that day and how Father Leonor told all the sisters and novices of the great need. Thirty-five of the sisters volunteered to go, to cheerfully go.

Shortly after the visit, Mother Marianne wrote her answer to the priest. On July 12, she wrote:
"I am hungry for the work. I am not afraid of any disease."

God's Spirit stirred the very depths of Mother Marianne's soul as she pondered God's design for her life. For her, it was more than schools and hospitals and the role of mother superior. The call of those people most in need in a faraway land spoke to her heart and mind and will.

Chapter 7: **Missionary to Honolulu, Hawai'i**

No one knows what went on in the heart and mind and soul of Marianne in making her decision. She must have felt that it was her true vocation to be mother to each person suffering with the dreaded disease, even when that meant letting go of her role as provincial superior in Syracuse.

"I am hungry for the work and I wish with all my heart to be one of the chosen ones, whose privilege it will be, to sacrifice themselves for the salvation of the souls of the poor islanders.

"I am not afraid of any disease, hence it would be my greatest delight to minister to the abandoned 'lepers'."
- Mother Marianne, July 12, 1883 / Unpublished Letters of Mother Marianne

The sisters worked out the details over the summer of 1883.

With their decision to take on the mission to Hawai'i, the Sisters of St. Francis of Syracuse became the first congregation founded in the United States to initiate mission work in foreign lands. Up to that point, missionaries had come from Europe to various world sites. Now, the U.S. had a homegrown Catholic presence venturing out to other peoples.

And though she told the sisters that she would be gone a short time, she might well have known she would stay. From a largely German group of women, Mother Marianne picked five sisters of Irish background and one of Dutch background.

Mother Marianne and the six sisters going with her made their final preparations in the early fall. After a farewell Mass, the sisters left Syracuse on October 22 with travel plans to Chicago, Council Bluffs, Omaha, Ogden, and San Francisco where they would meet their boat on November 1. The trip lasted six days and six nights and proved to be stressful and exhausting to the sisters.

A Moment in Buffalo

At the Buffalo station, Mother Marianne got off at the terminal and took a train back to Syracuse. In the excitement of goodbyes and leaving Syracuse, she had forgotten her purse. She walked back in to the convent while the sisters were still talking about her leaving. She got her purse and quickly got a train and caught up with her group in Chicago. The purse contained important letters of introduction, documents, and addresses of contacts.

San Francisco – before bridge

The sisters had a few days in San Francisco until time for the steamer. On November 1, they boarded the Mariposa, a hundred foot long vessel. With 32 steerage passengers below deck and 31 on the main deck, the boat also carried 1,330 tons of merchandise.

First glimpse of the Islands

Mother Marianne was seasick the whole time and ever after seasick on any boat. On their seventh day out to sea, they had their first glimpse of Hawai'i. They saw the mountains, the low Island of Moloka'i with its flat leaf peninsula known as Kalaupapa.

When they arrived in Honolulu, Father Leonor came to the dock to verify that they were on the boat and he rushed back to town to tell the queen and the king.

Aloha!
Many turned out to welcome the sisters.
Our Lady of Peace Cathedral, Honolulu

The cathedral bells rang out across the city. Five royal carriages carried the sisters past I'olani Palace and to the doors of Our Lady of Peace Cathedral where the Bishop Hermann Koeckemann welcomed them.

In a grand ceremony of blessing, the organist played beautiful hymns

Chapter 7: **Missionary to Honolulu, Hawai'i**

including the Te Deum. Benediction of the Blessed Sacrament completed the cathedral event.

Changes in Hawai'i's History

Mother Marianne and her companions arrived at Honolulu, Hawai'i, in November 1883. They lived through the years of Hawaiian monarchy and missionaries into the times of revolution and territory. The early sisters lived through the years of Hawaiian monarchy. The sisters that followed lived into the times of revolution and territory and eventually into the time of Statehood for Hawai'i.

Mother Marianne and the sisters settle in Honolulu

"For us it is happiness to be able to comfort, in a measure, the poor exiles, and we rejoice that we are unworthy agents of our heavenly Father through whom He deigns to show His great love and mercy to the sufferers."
-Mother Marianne, 1884 / http://www.stmariannecope.org/

"We bring no gift to Your Majesty except our service in behalf of your suffering people, whose infirmity we bear in our hearts."
-Mother Marianne, 1884 / http://www.stmariannecope.org/

On the day after their arrival, King David Kalakaua and Queen Esther Kapi'olani visited the sisters. Both felt great alarm at the rate of leprosy in their island kingdom and expressed gratitude to the sisters for coming.

Though promises had been made, nothing was really ready for the sisters. Construction of the convent had barely begun and wouldn't be ready for several weeks. At first, they stayed with the sisters at the cathedral convent.

Then Mr. Gibson rented a big house in the heart of town for the sisters and arranged for a carriage each morning to take them to and from Mass. The sisters set up their household and established a daily routine.

While fruits and vegetables remained inexpensive, anything imported came with a high price. The sisters set about setting up their household. Little by little, the sisters grew used to the language and absorbed the Pidgin English and island vernacular.

Though the queen and king attended St. Andrew's Episcopal Cathedral, they grew fond of the Catholic sisters. Mother Marianne and the sisters visited the queen's sick sister in her beautiful castle. Kapi'olani gave money to the sisters for building a home for healthy children and was quoted as saying:
"You are my Sisters. I love you and you will always be my Sisters."

Sights and Smells at Kaka'ako

Mr. Gibson took Mother Marianne and Sister Bonaventure to visit the Branch Hospital at Kaka'ako. Established in 1881 on a salt marsh, the facility served as a receiving station for people suspected of having leprosy. Sometimes other diseases, especially scabies and fungal infections, resembled leprosy. Doctors needed a place to sort things out.

Mother Marianne and Sister Bonaventure came face to face with the stench of the untended sores. They saw the overcrowded conditions where 200 lived in a place built for 100.

Not much grew there because the ocean salt water washed in and killed any vegetation.

Most of the people who had the disease felt abandoned by God and rejected by humans. Most countries simply exiled anyone with the disease and left him or her to fend for himself or herself. Hawai'i spent more money than any other country on improving conditions for those with leprosy.

Later, Sister Leopoldina wrote about Mother Marianne's memories of that first visit. She wrote:
"Mother Marianne could easily see what good the sisters could do there."

Chapter 7: **Missionary to Honolulu, Hawai'i**

This, after the sisters had noted the filth and flies, the lice and bed bugs, the faces of despair, the horrors of what they saw that day.

"To us it is shocking to see how poorly the helpless females are protected, and how much they are exposed to danger."
...
"Their pitiable condition appeals strongly to our sympathy."
- Mother Marianne, January 1884 / Unpublished Letters of Mother Marianne

The New Convent

The sisters moved into the new convent on January 3, 1884. In her letter home, Sister Bonaventure described the two-story house that was painted white inside and out. The convent sat near Honolulu Harbor at the edge of the hospital compound.

The day began at 4:30 a.m. with one sister ringing a hand bell to awaken the rest. By candlelight, they dressed and met for prayer in their small chapel. At 6:15 a priest came for Mass and some patients with leprosy also came for Mass. Breakfast followed.

On January 7, Mother Marianne sent word to Mr. Gibson that they were ready for work and that they saw much that could be changed.

The sisters worked at the hospital for the morning, came home for their main meal at noon, and went back to work until suppertime. In the evening, they did household chores and assembled for prayers before heading to bed.

Though they found the resident steward and the physician uncooperative, the sisters with quiet and cheerful efficiency went about providing better care for the patients along with improving sanitary conditions and morale.

The sisters, especially Mother Marianne, had to deal with "state" in the form of persons of royalty and government officials in this foreign land. Sister Angelyn Dries points out that "The Sisters mission mindset moved fluidly between their work and spirituality." (MM in AMCH, page 54) In their chapel they honored the Eucharistic Body of Christ. In their work they honored the bodies of the leprosy patients they attended.

(Dries, Angelyn, OSF. *The Missionary Movement in American Catholic History.* Maryknoll, N.Y. Orbis Books. 1998. Copyright by Angelyn Dries, 1998)

The sisters brought grace to the state of affairs in 1884 Kaka'ako Hospital.

Medicine Women

Over the next several months of work at the hospital, the sisters found that the men, Mr. Gibson and the Board of Health, the directors of the hospital, and others all wanted the sisters to serve as nurses in the wards. The men did not want Mother Marianne or the sisters to take on administrative roles.

Mother Marianne, used to being the administrator, found it hard to accomplish things like cleanliness and safe procedures when those over her thwarted her.

If the sisters felt their exile in this foreign and male dominated situation, the patients felt exile even more.

"For us it is happiness to comfort in a measure the poor exiles," Mother Marianne wrote to Mr. Gibson.

Godliness and Cleanliness

The sisters set about cleaning up the place, especially the hospital kitchen, the cookhouse, and the dining hall.

While Mr. Van Giesen, administrator, continued to be as uncooperative as possible, the sisters went ahead and housecleaned the residential cottages.

Chapter 7: **Missionary to Honolulu, Hawai'i**

The patients noticed the good example of the sisters and the good deeds that truly showed the old adage that "cleanliness is next to godliness". Father Leonor wrote his superiors about his approval of the sisters as he called them "our saintly Franciscan sisters."

Early on, Mother Marianne insisted that the sisters assign a sister as housekeeper and cook for the convent to prepare the meals for the sisters. None of the sisters who worked at the hospital were allowed in the kitchen. Mother Marianne also insisted on constant hand washing for the sisters as a way to not catch the disease.

At the time, over 200 persons with Hansen's disease resided at Kaka'ako Hospital. Doctors feared the disease and most would never touch a patient. The sisters willingly dressed the sores and did all in their power to improve the sanitary conditions of the entire complex of a hospital without walls.

In an 1887 report, Mother Marianne did admit to "many trials and difficulties in the first few months" but the sisters bore these with courage and prayer.

With the presence of the sisters and the improvements they wrought, the patients came to love the sisters and thought of them as angels, as "Sisters of Mercy" as they were often called.

Often, Mother Marianne would attach a note asking that a young person or a child heading to Kalaupapa would be taken to Father Damien.

Meanwhile, back in the states, the Diocese of Syracuse, also known as the Diocese of Central New York, came into being in November 1886. The Sisters of St. Francis now belonged to the Diocese of Syracuse, rather than the Diocese of Albany.

Branching Out

"We were not only willing but anxious to go and care for the poor outcasts."
- Mother Marianne, 1887 / http://www.stmariannecope.org/

"My heart bled for the children and I was anxious and hungry to help put a little more sunshine into their dreary lives."
- Mother Marianne, 1889 / http://www.stmariannecope.org/

"Her religious career, first as a sister, later as a mother superior, would show, from beginning to end, that she was an excellent teacher and administrator. She did not command: she led cheerfully, with tact and humor and grace, by example at all times, and with a most marvelous understanding of the feelings of her associates. After a while, when she grew older and more confident, she led her people with a dignity, a serenity, that subdued the most obstreperous adversary and soothed even the most weary sister."

- Hanley, O.S.F. Sister Mary Laurence; O. A. Bushnell (2009-11-01). *Pilgrimage and Exile: Mother Marianne of Molokaʻi* (Kindle Locations 465-468). Mutual Publishing, LLC. Kindle Edition.

Hospital in Maui

When Mr. Gibson invited Mother Marianne to go to Maui to work at a hospital there, she got caught up in the tensions between Protestants and Catholics. Mother Marianne had to come to an understanding of the politics involved.

Calvinists and Episcopalians wanted to outrival the Catholics by bringing some Episcopalian sister-nurses to the hospital at Wailuku on Maui. Protestants felt that Catholics already had Father Damien and Mother Marianne for their side.

Marianne did say "Yes" to the Maui hospital and also started a school at the same location.

Chapel at Kakaʻako

For the dedication of the convent chapel at Kakaʻako, a special celebration in January 1884 brought Father Damien to Honolulu. Mother Marianne met him in person for the first time. It is likely that he asked her to consider sending sister-nurses to Molokaʻi.

A statue of St. Philomena adorned the sisters' chapel. Also, the layout of the chapel included doors that could be opened to the other side where those with leprosy could attend Mass. Mother Marianne was putting into practice a philosophy that she expressed in letter to a benefactor of St. Joseph Hospital in Syracuse. She had written:
"The charity of the good knows no creed, and is confined to no one place."

In this respect, Mother Marianne was way ahead of her time in promoting ecumenism and good relations among the various religions.

In her book – *The Missionary Movement in American Catholic History* (1998), Angelyn Dries, OSF, writes of "the ecumenism of good works" of the "Sisters of Charity" as people in Hawai'i often called them, along with "Sisters of Mercy" and "Angels of Mercy". Sister Angelyn praised "Such an ecumenicity" and also explained the role that several ethnic situations – German, Irish, Italian with differing languages, foods, and devotions - played in the life of Mother Marianne before she even went to Hawai'i. (pages 51 to 54)

Malulani Hospital in Wailuku

The very next day after the chapel dedication, Mother Marianne and two sisters left for Maui, leaving four sisters in Honolulu.

As usual, Mother Marianne was sick at sea, especially during a storm that came up. Small boats came out to bring the passengers ashore and the storm nearly washed them all out to sea. However, they did reach land in midnight darkness. Sick, terrified, and exhausted, they travelled the seven miles on bad roads to the hospital in Wailuku.

Sister Antonella who accompanied Mother Marianne to Wailuku remained very sick for days after the arrival. She had pulmonary tuberculosis, which flared up. By year's end, she died.

By the 1860s the first sugar plantation along with its mill house and factory had grown up near the Catholic mission at Wailuku. On land given by the "Sugar King" the new hospital was clean but empty. The sisters had to gather what was needed and set it up for patients.

Princess Liliuokalani, sister of the king, visited the hospital in March 1884 and inspected it with Mother Marianne as guide. Mother Marianne invited the princess to select a name for the hospital and she called it - Malulani - meaning child of heaven - under the protection of heaven.

Mother Marianne gave Sister Antonella charge of the school, but by June she was too sick to continue. Sister Antonella died there December 12, 1884, at age 27. She was buried at the mission.

Mother Marianne and Sister Renata continued hospital work and lived in a tiny convent bungalow nearby

Franciscan sisters continued to operate this hospital until 1929. It was a general hospital, not a leprosarium.

Officially, still the mother superior of the whole province in Syracuse, Mother Marianne carried on her responsibilities via correspondence.

Father Leonor and Mr. Gibson continue to work in the background towards sending Mother Marianne and sisters to Moloka'i.

Malulani later became a state run hospital and still serves the people of the area.

Back at Kaka'ako

The sisters tried to reverse the "reign of terror" and cruelty to the patients under the leadership of Mr. Van Giesen. The bishop came and listened to the sisters. Mr. Gibson made promises that were never kept. He pretty much ignored the conditions under Mr. Van Giesen. To bring some solution to the conflict, the bishop asked Mother Marianne to come back to Honolulu.

Mother Marianne had left Sister Bonaventure as deputy. Mr. Van

Chapter 7: **Missionary to Honolulu, Hawai'i**

Diesen disliked the sisters and scorned them as well as the patients. Some of the stories written down by Sister Leopoldina years later derive from memories of the pioneer sisters.

Sister Leopoldina pictures this time as the greatest crisis that Mother Marianne handled. Caught in the cross purposes of the bishop and of Mr. Gibson and of Mr. Van Diesen, Mother Marianne told them all that she and the sisters would not stay unless certain conditions were met. One of those conditions stated that Mr. Van Giesen must be removed. Mr. Gibson, as prime minister at the time, sent Mr. Van Giesen to a job at Moloka'i and gave the sisters full charge of the hospital in April 1884.

Under the care of the sisters, the patients came to love them and the place. They felt more at home rather than in prison. Some preferred to stay there to being sent anywhere else.

"We have almost constantly 200 sick here afflicted with a horrible disease … "

"Sometimes our duties are very trying, but God is good to us and helps us out of all difficulties. I think it is all owing to the good prayers of our dear ones at home."

- Mother Marianne, August 1984 / http://www.stmariannecope.org/

Marianne's Bodhisattva Smile

In her book, *Pilgrimage and Exile*, Sister Mary Laurence writes highly of Mother Marianne's strengths. Sister Mary Laurence calls the faint smile as seen in the few photos of Mother Marianne "a bodhisattva's smile" of peace. In Buddhism, a bodhisattva is one whose motivation is compassion for others.

Sister Mary Laurence writes of Mother Marianne as a quiet woman with quiet purposefulness, a private person, with external serenity and peace and with a pure spirit of humility and deep spirituality.

Marianne must have come into contact with Asian patients with Buddhist beliefs and her compassion would easily have gone to them.

"Let us make the very best use of the precious moments and do all in our power for His dear sake and for His greater honor and glory."

- Mother Marianne, 1900 / http://www.stmariannecope.org/

"I do not think of reward; I am working for God, and do so cheerfully."
- Mother Marianne, 1902 / http://www.stmariannecope.org/

Mother Marianne at Kakaʻako

Once Mother Marianne became administrator at Kakaʻako, she put in place a new set of rules aimed at efficient and sanitary management.

Mother Marianne sent Sister Bonaventure to Malulani as superior along with Sister Renata and Sister Antonella to the hospital on Maui. Sister Bonaventure served in this place for the next 20 years.

By spring of 1884, at the Kakaʻako convent, Sister Rosalia grew ill. Sister Ludovica kept house and took care of Sister Rosalia. Mother Marianne and Sister Crescentia took care of the 200 patients, dressing their sores and keeping the dispensary clean. Sister Crescentia spent 10 hours a day attending to wounds, often outdoors on the veranda.

In June, the sisters held a fundraiser. In July, Mother Marianne visited every home in the settlement at Kakaʻako.

Mother Marianne remains general superior of Syracuse Sisters

With her term of office as general superior coming to an end in July 1884, Marianne sent word to Syracuse to excuse her from the upcoming chapter meetings. Meanwhile, the Franciscan father in charge of the Syracuse sisters decided to postpone the election for a year. This left Mother Marianne in charge of the whole province to administer from her faraway place in Hawaiʻi.

Chapter 7: **Missionary to Honolulu, Hawai'i**

When the king and queen asked for more sisters, none in Syracuse felt ready to come out to the mission. Rumors had circulated that the sisters were tending leprous wounds when servants should do that. Sisters in Syracuse also feared that they would all be sent to Moloka'i.

She moved a house

In the summer of 1884, Mother Marianne had the convent moved, dragged by horses to a higher place. She wanted better drainage for the house.

To do this, workers took down the fence and it never went up again. The six-foot fence had always made the sisters feel isolated. Marianne did have a wall put up to serve as a boundary between the women and the men. She included the convent with the women's side to signal the sisters' solidarity with the women patients.

Marianne also had every cottage refurbished. She oversaw landscaping and the planting of grass, shrubs, and trees.

Olinda Gomes – Sister Mary Elizabeth

In October 1884, a 17-year-old Portuguese young woman came to help the sisters. Olinda Louisa Gomes prepared meals and did housework for the sisters. The Portuguese Passenger Manifest of the Hawai'i State Archives shows that Olinda arrived with her family – her parents, two sisters, and a brother on the S.S. Bordeaux from Madeira on October 3, 1884.

Later, she entered the convent and became Sister Mary Elizabeth. She accompanied Mother Marianne on journeys among the islands. In the 1930s, she gave testimony based on her memories of times spent with Mother Marianne.

More sisters come to Hawai'i

In the spring of 1885, four sisters came to Honolulu – Sisters Benedicta, Martha, Carolina, and Leopoldina.

"Before she assigned the newcomers to duty, Mother Marianne granted them a period of eight days in which to recover from the fatigue of the journey and to adjust to the heat and humidity of Honolulu. Those days of grace also helped them to recover from the shock of seeing their first lepers, in the compound beyond the fence. "

-Hanley, O.S.F. Sister Mary Laurence; O. A. Bushnell (2009-11-01). *Pilgrimage and Exile: Mother Marianne of Moloka'i* (Kindle Locations 4440-4442). Mutual Publishing, LLC. Kindle Edition.

It never became exactly clear when Mother Marianne decided and knew in her heart that she must remain in Hawai'i. Sister Bonaventure seemed less than able to oversee the Hawaiian missions and this may have influenced Mother Marianne's decision to stay there.

For a long time, Mother Marianne and the sisters lived in some uncertainty about the future of the missions in the islands. They did not know if the next Franciscan priest protector might order them all home. They did not know if the Hawaiian government or the Catholic diocese would send them away or create an act that would establish them as a separate group in Hawai'i.

Commissary Provincial

When the Syracuse sisters held their chapter in August 1885, they elected Mother Delphine as the general superior. The sisters re-elected Delphine over the next several Chapters to a total of 22 years.
In 1885, the Syracuse leadership appointed Mother Marianne as commissary provincial of the Sandwich Islands (the term in use at that time).

Kapi'olani Home

"This Institution is called 'Kapi'olani Home' and is under the patronage of the queen. Her majesty the queen takes a deep interest in the suffering poor among her people."
- Mother Marianne, in her 1887 Account of the Mission
Seeing that healthy children, who could not stay with their sick parents,

needed care, Mother Marianne began planning an orphan home for them on the convent grounds.

One little girl, Ellen Davis, also called Snowdrop brought this need to light. The sisters placed Snowdrop with relatives. But often, no relatives would take such children.

When Kapi'olani home was ready, Mother Marianne tried to hire a matron, but no one came. Sister Martha took charge of the home and the children.

Queen Kapi'olani presented the keys to Mother Marianne on a red velvet pillow, which now rests at the Mother Marianne Museum in Syracuse.

At first, the girls resembled street urchins, but with time they settled in and thrived under the care of the sisters. One story tells how seven of the girls went missing one day and an all out search even into the city and the mountains did not find them. Then, the five-year-old Annie told the sisters that she knew where they were. And sure enough, they had hidden themselves under the foundation of the house.

Kapi'olani Home moved to three other locations in the Honolulu area until it closed in 1938.

On November 9, 1885, the king bestowed on Mother Marianne the Order of Kapi'olani with its related medal, which is now preserved at the St. Marianne Museum in Syracuse.

Changes in Hawai'i

The late 1880s brought many significant changes to Hawai'i. The owners of huge sugar plantations and the related merchants and businessmen became unsettled with the king and his officials who tried to unite all of the Polynesian Islands. The merchants resented the extravagances of the king's court and had no use for the king's revival of native dances, chants, rituals, and medical practices.

Mr. Gibson – Again

While Mother Marianne and the sisters appreciated gifts from Mr. Gibson, more and more he wanted attention from Mother Marianne. His diary reveals his egocentric desires for her attention. She and the sisters remained friendly with him, but Mother Marianne always saw him with another sister present.

Indicative of his undue attention is the gold ring he gave Mother Marianne on March 12, 1887, on the two-year anniversary of her decision to remain in the Islands. The Archives of the Franciscan Sisters in Syracuse now hold that ring.

Mr. Gibson became a Catholic late in life and died as a Catholic in 1888.

Reform Government

When the reform government appointed Dr. Nathaniel Emerson as head of the Board of Health, he requested that the sisters continue their work as before.

Charles R. Bishop, a philanthropist gave $5,000 towards the building of a home on Moloka'i, the Bishop Home for Girls.

During the late 1880s, much discussion took place about the Franciscan Sisters going to Moloka'i.

On June 15, 1888, the Hawaiian government made the decision that all persons of any age who were sick with leprosy would go to Moloka'i. The officials considered combining all care of them to one place.

Strength from God

"Creep down into the heart of Jesus. He alone can comfort you in your supreme hour of sorrow."
 - Mother Marianne, 1904 / http://www.stmariannecope.org/

"Try to accept what God is pleased to give you no matter how bitter-

Chapter 7: **Missionary to Honolulu, Hawai'i**

God wills it, is the thought that will strengthen you and help you over the hard places if we wish to be true children of God."
Mother Marianne, 1905 / http://www.stmariannecope.org/

"Let us make best use of the fleeting moments. They will not return."
- Mother Marianne, 1905 / http://www.stmariannecope.org/

Makanula - Northern peninsula of Moloka'i

Makanula Peninsula on the northern side of the Island of Moloka'i has come to be known as Kalaupapa because of the leprosy settlement there. The flat leaf peninsula was formed from flowing lava. The volcanic crater still sits near the center of the promontory and contains a lake inside. The sea cliffs behind the peninsula rise steeply to the upper area of the Island of Moloka'i.

In the 1800s, Hawai'i sent people with leprosy to this remote place with a salt marsh edge. Here, those people felt and literally were poor outcasts, banished, isolated, segregated, shunned and left to die. Lacking understanding of the disease, society at large feared those with the sores of leprosy, resented them, and wanted them gone. Many native Hawaiian families tried to hide and care for their own but officials tried to weed them out.

September 1888

Mother Marianne, accompanied by Olinda Gomes (later Sister M. Elizabeth) and by Dr. Emerson, travelled to Moloka'i. He got just as seasick as she did. He had a much greater dread of leprosy than she did. When the storm caused Mother Marianne's glasses to fall off and slide across the deck, it was Olinda who retrieved them and gave them back to Marianne.

Mother Marianne had previously insisted that the details of what work the sisters would do be put in writing. She had enough of verbal promises never kept.

Mother Marianne, like Father Damien, served as an early pioneer of social justice, of compassionate justice in the care and treatment of the physical needs of each person afflicted with leprosy as well as love for their souls and spirits.

When Father Damien came to Kakaʻako hospital for treatment, he and Mother Marianne had long conversations. Mother Marianne's plan to go to Molokaʻi came to birth at this time.

A white cross faces the sea and sits below the pali at Kalaupapa

Photo: Sister Barbara Jean Wajda

Chapter 8

Kalaupapa, Hawai'i
Kalaupapa on north shore of Moloka'i

Sister Leopoldina, in her account of this initial day, devised one of the most amazing understatements in the history of compassion when she wrote: "Mother Marianne could easily see what good the Sisters could do there.

Joseph Coudrin, founder of the Congregation of the Sacred Hearts of Jesus and Mary, explained in more elegant terms the insuperable power of Christian love: "Nature may shudder, but in the end grace will triumph."
-P&E

In this chapter

Five years after her arrival in Honolulu, Mother Marianne with two other sisters took the boat to Moloka'i to take care of women and girls at the Bishop Home in the settlement at Kalaupapa. During their first year there, Father Damien of nearby Kalawao died.

Mother Marianne and the sisters, as promised, took care of Baldwin Home for Boys until new arrangements could be made.

The Makanalua Peninsula holds three districts – Kalawao, Kalaupapa, and Makanalua in the middle.

Visitors including Robert Louis Stevenson, Edward Clifford, and Katherine Fullerton Gerould visited the area and their writings gave the world a better understanding of the place.

Priests including Father Pamphile de Veuster, brother of Father Damien, Father Paul Juliotte, and others came as pastors for the Catholic Church. Father Juliotte took many photos of the patients so they would have pictures to send to their families.

The Mormons, Protestants (Calvinists), Catholics and other religious groups worked well together in a convivenecia that lasted down through the years.

Mother Marianne died on August 9, 1918. Other sisters carried on the work and some also wrote their memoirs of their days in Kalaupapa.

Kalawao and Kalaupapa

Father Damien settled in one area of the peninsula, an area known as Kalawao. Mother Marianne and the sisters settled on the opposite side of the peninsula at Kalaupapa. The settlements sat on either side of the old volcanic crater. The distance between the settlements was about three miles.

The beach at Kalawao is more stone than sand and the endless rumbling and groaning of water on rock makes it a dangerous, even treacherous landing place. Small boats went out to meet the large steamers. Sometimes the captain and sailors dropped parcels and even passengers into the sea to ride the waves in or to drown in waves going out.

Kalaupapa offered a somewhat gentler shoreline.

As early as 1865, the Hawaiian government moved leprosy patients to this peninsula. Though some healthy Hawaiians, free of the disease of leprosy, still fished and farmed here, the government tried to move the

Chapter 8: Kalaupapa, Hawai'i

well people to the topside of Moloka'i.

By 1887, the reform government moved all persons known to have leprosy to the peninsula where they were surrounded by sea and cliffs.

Mother Marianne's visit around the peninsula took about three hours. She visited Father Damien at Kalawao and then went to Kalaupapa where the Bishop Home construction had begun. She noticed that the convent was nicely furnished. When Sister Leopoldina wrote about this convent where she had lived for 40 years, she told how she loved to watch the rough waters and the great high waves as the mighty power of God.

On her way back, Mother Marianne went to Wailuku on Maui to visit the sisters working there at the hospital.

Correspondence

Mother Marianne kept up a steady flow of correspondence with the sisters back in Syracuse as well as the officials of church and government in Hawai'i.

Deciding who goes

Mother Marianne talked with each sister in Hawai'i, at Wailuku and at Honolulu to determine her willingness to go to Moloka'i.

Sister Vincent said: "Willingly."

Sister Leopoldina said: "Yes, Mother, I can."

Sister Rosalia declared: "No indeed. I'll not go to Moloka'i."

Before they left, Sister Leopoldina received the blessing of Father Gregory who was dying of leprosy. He died the next day.

November 13 was set as the day for sailing to Moloka'i. About 40 patients travelled with the sisters. While the sisters boarded at

Honolulu, the patients were brought out to the steamer by small boats from the Kaka'ako Hospital.

"We had a pleasant moonlit night and a calm sea all the way but that did not prevent us from being sea sick."
- Mother Marianne, November 1888 / Unpublished Letters of Mother Marianne

Mother Marianne made the decision to take Sister Leopoldina and Sister Vincent with her as the pioneers. Mother Marianne decided who should stay at Kaka'ako and Wailuku. At Kalaupapa, Father Damien was among those who met and welcomed them. He offered Mass at the little church.

On day, when visiting Father Damien, Mother Marianne went with Brother Dutton to inspect some construction work. Meanwhile, Father Damien persuaded Sister Vincent and Sister Leopoldina to eat a meal with him. Mother Marianne had forbidden the eating of food with the patients and the eating of food prepared by the patients.

The two sisters confessed their transgression to Mother Marianne that evening. Early the next morning, Father Damien appeared to ask forgiveness also for having urged the sisters to eat at his home.

Edward Clifford visits Father Damien

Edward Clifford, from England, visited Father Damien in 1888 and sketched a portrait of the priest as well as scenes of the peninsula.

Mr. Clifford admired the quiet way that Damien so often sat down and prayed and how he prayed his breviary, even while the artist worked on the sketch.

Mr. Clifford wrote an account of his visit to Kalaupapa and his time with Damien in a book titled *Father Damien*.

Chapter 8: **Kalaupapa, Hawai'i**

Bishop Home

Once the sisters arrived at Kalaupapa, they took care of the patients of Bishop Home, so named for the donor who provided the funds. Women and girls resided here.

At the time, the water line was broken and not yet repaired so the sisters caught rainwater in a barrel. They referred to it as coffee because of its brown color tasting of paint and wood.

Later stories call this early convent the "hardship house" for its barren landscape, scarce food, and water problems.

Mother Marianne also observed the 25th anniversary of her profession in November of 1888, on the 19th, the feast, on the pre-1969 church calendar, of St. Elizabeth of Hungary, a Franciscan saint. On this day, the convent as well as the convent chapel was named and dedicated to St. Elizabeth of Hungary.

Arriving in Kalaupapa on November 14, 1888, Mother Marianne wrote a letter home to Syracuse on December 8th and said:
"Here I am at the Leper Settlement on the Island of Molokai, to which place we .... came on the 14th of November. And here it was that I spent the 19th, the twenty-fifth anniversary of my profession. On that day, the house we live in was blessed and placed under the patronage and protection of St. Elizabeth. I was happy to do something in honor of the dear Saint on whose feast 25 years ago, I have received so many and great graces."

Marianne - at age 50

If Kaka'ako offered Mother Marianne the greatest crisis of her life, Kalaupapa perhaps brought her the deepest joy and the fulfillment of her dream to minister to the patients in so much need.

At the time, more than a thousand patients resided on the peninsula. Most lived from six months to about four years.

When the sisters visited Kalawao, Father Damien showed them St. Philomena Church and his little house among the graves of the people he had buried. When Father Damien visited Kalaupapa, he knelt outside the sisters' chapel as he now had leprosy and dared not enter.

In her journal and in her correspondence, Mother Marianne noted that there are many hardships in the beginnings of all institutions. She had started enough to know this well.

One of the hardships of those early days was Sister Vincent who often sulked with fear. Mother Marianne put her in charge of the convent to clean and cook and thus Sister Vincent had no contact with the patients.

Sister Leopoldina also felt some fear and dread and asked Mother Marianne: "What will you do with me if I become a leper?"

Mother Marianne told her: "You will never be a leper nor will any sister of our order."

Mother Marianne seemed to have no fear of the patients or of their disease. She gave wholehearted service to them cheerfully. A visiting priest who was not sick did come for Mass in the convent chapel and for the sisters and the patients.

I wish you all the blessing you may stand in need of to become a perfect child of Saint Francis – that you may say with him in all sincerity – "My God and my All."
Mother Marianne, 1903 / http://www.stmariannecope.org/

"God giveth life; He will take it away in His own good time. Meanwhile it is our duty to make life as pleasant and as comfortable as possible for those of our fellow-creatures whom He has chosen to afflict."
- Mother Marianne, 1905 / http://www.stmariannecope.org/

Water

In time, a new pipeline for water and other improvements made life better.

Chapter 8: **Kalaupapa, Hawai'i**

Of the patients, 95% were native Hawaiians. A few immigrants from various places also contracted the disease.

The sisters had no breaks, no vacations as such, no retreats as such. They did enjoy occasional outings such as walks to the stream to wash clothes, walks to the edge of the crater, and walks to pick mountain apples and delicate ferns that grew nearby.

Sister Leopoldina liked to take girls to hike up the cliffs, the pali, but patients were not allowed to do so, so that stopped.

The sisters sewed clothes for the girls and taught the older ones to sew and bake. By 1905, all the girls wore wine colored uniforms.

Each sister received $20 a month for the convent treasury and the sisters spent much of the money on things for the patients.

Sister Leopoldina noted that Marianne was an artist, a "real artist" in her sense of blending colors and adding artistic touches to hats and dresses.

Mother Marianne found her joy in potted ferns and parlor plants. She used found items in her resourcefulness, such as using empty medicine bottles as candleholders and vases for the chapel.

Reports required by the Hawai'i Department of Health, as well as plans, letters, and other paper work often kept Mother Marianne up late into the night. She spent the day directly with the patients.

Christmas 1888

The sisters' first Christmas at Kalaupapa proved to be Father Damien's last Christmas. The several religions at the settlement worked together to arrange for gifts for the children and to decorate with greenery from the woods. Father Damien's Mass followed the midnight carols. One resident noted that the honeysuckle was in bloom.

Not long after Christmas, Father Damien visited Bishop Home for the last time. He noticed the beauty of the girls and women's pretty blue dresses and red ribbons. His heart felt peace that the Sisters had come and that they would take care of his boys after he was gone.

Devil Winds

With help from the patients of Bishop Home, Mother Marianne tended a kitchen vegetable garden. She planted trees as windbreaks to protect the convent that sat on a windy hill.

The settlement experienced the "devil winds" in February 1889 when a cyclone came and blew the Mormon chapel right into the sea.

Mother Marianne met this storm, which ripped the veranda right off the convent, with these words to the sisters: "Come, we must go to the children." (Jacks, page 112) The sisters rushed the children to the safest places and tended to those who needed first aid.

Mother Marianne and the sisters had a special calling to protect the women and girls of Bishop Home from the unwelcome advances of the men and male youths. This often meant night watchfulness as well as in the daytime. The sisters also dealt with a certain amount of "spring fever" restlessness among the girls and women. If the sisters were naïve about these areas of life, they soon got over it. They put forth every effort to make life comfortable and pleasant for those in their care.

Even in the 1970s, some of the elderly remaining patients remembered Mother Marianne's rules for one-hour visits with the men, for caution at social events, and for courtships. Anyone who persisted in ignoring the rules had to leave Bishop Home. Tough love prevailed.

There was about 10 kilometers between the men's area and the women's area.

Death of Father Damien

On April 15, 1889, the sisters received word that Father Damien had died. Mother Marianne and Sister Vincent had gone a few days earlier

Chapter 8: **Kalaupapa, Hawai'i**

and asked for his blessing.

"He also blessed the heroic daughters of St. Francis for whose coming he had so long prayed." (Law and Law book on Father Damien, page 104)

Father Damien died lying on a mattress on the floor. He never got around to building himself a bed.

Mother Marianne and the sisters lined the wooden casket with cloth, white satin with edges of white lace, and made it ready. The priests put Father Damien's vestments on him and placed him in the church. Many noted that his face was peaceful.

Mother Marianne wrote to her long time friend Mother Bernardina that Father Damien led "a grand and noble life of self-sacrifice" and had given "his life for his fellow creatures."

Two 12-year-old girls who came to Kalaupapa on the same boat as Mother Marianne and the sisters recalled 50 years later how Mother Marianne made black sashes for the girls to wear at Father Damien's funeral.

They buried Father Damien under the Puhala tree, the very same tree he had used as shelter when he first arrived.

"Our dear Father Damien died on the 15th of April …
…
"And standing at his bedside, one could image (sic) to hear the Voice of God calling him to come to his reward – his was a grand and noble life of Self Sacrifice …"
- Mother Marianne, May 1889 / Unpublished Letters of Mother Marianne

Brother Dutton and Father Conrardy

The brothers and priests at the Kalawao settlement and boys' home, especially Brother Dutton and Father Conrardy, grew very possessive of the place.

Mother Marianne knew that better care could be given the boys and young men and she had promised Damien that she would do what she could. The challenge for her was how to do this without giving offense to the brothers and priests. Another challenge came in how to get the sisters back and forth between the two settlements.

The Hawaiian Board of Health wanted Mother Marianne's presence and care at the boys' home and arranged to send horse, carriage, and driver to transport the sisters back and forth.

Sister Crescentia and Sister Irene came to Kalaupapa when the Branch Hospital in Honolulu closed down. Three sisters remained at the Kapi'olani Home for well children in Honolulu near the sisters' first convent.

Robert Louis Stevenson visits Kalaupapa

The driver and his wife left the Island of Moloka'i about the same time as Robert Louis Stevenson arrived. He too had pulmonary tuberculosis and spent a week at the settlement. He taught the girls how to play croquet, which brought great enjoyment.

He wrote a poem for Mother Maryanne (as he spelled it) and all the sisters - in which he said:
"... beauty springing from the breast of pain!"

A piano arrived at the settlement and provided many happy hours of music for the patients and the sisters. Mr. Stevenson sent a message that came with the piano – "so there will always be music."

Reverend Sister Maryanne
Matron of the Bishop Home, Kalaupapa

To see the infinite pity of this place,

The mangled limb, the devastated face,

Chapter 8: Kalaupapa, Hawai'i

The innocent sufferers smiling at the rod,

A fool were tempted to deny his God.

He sees, and shrinks; but if he look again,

Lo, beauty springing from the breast of pain!—

He marks the sisters on the painful shores,

And even a fool is silent and adores.

- Robert Louis Stevenson, Kalawao, May 22, 1889

Sister Death

The sisters and everyone at the settlement faced death frequently. The census from 1888 through 1900 ran about a thousand to eleven hundred patients at any given time. Of course, some of them died as the disease ravaged them.

By 1900, the census began to fall below one thousand.

Olinda Gomes enters the convent

A young woman named Olinda asked to join the sisters. She lived at Wailuku under the direction of Sister Bonaventure and was received into the Sisters of St. Francis as Sister Elizabeth. In 1891, she professed her vows and then came to Moloka'i.

Baldwin Home - New Boys' Home

Construction on the new Boys' Baldwin Home came to completion in the late spring of 1890. By the middle of May, a convent named Our Lady of Mercy was ready for the sisters. A cottage within the enclosure of the convent served as the home for very young boys.

The Baldwin Complex at Kalawao

Mother Marianne wanted all the sisters to spend their nights at the Kalaupapa convent so the house at Kalawao was used only in the daytime.

" … the Sisters and myself are willing to do what we can to make the boys' establishment a pleasant home for the poor children."
- Mother Marianne, May 1889 / Unpublished Letters of Mother Marianne

The division of labor never quite happened satisfactorily. Brother Dutton did not understand what Mother Marianne wanted and she felt he did not do his share of the work.

The sisters willingly took care of the boys during the daytime but they wanted the brothers and priests to supervise at night. In time, the sisters handed over the convent at Kalawao for the use of the brothers.

New Kapi'olani Home

When the Hawaiian government wanted to close the Kapi'olani Home for well girls in Honolulu, Sister Benedicta said: "No."

The involved parties did agree to build the new one in Kalihi, further away from Honolulu. Sister Benedicta possessed the strength of her convictions and the courage to carry them out. Later, in 1916, Mother Marianne sent for her to come as her successor at Kalaupapa.

Hawaiian History

On January 20, 1891, King Kalakaua died and his sister, Liliuokalani became queen. Two years later, on January 17, 1893, the Revolution deposed her and ended the monarchy.

This news slowly trickled to Kalaupapa.

The king had visited Kalaupapa in August of 1890. At that time, he

Chapter 8: **Kalaupapa, Hawai'i**

asked Mother Marianne about a place for a Father Damien memorial. She suggested a place close to Damien Road and close enough to shore that passengers on passing boats might see it.

The Celtic Cross memorial arrived in September 1893.

In 1892, Queen Liliuokalani came to the Bishop Home; the girls and women entertained the queen with recitations and songs.

Some other government changes included a provisional government for 1893 to 1894 followed by the establishment of the Republic of Hawai'i in August 1894. That lasted until 1898 when the United States annexed the islands as the Territory of Hawaiian Islands under the jurisdiction of the United States.

"We are Americans now, these Islands have been annexed – I hope for the best – The poor Natives feel very bad about losing their Country."
- Mother Marianne, August 1898 / Unpublished Letters of Mother Marianne

American flags went up as the native Hawaiians mourned the loss of their nation. The sisters made tiny U. S. flags but the Hawaiians did not like this.

In November 1892, two sisters, Sister De Sales and Sister Jerome (Hieronyma) and a novice, Sister Albina came out to the mission. Sister Albina made her profession on August 12, 1893 at the convent chapel at Kalaupapa and spent the rest of her life in that mission.

Mother Marianne still minded the smell of the leprous sores. It often gave her a sick headache. She also shuddered at shaking hands, but notes in her journal that "we just did it".

By 1893, Mother Marianne and the sisters cared for 103 girls and women at Bishop Home.

Mary and Rose

At one point, Mother Marianne took in two healthy babies, Mary in 1891 and Rose in 1893. The sisters raised the girls until they were eight years old and almost six years old. She then sent them to the Kapiʻolani Home for well girls.

In 1906, at age 15, Mary returned to Kalaupapa to assist in the convent. Later, Rose returned to Kalaupapa too.

Convivencia

Another aspect of life on the peninsula, both at Kalawao and Kalaupapa, shone forth brightly and warmly in the ways in which all the churches cooperated in the best interests of the patients and other residents of the area.

"Assisted by Mormon, Protestant, and Evangelical missionaries, as well as some courageous family members of patients, Father Damien grew crops; built homes, schools, and a reservoir for drinking water; and pleaded with the Hawaiian government and church officials to send more medical supplies, food, and clothing."
– *Exiled to Paradise* by Kevin Grange, in National Parks, Summer 2012.

Not unlike the convivencia of the Jews, Catholics, and Muslims of the 8th through 15th centuries in Spain, the sense of community on that north shore of Molokaʻi where Kalaupapa lies meant respect and inclusion of all. The Andalusian experience of the Iberian peninsula of the continent of Europe had its convivencia. So did that tiny peninsula on a small island of the Pacific archipelago.

And unlike that Iberian Peninsula's convivencia, which came to an abrupt halt in 1492 when Isabella and Ferdinand expelled by force the Jews and Muslims, the convivencia of Kalaupapa came down through the years as a strength and legacy of the two saints who walked the paths of that settlement.

The last remaining generation of the banished exiles still talk story about Mother Marianne and Father Damien. They tell how the hours of time donated to build a new Mormon place of worship in 1965 came to a higher count for non-Mormons than for the Mormon members. They talk story about the "best friends" that Father Damien and Jonathan Napela were to each other.

Convivencia at Kalaupapa

God granted one of the miracles required for the canonization of Marianne Cope to a woman not of the Catholic faith. Sharon Smith, a member of the Protestant Church of the Nazarene, lived through a bout with pancreatitis when an infection began to shut down all her organs. The doctors said they could do no more for her.

A Franciscan Sister visited her and prayed, asking Blessed Marianne to heal Sharon. That Sharon did not die but recovered to reasonably good health cannot be explained by medical science. That Sharon holds a faith other than Catholic links well to the way Mother Marianne and the sisters and also Father Damien went about their ministries in Kalaupapa and Kalawao on the Island of Moloka'i.

"The charity of the good knows no creed and is confined to no one place."
- Mother Marianne / http://www.stmariannecope.org/

Marianne wrote this in the 1870s while she served as administrator of St. Joseph Hospital in Syracuse, N.Y. She lived it then and she lived it along with her companion sisters at Kalaupapa. Under Marianne's leadership, the sisters cared for each person in their physical and spiritual needs with a sense of respect and equality. No matter their racial, ethnic, or religious background, each and every patient received the gentle ministrations of the sisters.

Festivities and funerals at any one of the settlement's churches, Protestant, Catholic, or Mormon, brought out members of all the churches congregations. The people sang in each other's choirs and helped each other in many ways.

Father Damien and Jonathan Napela

Father Damien too nurtured a sense of community that crossed the lines of church membership. While the rest of Hawai'i, and indeed the world, saw competition among the religions for the salvation of souls, two churchmen at Kalaupapa worked in harmony.

One of his best friends in his early days there arrived there just about the same time as Damien. Jonathan Napela, some 27 years older than Damien, came as a non-leprous kokua (helper) for his wife Kitty when she was banished because of the disease of leprosy.

Jonathan, a convert to the Latter Day Saints (LDS) also known as Mormons, took up a leadership role at the Mormon temple with about a hundred members of that religion. Both Father Damien and Jonathan shared a sense of service to all the patients and residents.

When donations of clothes and other items arrived, they distributed to all in need, to all.

Much of the incoming money for the Catholic mission for Father Damien to build cottages and to enlarge the church came from the efforts of Reverend Hugh Chapman, an Anglican churchman of England, because he greatly admired the heroic service of Father Damien.

When a certain Dr. Hyde wrote a scathing report against Father Damien and made it public, Robert Louis Stevenson, a Presbyterian, penned a rebuttal, pointing out the falsehood of every point. R. L. Stevenson had visited Kalaupapa and Kalawao shortly after the death of Father Damien and had heard first hand the stories that the people told about their beloved priest.

Robert Louis Stevenson also visited Mother Marianne and had conversations with her. He wrote the now famous poem about the work of Marianne and the Sisters.

Edward Clifford, a man of the Anglican Church, visited Damien, held long conversations with him, and made sketches of the priest whose face by then showed evidence of the disease.

Both Father Damien and Mother Marianne maintained good relationships with the king and queen of Hawai'i, members of the Anglican Church at St. Andrew's in Honolulu. Also, they worked well with Walter Gibson, president of the Hawaiian Board of Health, and a one time Mormon who converted to Catholicism in his later years.

If the name Kalaupapa means – flat leaf – and it does, the prevailing spirit of the settlement in the times of Mother Marianne and Father Damien leveled and flattened the status of all person coming there as exiles to an equality of survival in dealing with the illness they all suffered.

Soul of Kalaupapa

Fred E. Woods, who has studied the LDS history at Moloka'i, notes that "the place was unusually ecumenical" and how everyone worked together for the good of the patients with Hansen's disease. Woods visited Kalaupapa and interviewed several of the remaining patients. He noted that "… a settlement born in misery but redeemed by interfaith friendship." – referring to Father Damien and Jonathan – as "yokemates in charitable service" – led to a living sense of community among all the patients and residents.

Woods and Ethan Vincent co-produced – *The Soul of Kalaupapa: Voices of Exiles* – a film that tells the story via interviews with the last living patients. Woods who writes and lectures about the interfaith and intercultural collaboration at Kalaupapa also arranged for the film to be shown at the World Parliament of Religions in Australia in 2009.

Ecumenism in the 1980s
– a sister's point of view

"There are three religious groups in the settlement: Catholic, Protestant and Mormon. We were an ecumenical group. When there is a funeral or a celebration in any group, we would all attend and offer support. When we had Christmas or Easter Mass, members of the other groups would arrange their schedules and attend and vice versa. Kuulei Bell, a Mormon elder, had a very beautiful singing voice and sang with our choir.

"Because there was no embalming, a patient who expired in the morning was buried in the evening. If they died in the evening or night, they would be brought to the hospital and laid out in the first room next to the nurses' station. Each resident had a 'make box' or death box, which contain a blanket to line the coffin, clothes and shoes for the resident to be clothed in. My first death and funeral was Mary Sing, the wife of a Mormon elder. She was dressed in a white dress with a white veil over her hair. Since she died in the late evening, she was brought to the hospital. Some of the Mormon members kept vigil at her bedside and left at midnight. I happened to work the night shift. Yama, a very concerned woman, asked if I wanted to stay in her room for the night, of which I gladly accepted. (I am a scary cat.) The next morning, Mary was carried off to the cemetery and laid to rest after the entourage circled the settlement.

"A station wagon that opens in the back and sides was used as an ambulance, a hearse, and (to) transport patients to and from the hospital or clinic."

...

"Yana is Buddhist but she had a great devotion to St. Anthony. She had a little statue of him and once a month, she asked me to light a candle to him. Whenever she lost or dropped anything, she prayed to St. Anthony and she would find it. Her husband Shigemi died in Honolulu and his ashes were brought back to Kalaupapa. Unbeknown to me, there was this unfamiliar package wrapped in black cloth. I asked her if she received another care package and she said: "That's Shigemi's ashes and one day it will be sprinkled in the bay."
- From Sister Miriam Dionise's Memoirs, written in 2010

Chapter 8: **Kalaupapa, Hawai'i**

Quotes about interfaith sharing
– from Pilgrimage and Exile

Upon the arrival of the Sisters in Honolulu

"The king, keeping the promise he had given Father Leonor, sent five carriages of state. He himself decided not to attend, for reasons of policy, in which, for once, both Catholics and Protestants concurred."
- Hanley, O.S.F. Sister Mary Laurence; O. A. Bushnell (2009-11-01). *Pilgrimage and Exile: Mother Marianne of Moloka'i* (Kindle Locations 2069-2071). Mutual Publishing, LLC. Kindle Edition.

Sisters of St. Francis – often referred to as Sisters of Charity – as they set to work at Kaka'ako

"Even he recognized that most Protestants in town and legislature expressed both admiration for the Sisters of Charity and utmost relief because they had taken over the duties that no one else seemed willing to assume. But, His Lordship asked, would these same Calvinists, with their strange American notions about the complete separation of church and state, accept with equal complacence the delegating of Catholic sisters to operate a hospital that would not be receiving lepers as patients?"
- Hanley, O.S.F. Sister Mary Laurence; O. A. Bushnell (2009-11-01). *Pilgrimage and Exile: Mother Marianne of Moloka'i* (Kindle Locations 3095-3099). Mutual Publishing, LLC. Kindle Edition.

Why the sisters should go to Maui

"Gibson, unlike Bishop Hermann and Father Leonor, spoke with Protestants rather more often than he conversed with Catholics. He could discover no good reason why Father Leonor's wish to send Franciscan sisters to Maui would not be acceptable to Protestants in and out of the legislature. The legislators were practical men, Gibson knew, and always interested in getting things done, just as he was. Nor would they mind who did the work, as long as it was done well - and at the least possible expense to taxpayers. In these respects, the sisters commended themselves admirably: not only did they take care of lepers,

they also worked for love of God, rather than for love of money."
- Hanley, O.S.F. Sister Mary Laurence; O. A. Bushnell (2009-11-01). *Pilgrimage and Exile: Mother Marianne of Moloka'i* (Kindle Locations 3099-3104). Mutual Publishing, LLC. Kindle Edition.

Sharing the use of the organ

"When, in 1884, an organ was purchased for the sisters, the console was set outside the sliding partitions, so that Protestants too might enjoy its music. Sometimes a patient might play upon the flute, to accompany the hymns; or another would play the organ. In 1936 Sister Benedicta Rodenmacher (who arrived at Kaka'ako in 1885) would remember how the hymns, being sung in Hawaiian, were "strange to us, but very devotional."
- Hanley, O.S.F. Sister Mary Laurence; O. A. Bushnell (2009-11-01). *Pilgrimage and Exile: Mother Marianne of Moloka'i* (Kindle Locations 3197-3200). Mutual Publishing, LLC. Kindle Edition.

Mother Marianne's Thoughtful Arrangements

Mother Marianne probably was responsible for these thoughtful arrangements to share the one place in the whole hospital compound where religious services might be held. She saw that the inmates needed all the consolations of religion they could possibly receive, if only because the medicines they took into their devastated bodies were so useless, but most of all because, for them, more than for others, death was so imminent.

As mother provincial of the congregation of sisters that opened two hospitals in central New York to all people, regardless of race, color, sex, or creed, Mother Marianne could not possibly be possessive about the convent's chapel at Kaka'ako. In later years, on Moloka'i, she often repeated to the sisters, words written to a benefactor during her years at St. Joseph Hospital in Syracuse:

"The charity of the good knows no creed, and is confined to no one place."
- Hanley, O.S.F. Sister Mary Laurence; O. A. Bushnell (2009-11-01).

Chapter 8: **Kalaupapa, Hawai'i**

Pilgrimage and Exile: Mother Marianne of Moloka'i (Kindle Locations 3206-3207). Mutual Publishing, LLC. Kindle Edition.

Cooperation in setting up the hospital at Wailuku

"Father Gulstan Ropert and his fellow priests, with support from Protestant and Mormon clergymen of the district, involved the women of the whole community in the effort. "Some of the ladies from different parts of the [district], natives and part Hawaiians, came day after day to assist Mother," Sister Leopoldina reported. "I heard her say many times that she would be forever grateful to them and that she did not know what she would have done had it not been for their help." In this respect, as in others, the people of Wailuku showed that they were better Christians than were the residents of Honolulu."
-Hanley, O.S.F. Sister Mary Laurence; O. A. Bushnell (2009-11-01). *Pilgrimage and Exile: Mother Marianne of Moloka'i* (Kindle Locations 3269-3273). Mutual Publishing, LLC. Kindle Edition.

Bringing solace to the patients at Kaka'ako

"Bishop Alfred Willis of the Episcopal Church, or one of his vicars, held an occasional service for their communicants in the shared church. Presumably Anglican prelates, Catholic priests, and Mormon elders not only preached in the chapel but also entered the hospital wards when called, if only to take the last rites to dying patients. Congregationalist pastors did not have to do so, at least in 1885 and most of 1886: Reverend J. Kauwa, one of their native converts and ordained ministers, was an inmate, always on call."
-Hanley, O.S.F. Sister Mary Laurence; O. A. Bushnell (2009-11-01). *Pilgrimage and Exile: Mother Marianne of Moloka'i* (Kindle Locations 4966-4969). Mutual Publishing, LLC. Kindle Edition.

Welcoming other Faiths

" … the Franciscans did not bar Protestant pastors and Mormon elders from visiting patients belonging to their faiths who lived as wards of the Bishop Home."
- Hanley, O.S.F. Sister Mary Laurence; O. A. Bushnell (2009-11-01).

Pilgrimage and Exile: Mother Marianne of Moloka'i (Kindle Locations 7400-7401). Mutual Publishing, LLC. Kindle Edition.

A Mormon Kokua helped Sister Benedicta go for a nurse as Mother Marianne approached death.

"Early next morning, soon after daybreak, Sister Benedicta started upon her journey. Accompanied by George, a healthy kokua and a Mormon, "one of the best men in the Settlement," she climbed the cliff for the first time in her life. At the top of the trail she parted from George."
- Hanley, O.S.F. Sister Mary Laurence; O. A. Bushnell (2009-11-01). *Pilgrimage and Exile: Mother Marianne of Moloka'i* (Kindle Locations 7935-7937). Mutual Publishing, LLC. Kindle Edition.

Father Pamphile deVeuster, Father Paul Juliotte and other Picpus Fathers and Brothers

Father Pamphile deVeuster

At the time of the beatification and canonization efforts towards Damien's sainthood, his brother Auguste who was two years older, served as a main source of childhood stories about little Jef (Josef) as Damien was known before his ordination.

Auguste joined the Congregation of the Sacred Hearts in Belgium and did well with books and teaching. He also trained for and hoped to be a missionary. Josef, inspired by his brother's way of life, also joined the Congregation and hoped to become a priest.

When Father Pamphile (Auguste de Veuster) took ill in 1863, his younger brother Josef, not yet ordained in the congregation, volunteered to take Pamphile's place and go to the Hawaiian Mission. Pamphile had tutored his younger brother in the subjects needed for ordination to the priesthood.

Joseph reached Honolulu and was ordained with the name of Father

Chapter 8: **Kalaupapa, Hawai'i**

Damien at Our Lady of Peace Cathedral in Honolulu. He spent several years as a travelling missionary mostly on the big island of Hawai'i. In time, he went to Moloka'i, to the settlement at Kalawao on the northern peninsula of Moloka'i and lived and labored among the patients with the disease of leprosy.

Over the years, the two brothers sent many letters back and forth. Once he contracted the disease of leprosy, Father Damien pleaded with Father Pamphile several times to come to Moloka'i and help out. And Father Pamphile asked to do just that but the superior general did not agree to allow Father Pamphile to go to Moloka'i.

After Father Damien's death, Father Pamphile did travel to the Moloka'i Mission and served as resident priest. Visiting Father Damien's grave and living where Father Damien had lived must have cost Father Pamphile some strong emotions.

He found the climate very difficult and remained less than two years. Mother Marianne and the sisters benefitted from his priestly ministry there, from 1895 to 1897. Perhaps, Father Pamphile talked with the sisters about their memories of Father Damien.

Returning to Belgium, Father Pamphile compiled the letters he had received from Father Damien over the years and published them in 1889 in London. Earlier, he had agreed to not make them public, but with Father Damien's death and worldwide popularity, Father Pamphile decided that letters should be made known.

The text of this book titled - *Life and Letters of Father Damien* - by Father Pamphile De Veuster, SS. CC. – is out of print and hard to find. Pamphile died in 1909.

Father Paul-Marie Juliotte (1867 – 1956)
At Kalaupapa – a missionary and photographer

Father Paul Juliotte (Father Joseph) served the Catholic community at Kalaupapa from 1901 to 1907. During those years he took photographs for the patients to send home to their families. In the early years of the 21st century the glass negative slides resurfaced and some of these photos are now being made available.

The photos show the lovely dresses that Mother Marianne and the sisters made for the girls and women and other ways that the sisters encouraged beauty.

After his ordination to priesthood, Father Juliotte joined the Congregation of the Sacred Hearts and in 1901 he set out as a missionary to Hawai'i. At the time of his profession in the congregation, he became known as Father Joseph.

He went to Moloka'i and devoted himself to those afflicted with the disease of leprosy and he hoped to live and die doing that.

But, in 1903, he was appointed provincial superior of the Hawaiian Islands and travelled to Belgium in 1908 and 1912 for general chapters of the congregation. In 1912, he was sent to Paris for parish work there. In 191, he was sent to Spain to service as director of novices.

In 1923, Father Joseph departed Europe for the mission in China where he served as superior. As bishop of the Prefect Apostolic, Bishop Juliotte and his companions suffered a loss of freedom under the Communist rule of China in the 1950s. In 1953, the Communists forced the missionaries out of China. At age 85, Father Juliotte returned to France and devoted himself to the spiritual care of the novices. He died in 1956.

The Congregation of the Sacred Hearts of Jesus and Mary are also known as the Picpus Fathers because Rue de Picpus is the street in Paris, France, where they had their first house.

Visitors to Kalaupapa and their Writings

Many of those who visited Kalaupapa wrote about it. To read about these early accounts gives some sense of what life was like in those pioneer years, both during the lifetime of Mother Marianne, and in later years as the Franciscan Sisters carried on the work.

Chapter 8: **Kalaupapa, Hawai'i**

1908 – Jack London
1916 – Katherine Fullerton Gerould

Jack London (1876 – 1916)

Many remember reading Jack London in their student days – *To Build a Fire*, *Call of the Wild*, *White Fang*, and others.

When Jack London visited the settlements on the north coast of Moloka'i, he witnessed the presence of some 800 patients with leprosy and wrote about it in 1908. He made every effort to dispel the "yellow" journalism that had portrayed "the most cursed place on earth." Jack and his wife spent the Fourth of July at joyous races – of horses and donkeys – "and all the while nearly a thousand lepers were laughing uproariously at the fun."

Jack wrote of their time at the Settlement in an essay titled – *The Lepers of Moloka'i*.

Jack wondered if it was all right for to have fun in such a place of horror, but he declared the horrors do not exist there. He affirmed that "leprosy is leprosy and it is a terrible thing."

He also painted a scene in his words of bands playing music and groups singing serenades.

Though Jack never mentioned Mother Marianne or the sisters, he affirmed that "The precautions of simple cleanliness seem to be all that is necessary." Mother Marianne and the sisters would have agreed. Jack also saw the value of segregation as a precaution, but he said that leprosy is really not as contagious as once thought.

Jack described the mostly delightful climate of the windward location receiving "the trade fresh northeast trades." He told of the enterprising folks who fished and farmed and owned their own homes.

In concluding his travel tale, Jack exhorts philanthropists to continue the search for a cure of the disease of leprosy.

Mr. London did mention Father Damien, the "hero of the church" and how he somehow contracted leprosy and died from it. Damien would have been dead about 20 years by the time Jack visited. Jack probably heard about the beloved priest from the patients and residents. Marianne would have been in her late 60s when Jack visited. Perhaps, he spent no time with her.

Jack wrote a short story – Koolau the Leper – a rebel with an "indomitable spirituality." Jack made a return visit to Hawai'i in 1915.

(In the 21st century, it is no longer acceptable to call people lepers, but rather patients with leprosy. The early 20th century use was kept in this article, with sensitivity to contemporary use.)

Katherine Fullerton Gerould (1879 – 1944)

In his biography of Mother Marianne of Moloka'i (1935), L. V. Jacks mentions that Katherine Fullerton Gerould, as a woman traveller to the Hawaiian Islands, observed MM as the epitome of a superior in a convent – "blood-kin of all superiors" (page 167)

In Katherine Fullerton Gerould's own book about Hawai'i, Katherine writes of her 1916 visit to eight of the Islands of Hawai'i. She describes the attitude of residents of the other islands and their reluctance for her to visit Moloka'i. They seem to reveal an out of sight, out of mind attitude that did not want the whole world to know about their epidemic of the disease of leprosy.

Katherine observes the sisters at prayer, at work, and in social situations and finds them humble and gentle.

Katherine toured eight of the Hawaiian Islands and wrote travel essays, which appeared in Harper's in 1916, and which is now available as a book titled – *Hawai'i: Scenes and Impressions*.

In her Preface, Katherine said that her writing is a "wandering record of a month" and that the adventure and the record are as "a basket of summer fruit."

Chapter 8: **Kalaupapa, Hawai'i**

"My context is richer than my page;" she said, "my memory — than my manuscript."

In a three-part essay – *Honolulu, By Ways in Hawai'i, Kalaupapa* - she devoted a full third of the book to "a place that most islanders ignore – Moloka'i ..." – the settlement to which the government sent patients with the disease of leprosy. For Katherine, "that lone settlement of shuddering connotation proved to be "positively the finest of our memories."

She reported that her desire to visit Kalaupapa was going to make her unpopular, as the islanders did not like to think about the reason for its existence, namely, leprosy. While the islanders may describe the peninsula on the north coast of the Island of Moloka'i as "unbelievable beautiful" where happy people receive the care they need, these same islanders do not wish to think or talk about the place at all. She accuses the Islanders of "playing the ostrich about Kalaupapa" in their "sorry logic" and attitude about the situation.

While the author spoke of Honolulu as the "melting pot" and the Hawaiian curios as "chiefly ukuleles and bead and shell necklaces, and tapa cloth," she recalled how she had "trod the grassy 'streets' of Kalaupapa all in the celestial light of an August morning."

Katherine visited the convent of the Franciscan sisters and noted that the parlor was half filled with garments ready to be given out to those in need. She told how Mother Maryanne (spelling given in the essay) "confessed that the night had been hot and sleep difficult."

The essayist continues with a quote from the Mother Superior.

"You wouldn't think we'd be busy here," Mother Maryanne ventured, smiling, "but there is a good deal to do."

The author berated with her word the authorities for the lack of electricity in the hospital and other buildings and told of her hope that the authorities might give Mother Maryanne an electric fan before she dies.

Mother Marianne would have been in her late 70s and quite close to death at the time that Katherine visited.

In other scenes, Katherine described how "a sister waved her free hand at us from a porch and the other hand held the bandaged stump of …" a patient.

She wrote of how the sisters' tiny cottage, which faced out onto their green compound, held its authentic convent atmosphere. She explained that five sisters managed to care for about 80 patients, the youngest at five years and the oldest at 80 years.

As Katherine was leaving, she heard bells sounding faintly and saw the sisters heading toward the church. She called the Franciscan sisters "saintly poor-creatures" and "quiet heroes" with endearment.

Between pages 156 and 157 of the book, a photo depicts two sisters leading a group of women and girls in white in front of the church. One sister has her hand in front of her face, perhaps because she did not like her photo taken. It's probably not Mother Marianne as the sister looks young and spry. The photo is by R. K. Bonine who has other photos in the book.

At the very end of the book of three essays, Katherine includes a map showing the paths of her travels. Reading the book impresses the author's affirmation that Kalaupapa was indeed "positively the finest of our memories."

Early 20th century

By the time of her 61st birthday, Mother Marianne had attacks of pulmonary tuberculosis in which she coughed up blood. Extra rest helped her some, but she never again left the settlement for the last 20 years of her life. She feared and dreaded any further hemorrhages. She sent letters or had the sisters from Oʻahu or Maui come to her.

Mother Marianne avoided publicity and photos as best she could. One photo shows the five sisters with Mother Marianne in the middle.

Chapter 8: **Kalaupapa, Hawai'i**

Another, snapped by a Benedictine abbot, shows Marianne wearing an apron and talking to someone.

During 1899, Mother Delphine along with Sister Robertina and Sister Susanna came for visitation. They arrived in Honolulu on December 20. They left Honolulu just in time to avoid the quarantine because of Bubonic plague. Once in Kalaupapa, they had to stay for nine weeks, as boats did not travel during the quarantine. No one in Kalaupapa or Moloka'i got the plague.

The sisters held a discussion about a school in Hilo. By February 1900, the epidemic seemed finished and once again ships sailed to take mail and supplies to the outer islands. The three visiting sisters left on March 4th.

The three visitors tried to land at Lahaina to visit the mission at Wailuku. The citizens, fearful that the passengers might carry the plague, did not want the sisters to land. The captain said to them that if they wanted the supplies unloaded, they had to allow the sisters to come on land.

Mother Delphine injured her leg and had to stay at Wailuku until May. They initiated St. Joseph School for girls and had it ready for September 1900. Mother Delphine left June 13 and reached Syracuse in early July.

Devil winds - of the Sisters

Sister Mary Laurence in her research and writing does tell of the difficulties some sisters had in this particular mission field. Sister Mary Laurence compares one of those difficult times to the "devil wind" that blew hard across the islands. She also describes other bouts of pouting, depression, and madness on the part of the sisters.

Neither Mother Marianne nor Sister Leopoldina write about these situations in their journals and diaries.

Deputy Commissary

By 1910, the sisters at Syracuse in their Chapter meetings showed their concern about Mother Marianne and her inability to travel. The appointed Sister Helena as deputy commissary so that she could carry on business in the event of illness or death of Mother Marianne.

For a time, the sisters in Hawai'i were considered a separate but related group. By the 1910 Chapter, they were now again part of Syracuse congregation and the sisters could attend and vote at Chapter and they could do this by telegraph cable.

50th Jubilee

In October of 1913, Marianne celebrated her 50th Jubilee. She had asked to be relieved of office and asked again in 1916. Photos of these last few years of her life show her quite aged.

Ode St. Anne

In 1917, Captain Henry Berger composed the "Ode St. Anne" in honor of Mother Marianne and her patron saint – St. Anne. Mr. Berger wrote the music and Mr. Hughes the words.

"You will be surprised to hear that St. Ann has many devoted children on the Sandwich Islands, and that more honor is paid her here than in the United States, just because she is the dear Grand Mother of Jesus."
- Mother Marianne, August 1884 / Unpublished Letters of Mother Marianne

The Syracuse sisters had the practice of wearing a blue-and-white checkered work apron. At Kalaupapa, Marianne insisted that the sisters change their aprons and habits when coming from work. The sisters carried on this practice until 1969 when medical knowledge indicated that the disease was not as contagious as had been thought.

Chapter 8: **Kalaupapa, Hawai'i**

Spirituality and Philosophy of Life

L. V. Jacks who authored the first biography of Mother Marianne of Moloka'i (1925) wrote of her philosophy of life as one based on "her heritage of faith and study, charity and reflection, experience and suffering." (page 106)

And of her spirituality, he said: "... the spiritual element was the very factor upon which all her life and sacrifice hinged." (page 107)

Mother Marianne's preaching was more a matter of actions and deeds than words, though she did offer words of encouragement mostly, and admonitions as needed. Her tasks of preparing the medicines, washing and dressing the sore, making bed, bathing those who could not do it for themselves – these are her sermons. Mother Marianne's Franciscan life of true Gospel living expressed itself in so many practical and resourceful ways, some of which was to involve the girls in making a walkway, in making lace, and in planting gardens.

As an artist and thinker, Mother Marianne left an impression on visitors too. For 1916 publication, Katherine Fullerton Gerould wrote a description of her visit to Kalaupapa. She said of Mother Marianne "Mother Marianne in her little parlor, was the blood-kin of all superiors."
- As quoted in Jacks, page 167, from Scribner's Magazine of July 1916, Hawai'i Scenes and Impressions

" ... she seemed like an old, old woman who had seen many things ... the precise nature of those things which, in thirty years on Moloka'i, Mother Marianne had seen ..." (loc. Cit.)

In January 1918, the sisters helped Mother Marianne celebrate her 80th birthday. Though she experienced kidney and heart failure and had swelling from dropsy, she tried to be up and in her wheel chair every day.

Sister Leopoldina, a 30-year companion to Mother Marianne, as well as Sister Crescentia and Rose and Mary, took Mother Marianne to the veranda as often as possible.

Sister Leopoldina dreaded the day that fast approached. In the evenings, Sister Leopoldina smelled something very lovely and called it her "angels at twilight". She learned that Mother Marianne had planted some Japanese flowers just under Leopoldina's window and that's where the pleasant scent came from.

Sister Albina came for a few weeks in July and took several photos including one often seen of Marianne in her wheel chair.

On July 26, 1918, the girls from Bishop Home sang to Marianne outside her window.

Sister Benedict travelled by car, boat, and by climbing down the pali cliffs to bring Sister Magdalene, a nurse, to help with Mother Marianne's care, especially at night.

August 9, 1918

On August 9, 1918, Mother Marianne came to lunch and supper but did not eat. She asked to be taken to the veranda where she waved to a little girl.

Once in her bed Mother Marianne gave her parting blessing to the sisters gathered round. She remained conscious to the end and had no deathbed agony. She died quietly about 11 p.m.

At the sisters' request the patients made her coffin. Everyone seemed to feel an invisible presence of Mother Marianne.

They hoped to bury her near Father Damien, but the ground proved too rocky. The buried her on August 10 at the foot of the side hill in an orange grove that she had planted. Just about everyone in the settlement came to the burial. The patients knelt around her grave and continued to sing and pray for a long time.

Chapter 8: **Kalaupapa, Hawai'i**

Mother Marianne Passes On
Dr. A. Mouritz

"The Venerable Mother Superior Marianne died at 10:50 p.m. on Friday, August 9, 1918, at the Bishop Home, Kalaupapa, Moloka'i; then the waiting Angels most assuredly guided her Spirit, heavenward. She had devoted 29 years of her life [plus] caring for the women and girls of the Home, and also five years previously at the Kaka'ako Hospital [island of O'ahu] from November 8, 1883 to November 13, 1888. Her age at death was [80] years, 6 months and 17 days. The immediate cause of her death was kidney and heart disease...of several years standing."
- Dr. A. Mouritz, *A Brief World History of Leprosy* 1943
[Dr. Mouritz was Father Damien's physician.]
http://www.stmariannecope.org/

Part Three

In the Footsteps of Mother Marianne
The Sisters who followed her at Kalaupapa

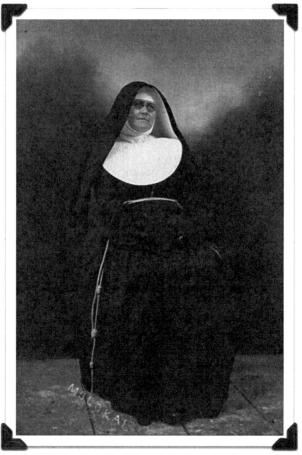

Sister Leopoldina Burns from the collection of Father Juliotte's from 1901-1907

Photo: Courtesy of the Congregation of the Sacred Hearts of Jesus and Mary

Chapter 9

Deceased Sisters and Graves

Not in any one of our houses in America are the Sisters so well cared for as here. The Board of Health supplies us with the best of food, and our house is furnished with everything that even the most exacting can wish for. We want for nothing but the Grace of God to perform our duties well, and to advance on the road of perfection according to the Spirit of our Order, and the Just Will of our Superiors in America...."
-P&E

In this chapter

Sister Leopoldina, Sister Crescentia, Sister Elizabeth, and other sisters carried on the ministry to the patients in the spirit and style of Mother Marianne.

Over the years, many more missionary sisters came to Kalaupapa on assignment or as volunteers known as na kokua.

Mother Marianne was the only sister buried at Kalaupapa. Others who died now lie in rest in cemeteries on Maui and Oʻahu. Some sisters lived their later years back in Syracuse and lie buried in that city.

A second Sister Marianne worked for some years at Kalaupapa and other places in Hawaiʻi.

A few of the Sisters worked at Kalaupapa both before and after the year of 1969, a year which marked significant changes in the treatment of patients with Hansen's disease and in the convent practices of the sisters, too.

Deceased Sisters who worked at Kalaupapa

"Sister Leopoldina, in her old age, remembered with smiles and happy tears the precious little mystery wrought for herself alone many years before 1918. "One beautiful evening after having spent the hot sultry day in the leper rooms where the air is anything but sweet I was tired when I went to my room. how surprised I was to be met, by the cool fresh air filled with the sweetest perfume…the little room seemed to be changed to a paradise, how can this be I thought…it must be the angels I will keep my secret and so I did, but every evening about the same time at twilight the room was delightfully perfumed, this is a mistry (sic) I can keep it no longer Mother surly knows somthing (sic) about it, and I went so ceriously (sic) to Mother and told her my secret. The angels are visiting my room every evening at twilight."
-Hanley, O.S.F. Sister Mary Laurence; O. A. Bushnell (2009-11-01). *Pilgrimage and Exile: Mother Marianne of Molokaʻi* (Kindle Locations 7835-7840). Mutual Publishing, LLC. Kindle Edition.

Note – Sister Leopoldina made many spelling mistakes, which have been handed down that way.

Heroic work – best recounted …

"The story of her (Mother Marianne's) heroic work there has been many times told, and in many ways. It is best recounted in the lives of the many souls touched by her charity and that of the sisters who followed her, spending themselves in the work of the schools and hospitals."

Chapter 9: **Deceased Sisters and Graves**

- Unpublished obituaries of Sisters of St. Francis in Hawai'i

In the obituary information of the sisters in Hawai'i for Mother Marianne, this paragraph tells of the lasting influence of Mother Marianne as the pioneer missionary to Hawai'i and especially to Kalaupapa.

"Having accompanied the sisters to this Missionary field, she remained with them until death called her to her eternal reward August 9, 1918."
- Unpublished obituaries of Sisters of St. Francis in Hawai'i

The Sisters of St. Francis –
Kalaupapa Community – 1888 to present

In early 2012, the Sisters in Hawai'i put together a display of ten frames, each 20 by 30 inches, of all the Franciscan Sisters who have ministered at Kalaupapa since 1888. The Sisters in Hawai'i also held a prayer service on January 21, 2012, to celebrate both the birthday and feast day of Mother Marianne (January 23) and to pay tribute to all the sisters who followed in her footsteps at Kalaupapa.

One sister struck a Tibetan gong as others read the name of each deceased sister. The gong provided a meaningful interfaith touch to the ceremony.

A booklet explains each of the ten frames and also lists the names of Kalaupapa sisters who still live in either Syracuse or Hawai'i. Three sisters, one of them a nurse, continue the work at Kalaupapa now and for the foreseeable future.

Sister Frances Therese Souza, a nurse, who currently lives at Kalaupapa, has ministered there for 21 years to date. Sister Rose Annette Ahuna and Sister Theresa Chow have lived there since 2009 and work as volunteers giving talks on Mother Marianne in the historic St. Elizabeth Chapel, and also in St. Elizabeth Convent.

Efforts are underway to also give recognition and tribute to the many sisters who came as na kokua (helpers) over the years to relieve the regular sisters so they could go on vacation or to retreat. Many school sisters spent part of their summer vacations to come as na kokua to Kalaupapa.

The first of the ten frames holds photos of King Kalakaua and Queen Kapiʻolani, who supported the building of Kapiʻolani Home in Honolulu, and Charles Reed Bishop, who gave a large sum of money, and all of whom played a major role in opening Bishop Home at the Kalaupapa Settlement in the 1880s. A photo of St. Elizabeth Convent with its wide verandas along with a lively description of the convent by Sister Leopoldina Burns sits at the bottom of that framed page. This first convent no longer stands. The sisters now use a newer one.

The framed pages continue with the photos and names of the sisters in residence and at work at Kalaupapa. At first, it is 1888 to 1899, and 1900 to 1929. Then it is by decades for the 1930s, 1940s and so on until the 1970s. The last framed page is for 1980 to the present.

Once sulfonamide drugs of the 1940s helped to contain the disease, fewer patients came to Kalaupapa. In 1969, the banishment was lifted and patients were free to choose where to live. Many felt that Kalaupapa was their home after so many years and chose to remain as residential patients. They are free to come and go and come back as they wish.

To date, 64 Sisters of St. Francis have lived and worked and prayed at the Kalaupapa Settlement. Some spent most of their lives there. Mother Marianne spent 30 years. Sister Leopoldina Burns, 40 years. Sister Crescentia Eilers, 40 years. Sister Elizabeth Gomes, 54 years. Sister Anne Adams, 22 years. Sister Marie Celine Wagner, 25 years. Sister Wilma Halmasy, 32 years. Sister Richard Marie Toal, 38 years. Sister Dativa Padilla, 28 years.

Burial places

Mother Marianne was the only sister buried at Kalaupapa. The Sisters of St. Francis made the decision to exhume her remains in 2005 and move them to the Shrine in Syracuse, N.Y.

Four sisters lie buried at on the Island of Maui. The remains of several others rest at Diamond Head Cemetery near Honolulu. Two lie buried at Hawai'i Memorial Cemetery.

20th Century
Before 1969 / Since 1969

Marianne's story – retold in lives of those who followed

In 1916, as Mother Marianne neared age 80, Sister Flaviana Engel was appointed Vicaria. In 1918, after Marianne's death, Sister Flaviana became the Commissary General for the Region of Hawai'i. She spent time at Kapi'olani Home and St. Francis Hospital, both in Honolulu, as well as time at Bishop Home at Kalaupapa.

Sister Leopoldina Burns (1855 – 1942)
Kalaupapa – 1888 - 1928

Sister Leopoldina Burns came to Honolulu in April 1885 to work at Kaka'ako Hospital. In 1888, Sister Leopoldina and Sister Crescentia travelled with Mother Marianne to Kalaupapa and worked alongside her all those many years. Sister Leopoldina took good care of Mother Marianne in her later years, and often took her out in a wheel chair to the veranda where she could see the yard and the girls and women at Bishop Home. Sister Leopoldina also wrote extensively about those early pioneer years.

Sister Albina Sluder (1869 – 1946)
Kalaupapa – 1892 - 1895

Sister Albina Sluder professed her vows at Kalaupapa and lived there from 1892 to 1895. Sister Albina wrote about her years there as well as about Kapi'olani Home where she spent many years.

Sister Elizabeth Gomes (1866 – 1947)
Kalaupapa – 1891 - 1945

Sister Elizabeth Gomes, an immigrant with her family from Portugal, came as a laywoman to help the sisters, decided to enter the congregation, took her training and lived at Kalaupapa as a sister from 1891 to 1945.

Sister Crescentia Eilers (1846 – 1931)
Kalaupapa – 1889 - 1929

Sister Crescentia Eilers went to Kalaupapa a year after the first three sisters. She stayed for 40 years until 1929.

Sister M. Vincentia McCormick (1853 – 1919)
Kalaupapa – 1888 - 1900

Sister Vincentia, the third of the three who went to Kalaupapa in 1888, stayed for 12 years until 1900. She was born in Oswego, N.Y. the city where Mother Marianne ran the school for three years. Sister Vincentia entered the convent in 1883.

A second Marianne – Sister Marianne Carvalho (1906 – 1995)
Kalaupapa – 1932 – 1948

Who is the Sister Marianne listed as living at Kalaupapa in the 1930s?

Well, Bessie (Elizabeth) Carvalho, daughter of Ida Alves and Joseph Carvalho, Portuguese parents who had lived in Japan, was born in Makawao, Maui, Hawai'i, in 1906.

Much like the first Sister Marianne, Bessie helped with the care of her siblings, two sisters and two brothers, after the death of their mother. Bessie entered the Sisters of St. Francis in 1924 and completed her novitiate training in Hawai'i.

With the name of Sister Marianne, she professed her final vows in 1929. She took care of children at Maui's Children's Home and Kapiʻolani Home in Honolulu.

Sister Marianne Carvalho spent many years during the 1930s and 1940s at Bishop Home at Kalaupapa. Surely, she absorbed some of the spirit of St. Marianne in those years following the 1918 death of Mother Marianne.

Sister Olivia Gibson who knew the second Marianne in the 1940s told how "she would cook for the girls in the convent school." One of the resident students of those years, Sister Candida remembered that the second Marianne always asked: "May I help you?" when anyone entered the house.

In 1949, Sister Marianne moved to St. Francis Convent in Manoa.

She loved to watch TV, especially soap operas and kept track of the characters and their doings. While watching TV, she crocheted leis, which she graciously gave to every visitor.

In 1976, she retired from active duty. After many years of illness, she died on December 27, 1995.

Sister Vera O'Brien (1918 – 2007)
Kalaupapa – 1954 - 1958

Born in 1918, the year that Mother Marianne died, Catherine completed the Registered Nurse Program at Auburn Memorial Hospital at Auburn, N.Y. before she entered the Sisters of St. Francis at Syracuse, N.Y. As Sister Vera, she spent four years at Bishop Home at Kalaupapa and several years at St. Francis Hospital in Honolulu.

In her later years, Sister Vera served as receptionist at St. Anthony Motherhouse in Syracuse.

Sister Mary Benedicta Rodenmacher (1855 – 1942)
Kalaupapa – 1916 - 1929

After entering the Sisters of St. Francis in Syracuse, Sister Benedicta volunteered for Hawai'i and served at Kapi'olani Home from 1888 until 1916. At that time, she went to Kalaupapa to assist Mother Marianne in her last years. Sister Benedicta stayed on at Kalaupapa until 1929, at which time she returned to Kapi'olani Home.

Mother Jolenta Wilson (1895 – 1968)
Kalaupapa – 1935 - 1939

In 1933, Sister Jolenta at age 38, travelled to Hawai'i to take up the role of supervisor of nurses at St. Francis Hospital in Honolulu. She spent four years at Bishop Home in Kalaupapa. In 1946, she returned to St. Francis Hospital in Honolulu as superior and superintendent.

In 1946, the Sisters of St. Francis named her as superior of all the Hawaiian missions. In 1953, the Sisters at Syracuse elected her as mother general of the congregation. The Sisters re-elected her to a second term in 1959.

While visiting Kalaupapa as Mother Jolenta in the late 1950s – early 1960s, she contemplated the removal of the remains of Mother Marianne to Syracuse, but the pleading of the patients and residents persuaded her not to do that.

From the Blessed Marianne Cope website - Late 1950s-60s

Rev. Mother M. Jolenta Wilson's planned to exhume Mother Marianne's remains. The process is suspended temporarily after she visits Kalaupapa to make arrangements and meets with patients who knew Mother Marianne and care for her grave. Patients ask for the exhumation not to be done while they are alive.

Chapter 9: **Deceased Sisters and Graves**

Sister Margaret Mary Bennis (1881 – 1975)
Kalaupapa – 1935 - 1947

Elizabeth Bennis trained as a nurse and served overseas as an army nurse during World War I. Then she entered the convent.

In 1929, she went to Hawai'i where she did both teaching and nursing on the islands of Maui, Hawai'i, and O'ahu. In 1935, she went to the Island of Moloka'i where she did nursing care of the patients with Hansen's disease until 1947.

Her funeral in 1975 included the liturgy of the Church, the homage of her community of sisters, and the United States flag on her casket because of her years as an army nurse.

Sister Mary Berchmans Schack (1909 – 1995)
Kalaupapa – 1938 - 1946

Born in Germany, Sister Mary Berchmans entered the Sisters of St. Francis in Rome, Italy. She came to the United States and learned English. When she went to Hawai'i, she worked at both the Kapi'olani Home in Honolulu and Bishop Home in Kalaupapa where she served as a practical nurse and x-ray technician.

Sister Lucy Wessner (1902 – 1969)
Kalaupapa – 1938 - 1941

In the late 1930s, Sister Lucy worked at Kapi'olani home and then at Kalaupapa at Bishop Home.

Sister Carmela Chmeilewska (1894 – 1953)
Kalaupapa – 1938 – 1942, 1948 - 1958

After entering the Sisters of St. Francis, Sister Carmela trained as a nurse. In 1938, she travelled to Kalaupapa and devoted herself to the care of the patients. When she assisted a young mother who had leprosy and was in labor, Sister Carmela suffered a heart attack from the exertion. She died soon thereafter.

Sister Julia Albicker (1900 – 1949)
Kalaupapa – 1945 - 1946

After spending her early years in the convent as a teacher, Sister Julia went to Hawai'i to serve as director of novices. She taught school and served as convent superior at Lahaina on the Island of Maui.

In 1945, Sister Julia moved to Kalaupapa as superior of St. Elizabeth convent at the Bishop Home complex.

Sister Antonia Brown (1859 – 1945)
Kalaupapa – 1905 – 1918, 1928

When Sister Antonia first moved to Hawai'i, she taught at St. Anthony School in Wailuku, Maui, and St. Joseph School in Hilo, on the Island of Hawai'i.

In 1905, she moved to Kalaupapa and worked along side Mother Marianne until 1918. After that, she went to Kapi'olani Home and later to St. Francis Hospital.

Sister Antonia would have come to know Mother Marianne in those 13 years.

Sister John Vianney Murdy (1904 – 1991)
Kalaupapa – 1947 - 1955

With teaching catechetics as her specialty, Sister John Vianney spent eight years (1947 to 1955) at Bishop Home in Kalaupapa.

Chapter 9: **Deceased Sisters and Graves**

Sister Joseph Marie Brager (1896 – 1969)
Kalaupapa – 1940 – 1945, 1948 - 1958

As a young sister, Sister Joseph Marie taught schools and then began training as a nurse. As a nurse, she moved to Hawai'i where she cared for children at Kapi'olani Home and at Bishop Home at Kalaupapa.

She taught at several island schools and then returned to Kalaupapa as superior of the sisters' convent.

Sister Mary Teresa Talbott (1899 – 1969)
Kalaupapa – 1945 - 1948

Sister Mary Teresa taught small children in Syracuse and Albany before her assignment to Hawai'i, where she taught at several schools. After a year of nursing school, she moved to Bishop Home at the Kalaupapa Settlement on Moloka'i where she worked with the children and served as superior of the convent.

Sister Hermina Wameling (Mary Magdaline) (1884 – 1972)
Kalaupapa – 1942 - 1947

Sister Hermina entered the convent at age 15 and taught in parish schools in New Jersey, New York, and Ohio. She studied for and received her RN and worked in the nursing field for 30 years, five of which she devoted to the care of patients with leprosy at Kalaupapa's Bishop Home.

Sister Marie Celine Wagner (1894 – 1991)
Kalaupapa – 1939 - 1964

For 63 years, Sister Celine devoted her time to serving the people of Hawai'i. She decided to become a Sister of St. Francis after reading an article about the plight of people with the disease of leprosy on Moloka'i in the Universe Bulletin of the Cleveland Diocese.

"I wanted to enter," she said, "because I did not want to risk not being sent to Moloka'i."

In 1928, she moved to St. Francis Hospital in Honolulu where she trained as a nurse and received her degree. As superintendent of Kapi'olani Home, she oversaw the care of the healthy babies born to parents with Hansen's disease.

When Kapi'olani home closed once people knew that leprosy was not inherited, Sister Celine moved to Kalaupapa where her skills as a practical nurse kept her busy for 25 years. She did pharmacy work and took charge of fumigation procedures.

Sister Mary Francis Kostka (1903 – 1950)
Kalaupapa – 1947 - 1950

Sister Mary Francis spent three years at Bishop Home at Kalaupapa as well as some time at Kapi'olani Home and schools on the Islands.

Sister Francine Greis (1921 – 2007)
Kalaupapa – 1955 – 1956, 1957 - 1964

The last 26 years of Sister Francine's ministry saw her develop the first and largest hospice program in Hawai'i. She began it in 1978 and served as the executive director until 2004.

Sister Francine, in her younger years, earned a BS as a nurse and then an MS in nursing administration. She used her skills at St. Francis Hospital in Honolulu and at Kalaupapa, Moloka'i.

Sister Dativa Padilla (1932 – 2003)
Kalaupapa – 1964 – 1967, 1979 - 2003

Born of parents from the Philippines, Euphemia earned her nursing degree from St. Francis Hospital, Honolulu, School of Nursing before she entered the Sisters of St. Francis. She pursued graduate studies at the Catholic University of America.

Chapter 9: **Deceased Sisters and Graves**

Her ministry took her back to St. Francis Hospital in Honolulu as well as St. Elizabeth Hospital in Utica, N.Y. and then to Bishop Home and Hospital at Kalaupapa from 1964 to 1967 and again from 1970 to 2004. In 1992, she became the assistant supervisor of Kalaupapa Care Home.

The people of Hawai'i honored Sister "Tiva" as an "Island Treasure" at a Catholic Charities recognition event in 2002.

Sister Dativa is one of the few sisters who worked at Kalaupapa both before and after the 1969 lifting of the isolation.

http://www.youtube.com/watch?v=EbdWsNJm83U&feature=youtube_gdata_player

Sister Mary Claudia Cabral (1925 – 1987)
Kalaupapa – 1960 - 1966

Since the age of 4, Sister Claudia loved to climb trees. She met her death from neck injuries she suffered when she fell from a mango tree on the convent grounds in Lahaina, Maui.

In between those times, Sister Claudia served as teacher and principal at Island schools. She worked at Kalaupapa from 1960 to 1966.

Sister Cyrilla Erhart (1860 – 1947)
Kalaupapa – 1929 - 1931

Shortly after her profession, Sister Cyrilla arrived at Kaka'ako Receiving Station in Honolulu where she worked alongside Mother Marianne. Less than a year later, she went to the new hospital named Maululani at Wailuku, Maui.

In 1929, Sister Cyrilla started a two-year stretch at Kalaupapa's Bishop Home. In her 42 years of providing nursing care, she ministered to each patient's spiritual needs as well as physical needs.

Sister Cordis Marie Burns (1939 – 1999)
Kalaupapa – 1967 - 1968

Sister Cordis Marie received her BS in nursing form D'Youville College in Buffalo, N.Y. and her MS in nursing from the Catholic University of America. In the broad range of her ministry as nurse, Sister Cordis Marie also counseled patients with addictions. She also created Serenity House for those with addictions. She worked for a time at Kalaupapa Hospital, Moloka'i.

Sister Martina Feichtner (1897 – 1992)
Kalaupapa - 1947 - 1952

Born in Germany and having trained there as a practical nurse, Carolina came to the United States to enter the Sisters of St. Francis at Syracuse. As Sister Martina, she taught at several parish schools.

In 1948, she went to Bishop Home in Kalaupapa for five years and then to other Hawaiian missions for a span of 32 years.

Sister Columba O'Keefe (1886 – 1968)
Kalaupapa – 1915 - 1916

This Irish born sister entered at Syracuse and finished her novitiate in Honolulu. She worked at the hospitals in Kalaupapa, Hilo, and Honolulu.

Sister Mary Louis Warth (1867 – 1952)
Kalaupapa - 1930 - 1931

After teaching in several mainland parish schools, Sister Mary Louis taught at schools in Hilo, Lahaina, and at Kapi'olani Home where she also served as superior. In 1930, She spent a year at Kalaupapa.

Chapter 9: **Deceased Sisters and Graves**

Sister Anysia Adler (1899 – 1991)
Kalaupapa - 1945 - 1951

Theresa spent her childhood at Assumption Parish in Syracuse, and entered the convent at age 15. She cared for children and for the elderly as well as teaching and tutoring in various places. She trained as a nurse and worked at hospitals in New York State and later in Hawai'i at St. Francis Hospital in Honolulu, and then at Bishop Home Hospital at Kalaupapa, Moloka'i, for six years.

Sister Wilma Halmasy and Sister Mary Laurence Hanley

See Chapter 2 for Sister Wilma and Sister Mary Laurence

Some sisters who worked at Kalaupapa died in other places and lie buried at Syracuse, N.Y. or elsewhere.

List of Sisters on assignments at Kalaupapa
1888 to present

Mother Marianne Cope	1888 to 1918	30 yrs.
Sr. M. Vincentia McCormick	1888 to 1890	2 yrs.
Sr. Leopoldina Burns	1888 to 1928	40 yrs.
Sr. M. Irene Schorp	1889 to 1895	6 yrs.
Sr. M. Crescentia Eilers	1889 to 1929	40 yrs.
Sr. M. Renata Nash	1890 to 1891	1 yr.
Sr. M. Elizabeth Gomes	1891 to 1945	54 yrs.
Sr. M. Albina Sluder	1892 to 1895	3 yrs.
Sr. M. Bonaventure Oechtering	1900	1 yr.
Sr. Antonia Brown	1905 to 1917	12 yrs.
Sr. Columba O'Keefe	1915 to 1916	1 yr.
Sr. M. Benedicta Rodenmacher	1916 to 1929	13 yrs.
Sr. M. Magdalene Miller	1921 to 1926	5 yrs.
Sr. M. Cyrilla Erhart	1929 to 1931	2 yrs.
Sr. M. Flaviana Engel	1929 to 1935	6 yrs.
Sr. M. Praxedes Lynch	1929 to 1945	16 yrs.
Sr. Mary Louis Warth	1930	1 yr.
Sr. Marianne Carvalho	1932 to 1948	16 yrs.
Mother M. Jolenta Wilson	1935 to 1939	4 yrs.
Sr. Margaret Mary Bennis	1935 to 1947	12 yrs.
Sr. M. Lidwina Mitsch	1938 to 1939	1 yr.
Sr. M. Lucy Wessner	1938 to 1941	3 yrs.
Sr. M. Carmelita Chmeilewska	1938 to 1942 1944 to 1953	13 yrs.
Sr. M. Berchmans Schack	1938 to 1946	8 yrs.
Sr. M. Anne Adams	1938 to 1960	22 yrs.
Sr. Mary Joseph Cotleur	1939 to 1950	11 yrs.
Sr. Marie Celine Wagner	1939 to 1964	25 yrs.
Sr. M. Joseph Marie Brager	1940 to 1945 1948 to 1958	15 yrs.
Sr. M. Hermina Wameling	1942 to 1947	5 yrs.
Sr. M. Julia Albicker	1945 to 1946	1 yr.
Sr. M. Teresa Talbott	1945 to 1948	3 yrs.
Sr. M. Anysia Adler	1945 to 1951	6 yrs.

Chapter 9: Deceased Sisters and Graves

Sr. M. Wilma Halmasy	1946 to 1955	
	1962 to 1969	32 yrs.
Sr. M. Francis Kostka	1947 to 1950	3 yrs.
Sr. M. Martina Feichtner	1947 to 1952	5 yrs.
Sr. John Vianney Murdy	1947 to 1955	8 yrs.
Sr. M. Rosanne La Manche	1949 to 1952	
	1955 to 1961	9 yrs.
Sr. M. Vera O'Brien	1954 to 1958	4 yrs.
Sr. M. Francine Greis	1955 to 1956	
	1957 to 1964	8 yrs.
Sr. M. Norma Mihalko	1955 to 1960	5 yrs.
Sr. M. Gaudentia Muchlinski	1958 to 1959	
	1968 to 1977	10 yrs.
Sr. M. Christopher Dixon	1959 to 1966	7 yrs.
Sr. M. Claudia Cabral	1960 to 1966	6 yrs.
Sr. Richard Marie Toal	1960 to 1971	
	1973 to 2000	38 yrs.
Sr. Mary Philip Alijado	1964 to 1966	
	1973 to 1974	3 yrs.
Sr. M. Dativa Padilla	1964 to 1967	
	1979 to 2004	28 yrs.
Sr. Frances Cabrini Morishige	1966 to 1968	
	1996 to 1997	
	2002 to 2007	8 yrs.
Sr. Hilary Tindall	1966 to 1974	8 yrs.
Sr. M. Andrew Bomba	1966 to 1975	9 yrs.
Sr. Cordis Marie Burns	1967 to 1968	1 yr.
Sr. Particia (Mary Edmond) Clark	1969 to 1975	6 yrs.
Sr. Emmett Ann Geary	1970 to 1973	3 yrs.
Sr. Eligia Eiholzer	1971 to 1974	
	1983 to 1990	10 yrs.
Sr. Corita Miura	1974 to 1979	5 yrs.
Sr. Mary Ann (Timothea) Kane	1975 to 1977	2 yrs.
Sr. Gertrude Martin Delaney	1975 to 1979	4 yrs.
Sr. Mirian Dionise Cabacungan	1980 to 1983	3 yrs.
Sr. Agatha Perreira	1988 to 1989	1 yr.
Sr. Frances Therese Souza	1989 to 1994	
	1995 to Preset	21 yrs.

Sr. Rose Annette Ahuna	2009 to Present
St. Theresa Chow	2009 to Present

Chapter 9: **Deceased Sisters and Graves**

Mid 20th Century Visitor

Ernie Pyle (1900 – 1945)
Kalaupapa – "surely spiritual, almost heavenly"

Ernie Pyle, a journalist who served as a war correspondent during World War II and spent time in the Pacific arena. People loved his writings, which read as letters from the field to those at home.

He died on Okinawa as Japanese machine gunfire attacked him. He lies buried at the National Cemetery on the Hawaiian Island of O‘ahu.

In 1937, he visited Kalaupapa and left with a very favorable impression of the people and their lives there. His narrative about his impressions appeared as Chapter 16 – The Leper Colony – in the posthumous book titled *Home County* (1947).

Pyle's introductory paragraph labels the "leper colony" as "the martyring place of Father Damien." Arriving by airplane, Pyle noticed "cemetery after cemetery" and expected to find a gloomy place.

He describes the great consciousness of both patients and non-patients to take the necessary precautions such as not shaking hands, not touching things, and the use of alcohol and other disinfectants.

He also takes notice of the flowers and vines and shrubs and gardens everywhere – around the private cottages as well as around the group homes at the settlement.

Writing that the word "leper" is "a word that is in disfavor in Kalaupapa" – (remember this is the 1930s) – and the word "patient" is the current phrase used at the time.

About 500 people lived at Kalaupapa at the time of Pyle's visit – about 400 with the disease of leprosy and about 100 well people.

Pyle writes about the babies born to parents with leprosy and how they babies are taken away and placed with adopting families or placed at homes like Kapiʻolani.

In a poignant paragraph, this writer tells of only four leprosy cases among those who came to serve, and this mainly because of a lack of precautions.

He states: "Some of the nuns had been there even longer." This, in reference to Brother Dutton who served there for 44 years and never got leprosy. None of the nuns ever got leprosy.

Those who did include Father Damien, Brother Van Lyl, a doctor whose name is not given, and Father Peter, who had the disease but with treatment had a cure or remission. Father Peter lived at Kalaupapa at the time of Ernie Pyle's visit and the two men shared conversations.

Pyle devotes several paragraphs to Father Peter d'Orgeval-Dubouchet, a missionary from France. Father Peter arrived in Kalaupapa in 1925 and two years into his time there, he contracted leprosy. Early treatment saved him and he tended to the spiritual needs of the people of the settlement for many years.

Pyle also devotes several paragraphs to his time and conversation with Shizuo Harada, "a full-blooded Japanese." The two men shared ideas about the need for more doctors to do leprosy research and also the ways that leprosy affects people – "their minds, their attitudes, their whole remaining lives."

"My stay at Kalaupapa was one of the most powerful adventures of my life, " Pyle wrote, toward the end of his essay. He felt an atmosphere of calmness, "an atmosphere that was surely spiritual, almost heavenly."

Listening to ten men sing "Aloha ʻoe" to him as he left the settlement brought " tears in his eyes."

21st Century visitors to Kalaupapa, as well as those of earlier times, get to see the cliffs and peninsula, the high valleys and pali zone, the intertidal and reef zone, the coastal scrub zone, the Kauhako Crater zone, and the coastal beach zone.

Chapter 9: **Deceased Sisters and Graves**

Rainbows and sunsets offer special natural beauty.

As they visit the settlements of Kalawao and Kalaupapa settlements on the Makanalua Peninsula, they visit the areas associated with Mother Marianne and Father Damien as well as some of the prehistoric and early historic aspects of the land and sea. They come to know the living historical community of the last remnants of those whose disease quarantined them in that place until 1969 and who choose to remain there and call Kalaupapa their home. They become aware of the natural resources and resource stressors and the sad history of some 8,000 persons who lived and died throughout the quarantine years of 1866 to 1969.

Sister Rose Annette Ahuna of Kalaupapa tidies the site of St. Marianne's grave.

Photo: Sister Barbara Jean Wajda

Chapter 10

Na Kokua - the Helpers

Sister Cyrilla, in Wailuku since July 1887, said she had always wanted "to nurse the poor lepers.... Therefore, dear Mother, I am ready to go with God's grace whenever you call me."
-P&E

In this chapter

Many of the sisters who spent time at Kalaupapa, on assignment as well as on a volunteer basis shared their stories in writings and in taped oral histories. Their experiences tell of the great variety of ways in which God's presence lives in the relationships between patients and caregivers.

Three sisters, a nurse and two volunteers for tours and talks, reside at Kalaupapa at the time of St. Marianne's canonization.

Voices of the Sisters of St. Francis

"We want to include anyone who may have something to share about

their time in the mission at Kalaupapa - since multiple perspectives will give a richer picture of life on this little piece of land that is giving the world two saints."
- Sister Barbara Jean Wajda, iNews of Sisters of St. Francis, June 2012

An invitation asked for input from the sisters who served in Kalaupapa over the years, either as an assigned ministry or as volunteer ministry (na kokua) - those who helped out during summers, holidays or weekends so the resident sisters could go for home, doctor, and other visits, or who took part in any other aspects of life on the peninsula.

Living Sisters – interviews and stories
Both regular assignments and na kokua

Name of Sister	at Kalaupapa
Sister Norma Mihalko	1955 to 1960
Sister Christopher Dixon	1959 to 1966
Sister Richard Marie	1960 – 1971, 1973 – 2000 Both before 1969 and after
Sister Dativa	1964 – 1967, 1979 – 2004 both before 1969 and after
Sister Frances Cabrini	1966 to 1968 and 1996 to 1997
Sister Ruth Esther	both before 1969 and after
Sister Mary Andrew	1966 – 1975, 1992 – 1995 both before 1969 and after

1969 – a Turning Point

Sister Patricia Clark	1969 to 1975
Sister Laurenza	after 1969

Chapter 10: **Na Kokua - The Helpers**

Sister Anonymous	after 1969
Sister Agatha	1988 - 1989
Sister Roseanne	after 1969
Sister Gwendolyn	after 1969
Sister William Marie	after 1969
Sister Miriam Dionise	1980 - 1983

Sisters currently at Kalaupapa

Sister Frances Therese	2009 – present of 2012
Sister Rose Annette	2009 – present of 2012
Sister Theresa Chow	2009 – present of 2012
Sister Frances Cabrini	1966 – 1968, 1996 – 1997, 2002 - 2007

Sisters who work at Kalaupapa

Among the many, many Sisters of St. Francis who brought Gospel living to Kalaupapa as they carried on the work begun by Mother Marianne and the pioneer sisters, several still live either in Hawai'i or in Syracuse, N.Y. Sister Barbara Jean Wajda, a native of Western New York, lives in Honolulu and interviewed several of these sisters, both those who had served as long time caregivers at Kalaupapa and those who went there as part time volunteers, often in the summer months, to allow the others to leave for vacation, retreat, family visits, and appointments. Sister Alicia Damien Lau, also of Honolulu, interviewed and recorded on tape several sisters who had formerly been assigned to Kalaupapa.

Actually, the Kalaupapa National Historic Park now considers all non-patients who help at Kalaupapa as na kokua.

Sister M. Norma Mihalko
At Kalaupapa from 1955 to 1960

Sister Norma, who served as convent cook at Kalaupapa in the days before 1969, told how any mingling with the patients required a bath and all clean clothes.

She prepared meals three times a day, seven days a week, and also meals for visitors. She also cooked the main meal for noonday for the priests who ate apart from the sisters.

During Sister Norma's time at Kalaupapa, six sisters lived at the convent, as the Hawaiian government required no less than six.

Following directives from the time of Mother Marianne, the sisters ate no food grown by the patients on the peninsula, but rather obtained their food from Topside Moloka'i brought down on mules or from the occasional barge from Honolulu.

Before 1969, even the fish that the sisters caught off Kalaupapa shores

Chapter 10: **Na Kokua - The Helpers**

went to the patients.

Someone gave Sister Norma a camera and she took many photos, which she showed to the interviewer. The listener of the taped interview had to imagine the pictures as Sister Norma talked about them and showed them to the interviewer.

From time to time, tidal waves hit the Hawaiian Islands and came ashore at Kalaupapa. The helpers moved the patients to higher ground and soldiers came to help restore things. Sister Norma remembered that she had prepared meals for these soldiers. To her delight, one time, the soldiers took her for a ride in their airplane.

When she asked, they told her: "You have to work for the government to ride in the plane."

"I do," she told them.

Yes, the Hawaiian government employed the sisters for the care of people afflicted with Hansen's disease.

One of Sister Norma's memories told of a student pilot who flew in with a load of eggs. He somewhat crash landed and all the eggs shattered. The sisters had no eggs for over a month.

Sister Norma said that she felt "doubly isolated" as she was not allowed to mingle with the patients and also she had to keep her distance from the sisters who worked with the patients. None of the sisters were allowed to enter or use the kitchen. This too dated back to the time of Mother Marianne, who protected the sisters from the disease by guarding well the food they ate.

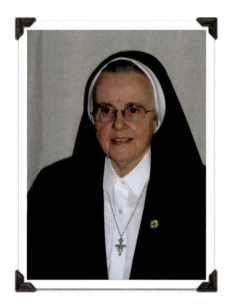

Sister Mary Christopher Dixon
At Kalaupapa from 1959 to 1966

From her girlhood on a farm near Syracuse, N.Y. Sister Mary Christopher holds only good memories of her time at the Kalaupapa mission. At St. Elizabeth Hospital, Utica, from which she graduated, Sister Mary Christopher made the rounds with Sister Regina and learned by doing.

She professed her final vows on August 18 and by August 22, she was on her way to Kalaupapa. At that time in 1959, about 500 patients resided at Kalaupapa, about half the number of Mother Marianne's time.

Sister Mary Christopher talked about the frequent change of clothing from black habit at the convent to white habit for going to the hospital and to hospital gown for procedures in the hospital. And, the sisters made the change of clothes in reverse, for going back to the convent. She cherished the walk from convent to hospital and back because it gave her a chance to pause at the gravesite of Mother Marianne.

At the hospital, Sister Mary Christopher worked in the surgery unit

Chapter 10: **Na Kokua - The Helpers**

and in the dressings room where she tended the open wounds of the patients.

She did IVs and syringe doses. She worked on a rotation basis, taking turns at the three shifts that covered 24 hours. She mentioned how international the hospital staff became as doctors and nurses came from other countries as well as from Hawai'i.

The sisters and patients celebrated Damien Day each year with picnics at Kalawao. They played cards, volleyball, and other games "just to be with the people" for recreation times.

Sister Mary Christopher told of one patient who placed several fish bones in her hair with the belief that this would dislodge a fish bone caught in her throat. By the next day, the patient was fine.

"Mother Marianne's scale was still in use," Sister Mary Christopher said, "to measure out the medicines. A drawer underneath the scale contained the weights."

Hiking became a favorite way to spend a day off. The sisters, often with patients, would walk for three hours to Waikolu Valley and eat lunch near the stream where Father Damien had first found fresh water for the settlement. In the afternoon, they would walk back.

Sister Mary Christopher spoke of Mother Marianne as "a woman ahead of her time" – especially about infections and preventing them. She said that the sisters still lived by the rules and boundaries of behavior set by Mother Marianne. They washed their hands before and after procedures.

"I didn't do it because I was scared," Mary Christopher said, in reference to sanitary measures at Kalaupapa.

"I did it because it was truly the right thing to do. We could have also given the patients our diseases too."

Sister Richard Marie Toal
1960 to 1971 and 1973 to 2000

In the interview with Sister Mary Andrew Bomba, Sister Barbara Jean also learned some stories about Sister Richard Marie.

Sister Mary Andrew had stories to tell of Sister Richard Marie, who resides at St. Francis Convent in Honolulu.

"Sister Richard Marie did not know anything about plants," Sister Mary Andrew said.

"Sister Richard Marie wanted to do something to help, so she went out to pull weeds at Mother Marianne's gravesite. A lady came to the convent to ask who had pulled all the mums from the garden at the gravesite."

"Another time, Jimmy Davidson, the gardener, planted anthurium, also known as flamingo flower for its bright red, deep pink blooms. Sister Richard Marie uprooted them from where they were and planted them

Chapter 10: **Na Kokua - The Helpers**

where they should not be. After that episode, she stayed away from plants and stuck with fishing."

Often, Sister Richard Marie went fishing for the day and Paul Harada, a resident, went along to keep her safe. They would bring home fish for the cat. The dog waited outdoors all day for their return.

Sister Richard Marie also cooked some fish for Father Gustave who enjoyed it right down to the skeleton.

Thinking about cooking, Sister Mary Andrew noted, Sister Richard Marie had a favorite meal and that was spaghetti and meatballs.

"She made enough for two days worth of eating."

In the interview with Sister Alicia Damien, Sister Richard Marie remembered the "good days" of her nearly 40 years at Kalaupapa.

Sister Richard Marie talked about all the walking she did to the various buildings in those days before the sisters had a car. She explained the eight-hour work shifts of morning, afternoon into evening, and night.

Her reputation as a "fisherwoman" remains and once found its way into a magazine.

The interviewer observed how much Sister Richard Marie loved the people of Kalaupapa and how much they loved her. Sister Richard Marie admitted that she felt sad when she left Kalaupapa in 2000. She so loved the Kalaupapa mission.

"Those days are gone now," Sister Richard Marie said as the interviewer praised her for her "ministry to suffering people … whatever their different needs."

While no special highlights came to mind for Sister Richard Marie, she said that she enjoyed the daily routine of hospital and school – where she taught adults.

Sister Frances Cabrini Morishige
At Kalaupapa from 1966 to 1968 and 1996 to 1997

Witness to dramatic changes

Sister Frances Cabrini worked at Kalaupapa in the 1960s and in the 1990s and saw significant changes in those decades.

During her first time there – 1966 to 1968 – "isolation was a key issue," she said.

"Clothes needed to be changed upon entry into the convent. The sisters were not allowed to socialize with the patients. Outgoing mail needed to be fumigated.

"The setting remained very strict even though sulfonamide drugs had been proven effective," she remembered.

"I was not afraid of going there," she said. "I went out of obedience. The isolation and the disease were very much like going to another hospital."

Chapter 10: **Na Kokua - The Helpers**

By her second time – 1996 to 1997 – the situation had become "totally different," she said. "Socializing was allowed and the changing of clothes after work was no longer required."

(Hawai'i lifted the isolation laws in 1969.)

Sister Frances Cabrini said that "the isolation from my Honolulu family, the sisters and friends there, did not bother me. It was not an issue."

From 2002 until 2007, Sister Frances Cabrini worked in Kalaupapa as a volunteer, a kokua.

In a June 2012 visit to Kalaupapa, Sister Frances Cabrini toured the archives and said: "I am amazed at the newness of the archives building, which was not paneled or painted when I worked here earlier.

"I remember climbing up and dusting all the shelves and all the artifacts, which at that time were piled on shelves awaiting cataloguing.

"The order and tidiness of the room, just recently paneled, painted, and air-controlled, is such a delightful sight to me," she said.

Cradle to Convent
Sister Ruth Esther Sherman
Kalaupapa in the 1950s, 1960s, and 1990s

Sister Ruth Esther spent summers at Kalaupapa in the 1950s, 1960s and again in the 1990s. Her experiences there crossed over the year of 1969 when Hawai'i lifted the isolation of persons with Hansen's disease.

In writing her autobiography, Ruth Esther titled it *Cradle to Convent*. She told how she was baptized Catholic at age 12 and entered the convent at age 18 after a couple of years in the Sisters of St. Francis Juniorate high school program. Her early missions took her to convents where she cooked and taught primary grades in New Jersey and New York State.

Her overseas missionary life over the years encompassed both Hawai'i and Peru.

Chapter 10: **Na Kokua - The Helpers**

Damien Statues

In the 1960s, Sister Ruth Esther and her mother Bessie began making bust statues of Father Damien. At first, Sister Ruth Esther worked with students at Manoa's St. Francis School's Art Department, which she founded, to make statues of Father Damien, as part of the effort to get a statue of Father Damien into the Hall of Fame at Washington, DC. Her efforts helped and Father Damien was chosen to stand in the Hall of Fame.

The Damien Council YMI (Young Men's Institute) in Honolulu paid the way for Sister Ruth Esther to go to Kalaupapa to teach the patients there how to make the statues. In all, they made 500 Father Damien statues.

Marianne Statues

In 1968, Mother Viola asked Sister Ruth Esther for a Mother Marianne bust statue. Working with her mother Bessie at a mission in Mexico, they sculptured the original image in Mexican clay. Then Sister Ruth Esther made rubber molds from the sculpture and began making Mother Marianne statues.

In the 1990s, the Kalaupapa Arts and Crafts Group paid Sister Ruth Esther's way for her to come and teach them to make Father Damien and Mother Marianne statues. Sister Ruth Esther still had one Father Damien rubber mold, now 30 years old, and it still worked well with PermaStone. Some of the other molds had been lost in a fire.

In 1998, Sister Dativa got involved in making Mother Marianne statues of PermaStone , which she dressed with a cloth veil.

In 2004, Sister Ruth Esther took her final visit to Kalaupapa to celebrate her diamond jubilee. She also visited her former mission in Peru.

Mission in Peru

Sister Ruth Esther had worked in Peru in the early 1970s at Paramonga.

Sister Ruth Esther, her mother, and other sisters helped out in rescue clinics when the May 1970 earthquake brought havoc to the area. From 1973 until 1979, Sister Ruth Esther continued her missionary work in Pativilca, Peru, until a car crash seriously injured her.

When she could travel, she was brought to St. Joseph Hospital in Syracuse and went through 15 surgeries to remedy her injuries.

Back to Hawai'i

Sister Ruth Esther returned to Hawai'i to St. Joseph School in Hilo. She had earlier worked in Hawai'i at St. Joseph in Hilo and also St. Francis School at Manoa.

Sister Ruth Esther, daughter of Bessie, an ordained Methodist missionary, entered the Sisters of St. Francis Juniorate in 1941 and completed her high school education. At her reception ceremony, she received the name of Sister Mary Clarence. Another in her group received the name of Sister Mary Laurence, later the author of *Pilgrimage and Exile.*

Sister Mary Clarence professed her first vows in 1946 and final vows in 1949, at which time she moved to Hawai'i. While teaching at the schools, Sister Ruth Esther spent her summers at Kalaupapa where she did convent cooking and assisted patients in their personal and home care in their cottages.

Later, she returned to her birth / baptismal name of Ruth Esther. Sister Ruth Esther returned to Peru from 1984 to 1989.

Ruth becomes a Catholic

In her autobiography, Ruth tells of the time a young Irish Catholic boy came to live with her family after his parents both died. Ruth's mother Bessie began to read the Catholic paper that came to the house for the boy. Bessie became interested in the Catholic faith and she with her three children, one of them Ruth, received (provisional) baptism at the local parish church. They had all been previously baptized in the

Chapter 10: **Na Kokua - The Helpers**

Methodist faith tradition.

About the same time, Ruth met two Sisters of St. Francis at the church and with their encouragement, Ruth went to Syracuse to the Juniorate for her high school years. Later, her father also became Catholic and both parents came often to visit Sister Ruth Esther.

Sister Ruth Esther's story is online at a family website.

http://atwaterpress.com/family/1926.1.info.html
http://atwaterpress.com/family/1926.1.auto.html

Her mother Bessie's story
http://www.atwaterpress.com/family/1899.1.auto.html

Sister Dativa Padilla (1932 – 2003)
Kalaupapa – 1964 to 1967 and 1979 to 2003

The ministry of Sister Dativa took her to St. Francis Hospital in Honolulu and then to Bishop Home and Hospital at Kalaupapa from

1964 to 1967 and again from 1970 to 2003. In 1992, she became the assistant supervisor of Kalaupapa Care Home. Sister Dativa, though now deceased, is one of the few sisters who lived in Kalaupapa both before and after the ban, which was lifted in 1969.

Although Sister Dativa is deceased, she appears in this section because her ministry in Kalaupapa lasted until 2003.

The people of Hawai'i honored Sister "Tiva" as an "Island Treasure" at a Catholic Charities recognition event in 2002. She died in 2003.

Sister Mary Andrew Bomba
1966 to 1975 and 1992 to 1995

At age 11 in her hometown in Texas, some 70 years ago, Sister Mary Andrew heard a sermon about the charity of Father Damien. Now in her 80s, Sister Mary Andrew still remembers that sermon.

In the 1940s, two young women in Texas considered entering religious life. When a Q and A appeared in a magazine that they both read, they thought that each other had sent in the question. Sister Mary Andrew

Chapter 10: **Na Kokua - The Helpers**

wanted to know what sisters worked where Father Damien had worked and here was her answer in the magazine.

"I thought she (the other young woman) had sent in the question and she thought I had. Anyway, I now had my answer to what I had wondered since age 11," Sister Mary Andrew said.

As a young adult, much like Mother Marianne, Sister Mary Andrew helped out at home by caring for the aged and the young and those who took ill. Also, much like Mother Marianne, Sister Mary Andrew was in her mid 20s when she entered the convent in 1947 and became a Sister of St. Francis at Syracuse. As a young sister, Sister Mary Andrew learned the story of Mother Marianne.

"I wanted to help people with my hands," Sister Mary Andrew said.

In 1966, Sister Mary Andrew went to Kalaupapa for a nine-year assignment at the mission there. She lived with six other sisters, all nurses, who took turns with night duty at the hospital. Sister Mary Andrew, who had taught in the schools for 17 years prior to this, now cooked, sewed, cleaned, and laundered for the sisters at the convent. For special occasions she also cooked along with members of the other church groups in the settlement.

Sister Mary Andrew spoke of the day she arrived at Kalaupapa and how Sister Richard Marie, a nurse on night duty, would come home around noon, have lunch, and go to bed. Sister Richard Marie helped the newly arrived sisters get adjusted.

"Sister Wilma," Mary Andrew recalled, "served as hospital supervisor in the late 1960s and early 1970s and used her artistic and creative skills for drama and crafts with the patients."

"One time, the sisters got a recipe from my aunt for making wine," Sister Mary Andrew explained. "We put yeast in some juice and put it in the closet of the guest room so no one could find it and criticize us. Sister Frances Cabrini was in on this."

Sister Mary Andrew recalled that Sister Frances Cabrini and Sister

Celine took care of the pharmacy in those same years.

Sister Mary Andrew recalled that Kenso Seki, a patient with fingerless hands, "kept after the boys to drink their milk and eat their vegetables."

Kenso knew how easy it was to get tuberculosis and "the boys gave credit for their good health to Kenso."

During her years at Kalaupapa, Sister Mary Andrew loved to hear the choir under the direction of Father Gustave Fierens, SSCC, and she still has a 33rpm record they made at the time (1961).

Some of the selections of the recording – A Tribute to Father Damien, with 13 tracks, may be heard (with a slide show of photos) at YouTube.

She recalled how Father Gustave came every day for Mass and how he so kindly visited the patients.

As with many who begin a new ministry, Sister Mary Andrew wondered how she would learn all the names of the patients and be able to tell them apart. "They all look alike, at first," she said.

Sister Mary Andrew had a knack for making jelly from whatever fruits she found available. She made jars of apple jelly for the patients at Christmas and she reminisced, "Oh, how they always wanted more."

She thinks that her recipes are in a book that might still be at Kalaupapa.

When they could, Sister Mary Andrew and the other sisters liked to go over to the other side of the peninsula, to Kalawao, to watch the sunrise, and in the evening to the pier at Kalaupapa to "watch the fish of many colors."

"To go to the dentist with Sister Hilary," Sister Mary Andrew narrated, "we would climb the pali to topside."

Residents of topside "would look down the pali at Christmastime" Andrew noted, "to see all the lights on the guava trees." Contests encouraged everyone to decorate the trees and bushes.

Chapter 10: Na Kokua - The Helpers

"At Christmas, the sisters held an open house at the convent for all the patients," Sister Mary Andrew explained. "Before that year (1969), visitors sat on a bench outside the gate and the sisters inside the gate."

Sister Mary Andrew lived at Kalaupapa when the Hawaiian rules for mandatory residency changed in 1969. The sulfonamide drugs, in use since the 1940s, gave patients with Hansen's disease relief from the effects of the illness and made them no longer in danger of transmitting the disease.

When all the residents, patients and na kokua alike, celebrated Damien Day (formerly April 15, now officially May 10) each year, all the churches invited everyone to all the parties.

"We had good relations among the Mormons, the Presbyterians, and the Catholics," Sister Mary Andrew said.

"Protestants had midnight services at 11 p.m. for Christmas, and then at 12 midnight all went to St. Francis Church for Midnight Mass. Then the Protestants invited everyone to their hall for food and social time."

Sister Mary Andrew mentioned in the interview that Sister Richard Marie Toal, a sister now in her mid 90s and living at St. Francis Convent in Honolulu, always thought that St. Francis Church at Kalaupapa was named for St. Francis de Sales. Karen Lucas created a St. Francis of Assisi mosaic that stands on the grounds. Others have said that St. Francis Xavier, patron of missionaries and a favorite saint of St. Damien, gave the church its name.

(Stuart Ching, archivist for the Sacred Hearts fathers in Honolulu, affirmed that the church was named for St. Francis of Assisi.
"Bishop Ropert dedicated the first church and Bishop Boeynaems the second church at Kalaupapa to St. Francis of Assisi and not St. Francis Xavier.")
-Stuart Ching, email of July 24, 2012

Fire destroyed the first church in 1907. The second church, built in 1908 with Gothic windows and a rear tower, sits close to the historic landing at Kalaupapa. The spires of the church reach to the sky along with the coconut palms of the peninsula that so distinguish the skyline. While talking story, Sister Mary Andrew told how "the sisters and Father Gustave got along so well with the minister and his wife, Herman and Miriam Miller, who led the Presbyterian congregation."

Also, Sister Mary Andrew spoke of David Kupele, a Mormon, and Annie Kupele, a Catholic, who raised 12 children. When the couple celebrated their golden anniversary, both Jack, the Mormon minister, and Father Gustave blessed Annie and David.

Sister Mary Andrew also talked story with the interviewer about Bernard who lived near a house where a lady died in a house fire and how "he kept looking over his shoulder to see if the lady would appear." Sister Mary Andrew also spoke of Olivia, who raised, dressed, and sold chickens and how her husband John "was the most enterprising young man she'd ever seen."

Sister Patricia Clark
At Kalaupapa from 1969 to 1975

Because she had often taken care of patients with various contagious diseases elsewhere, Sister Patricia had no fear of Hansen's disease. She

Chapter 10: **Na Kokua - The Helpers**

felt that the same precautions should be taken.

Sister Patricia arrived at Kalaupapa in 1969, the year that the government of Hawai'i lifted the isolation of persons with Hansen's disease and no new patients needed to be banished to Kalaupapa on the Island of Moloka'i. The one hundred or so remaining patients would live out their lives at Kalaupapa or elsewhere as they chose. The Sisters of St. Francis would continue their care and concern and compassion for those remaining.

Sister Patricia made a point of saying that she used no gloves when applying ointments. She used her bare hands. She thoroughly washed her hands before and after. She lived by the philosophy and practices that she shared with Mother Marianne – use hands, wash hands.

Sister Mary Laurenza Fernandez
At Kalaupapa during Summers

This sister talked with Sister Barbara Jean Wajda in late May 2012 and explained her role as a kokua.

Sister Laurenza now resides at St. Francis Convent in Honolulu. She readily calls to mind seven summers when she served as a kokua (helper) at Kalaupapa. She taught at schools on the Big Island and at Lahaina on Maui during the regular school year and then attended classes at Chaminade University in Honolulu.

Once school was out, she was picked up and taken to the airport and off to Kalaupapa where she put her nursing skills to use in the hospital for the summer months. She returned in time for the start of the new school year.

Several people come to her mind when you ask Sister Laurenza about her memories of those years. She recalls that Kuulei Bell worked in the post office and that Bernard Punikai'a, the singer, wrote "The Sunset of Kalaupapa."

Bernard, a patient at Kalaupapa since age 14, turned activist in the 1980s when he led the resistance efforts to save the Hale Mohalu treatment center on O'ahu. He strongly felt that the patients should have some say in the decision to close the place.

Kuulei later served as the first president of Ka'Ohana O Kalaupapa, a program founded in August 2003 to preserve "the dignity of every individual who was exiled to the Kalaupapa peninsula beginning in 1866."
-Ka'Ohana website
http://www.kalaupapaohana.org/

Sister Laurenza remembers that Sister Claudia, much like a mountain goat, loved to climb the pali, and would call out to Sister Laurenza, a somewhat slow climber: "Are you coming?" They oftentimes found wild pigs along the pali trail.

Over those summers, Sister Laurenza worked with Sister Richard Marie, Sister Rose Ann, Sister Claudia, and Sister Mary Andrew, and maybe others she doesn't call to mind.

She does remember Happy, the convent dog, who met her each time she came home from night duty at the hospital. "Sister Richard Marie had a cat," Sister Laurenza mentioned. At night, the wild deer came out and sometimes ate the plants on the grounds of the convent and settlement.

One of the joys at Kalaupapa happened in fishing expeditions. Sister Richard Marie and Paul Harada, a patient, taught Sister Laurenza how to fish and they would go for shore fishing of small fish. Paul always accompanied the sisters to keep them from harm.

In her sunset years, Sister Laurenza likes to call to mind the lovely song of "The Sunset of Kalaupapa."

Sister Anonymous

This sister, who talked with Sister Barbara Jean Wajda on May 28, 2012, in Honolulu, tells how she became a kokua.

A sister, who wishes to remain anonymous, recalls her summons to Kalaupapa.

Among the native Hawaiian population, many families feared Hansen's disease and had no desire to go to Kalaupapa, according to the interviewee. When Sister Anonymous entered the convent, she made it very clear that she did NOT and would NOT ever go there.

One day, while sitting at table with her superior, whom she admired, the superior asked sister if she would go to LUP (Kalaupapa) for two weeks so the other sisters could come back for visits, retreats, and appointments. All the sisters of that convent were sitting at the table when the request was made, so what was a person to do? She couldn't say no in front of everyone; so she said: "Yes."

When sister arrived at Kalaupapa, upon entering the laundry room, she saw two tubs filled with white habits soaking. Only two sisters remained at the convent at the time - Sister Richard Marie and Sister Anonymous.

Sister Anonymous had to scrub the habits every day - still the practice from the days of Mother Marianne – plus, cook the meals and clean the house. Although she worked every waking minute, this sister survived and is still around to tell the tale.

She lasted for those two weeks. And, despite her fears, she did not contract leprosy.

Sister Gwendolyn Larkins
A Kokua during the Summer

Sister Gwendolyn Larkins, now living at Jolenta Convent in Syracuse, remembers going to Kalaupapa for the month of August in the early 1970s. While there, she did the cooking. She also spent some days in retreat in this hallowed place.

She recalls that Sister Richard Marie invited her to go fishing. Although Sister Gwendolyn felt reluctant, she decided to go as long as someone would put the bait on the hook. And that must have happened, as that day, Gwendolyn caught 14 fish, seven of which they cooked and ate for breakfast.

Chapter 10: **Na Kokua - The Helpers**

At first she did not like the dog, but she got used to it. "One day, while walking outside, I felt something cold and wet on my hand," she said. "It was the dog giving me a kiss."

To replace someone retiring, the local post office offered her a job just as she was ready to leave, but "I was concerned that the hours of 7 to 5 would not leave me time to pray," she said.

Sister Barbara Jean, in this interview, asked Sister Gwendolyn about the hygiene of washing habits and aprons. Sister Gwendolyn said: "There were two sinks in a front room where the aprons and covers that the sisters wore to work were taken off and deposited in wash tubs. The sisters also washed their hands thoroughly there before entering the convent."

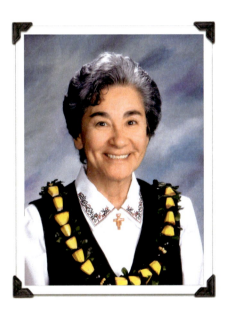

Sister Agatha Perriera
At Kalaupapa from 1988 to 1989

Peacefulness of the Place

Born on the Big Island of Hawai'i, Sister Agatha liked to voice her identity as "a Sister of St. Francis – as was Mother Marianne."

While on retreat at St. Francis Convent in Manoa, near Honolulu, Sister Agatha and Sister Dativa (Padilla) held a conversation while swimming in the pool. Sister Dativa said to Sister Agatha: "I wish we could get another helper (in Kalaupapa) as Sister Eligia (nursing supervisor) is so overwhelmed with work."

Sister Agatha said that she would "love to go," but explained that she had her mission in Maui as coordinator and first grade teacher. Also, Sister Antoinette (Almedia) needed her as a driver in Lahaina, Maui.

After retreat and back at Maui, Sister Agatha wrote to Mother Alicia Griffin, mother general, who received the offer with gratitude and gave Sister Agatha permission. Sister Agatha filled out the paperwork and signed on as a clerk-stenographer. Sister Dativa felt thrilled to hear this news.

Sister Agatha knew that she would need on-the-job training. As she began work at Kalaupapa hospital, she learned how to do POs (purchase orders) and how to record the information of the patients from Hale Mohala, a hospital for patients afflicted with Hansen's disease at Leahi, Oʻahu. She made arrangements for patients' off-island visits and returns. She also did transfer sheets and scheduled dentist and eye doctor visits, which required typing and posting in several areas on the peninsula for the patients to see. She also recorded blood work and other lab results.

When doing lab technician reports, to gain accuracy, Sister Agatha often had to check what the technician meant because of scribbled notes. She typed notes for a young doctor and also did nursing reports.

Sister Agatha spent evenings learning from Pearl how to do purchase orders. She also learned the abbreviations for the various medications.

And this is how Sister Agatha came to work for the state of Hawaiʻi as a clerk and stenographer at Kalaupapa.

Sister Agatha considered it an honor to walk past the grave of Mother Marianne at lunchtime. Her companions at the convent included Sister

Chapter 10: **Na Kokua - The Helpers**

Dativa, Sister Richard Marie, Sister Wilma, and Sister Eligia.

Sister Agatha loved to go swimming while Sister Richard Marie went fishing. The sisters enjoyed the peacefulness of the place. Because, Sister Agatha worked for the state, she could go anywhere at the settlement. She enjoyed long walks all over the area. She also enjoyed writing letters.

In 1988, when the state began renovations on St. Elizabeth Convent, Sister Agatha lived at the nursing residence. She lived and worked at Kalaupapa for one year, August of 1988 to August of 1989.

Sister Roseanne LaManche
At Kalaupapa from 1949 to 1952 and 1955 to 1961

Direct line to Mother Marianne

While Sister Roseanne worked at St. Elizabeth Hospital, Utica, N.Y. she met Sister Magdalene Miller, the sister who went to Kalaupapa to take care of Mother Marianne in the last days of her life. Sister Magdalene felt honored that Mother Marianne died in her arms.

From Pilgrimage and Exile

Sister Magdalene's own account of Mother Marianne's last days, which appears in an undated clipping from a Utica newspaper of the 1940s, adds perspective. "She knew that the end was near," says the sister, "but on that day she insisted on joining the nuns at mealtimes. 'No tears' she said, 'Of course, I'm coming to the table. Why not?' That night she died, slept away, while we sat by her bedside." As a result of the interview with Sister Magdalene, the reporter concluded that Mother Marianne was a "valiant" woman to the end.

- Hanley, O.S.F. Sister Mary Laurence; O. A. Bushnell (2009-11-01). *Pilgrimage and Exile: Mother Marianne of Molokaʻi* (Kindle Locations 7981-7985). Mutual Publishing, LLC. Kindle Edition.

Some time after Mother Marianne died, Sister Magdalene went to St. Elizabeth in Utica. That's where Sister Roseanne did her nurse's training and where she heard this story right from Sister Magdalene.

In 1949, Sister Magdalene and Sister Roseanne along with five other sisters – Sister Laurenza, Sister Frances Cabrini, Sister Mary Denis, and two others, left to serve in Hawaiʻi. Not all went to Kalaupapa. Sister Roseanne did go to Kalaupapa.

"I arrived just two years after sulfone (sulfonamide) drugs were introduced," Sister Roseanne said.

"I gave IVs and other medicines orally. We did biopsies every three months and stained and coded the slides for the number of bacteria present. We looked for the decrease of organisms and the diminishment of symptoms.

"Once a patient improved to the point of remission, he or she could travel and come back. The fumigation of clothes was still in effect," Sister Roseanne pointed out.

Sister Roseanne said: "I believe that Mother Marianne should have been canonized the day she died."

Chapter 10: **Na Kokua - The Helpers**

Each day on the way home from her work at the hospital, Sister Roseanne passed Mother Marianne's gravesite and prayed there.

Sister Roseanne served in Kalaupapa from 1949 to 1952 and 1955 to 1961. She lived with Sisters Martina Feichtner, Francine Greis, Norma Mihalko, Wilma Halmasy, Francis Kostka, John Vianney Murdy, Vera O'Brien, Gaudentia Muchlinski, Christopher Dixon, Richard Marie, and Claudia Cabral.

Sister Roseanne worked at the old hospital building, which later burned down in 1990.

http://www.nps.gov/kala/historyculture/firedept.htm

"An RN has to use good judgment and common sense," Sister Roseanne said.

"Physicians are not always available when a patient comes in for medical help. This calls for the nurse to assess the medical situation and respond in a professional manner.

"So, emergencies such as overdoses, for example, would be responded to with apomorphine to make the patient vomit the ingested substances.

"I know of at least one life was saved in this way," she said.

Sister Roseanne hiked up and down the pali trail many times. At times, Father Elbert would meet the sisters including Sister Carmelita and take them touring topside.

Sister Roseanne did not think of herself as a fisher person so she would sit on the shore while other sisters did the fishing.

Because Sister Roseanne worked at Kalaupapa before the 1969 lifting of the isolation law, she remembers the fumigation process.

"They used potassium permanganate to fumigate clothing," Sister Roseanne said. "Sister Celine, who was in charge of ordinary drugs for distribution, used to boil dollar bills before patients traveled off the peninsula."

Father Patrick Logan gave Sister Roseanne a Mary and Infant statue, which she treasures to this day.

A Spooky Story

At one time, Sister Roseanne had to escort one of the patients in a straight jacket to Hale Mohala Hospital in Honolulu. He had begged sister to remove the straight jacket. She said she would, once the plane wheels touched the ground. He was admitted to the hospital and sister took the plane home. When she arrived at Kalaupapa, the man admitted to the hospital greeted her. He had escaped from the hospital, flown back to topside and hiked down the pali trail.

Another Spooky Story

Sister Frances Anthony Sochor tells the story of a young sister who went to Kalaupapa to serve as a nurse. She, being the latest arrival, was assigned to night duty. She asked her supervisor what she should do.

"Whatever the patient asks." the supervisor replied. "Just make sure the patient signs the log book."

That night at about 3 a.m. a man came in and requested that the nurse change the dressings on his legs. She said she would, but asked him to sign the log, which he did.

The next morning, the supervisor inquired as to whether anyone came in for treatment, and the young sister told about the very early morning visit. The supervisor checked to see if the patient had signed in. The young sister said he had and showed her the signature.

The supervisor, acquainted with the history of the hospital, saw the signature, and told the young sister nurse that that patient had died 30 years ago.

Sister Roseanne LaManche, now living in Syracuse at Jolenta Convent, said that she had heard that story before and it was about Sister

Chapter 10: **Na Kokua - The Helpers**

Francine Greis, who worked at Kalaupapa from the mid 1950s through the mid 1960s.

When asked about the most difficult thing at Kalaupapa, Sister Roseanne remembered her first week and warnings about termites.

"Be sure to shake the termites out of your bedding," the other sisters told her.

Roseanne did find joy in the plumeria and watercress that grew along the stream in the Halawa Valley – a joy that Mother Marianne also experienced in her walks to the stream.

Sister William Marie Eleniki
One of the Na Kokua (helpers) at Kalaupapa

When Sister William Marie went to Kalaupapa, it was usually for a week to help with the cleaning. Her father would come with her and mow the lawn and do other chores. Then he would go fishing with the local guys.

Sister Miriam Dionise Cabacungan
At Kalaupapa from 1980 to 1983

"I guess I passed inspection"

After Sister Miriam Dionise graduated from St. Elizabeth Hospital, Utica, as a nurse in 1958, she worked at St. Joseph Hospital, Syracuse. Mother Marianne helped in founding both of these hospitals in central New York. She also worked at St. Francis Hospital in Honolulu and wrote of the way patients with Hansen's disease came from Kalaupapa to the hospital.

Isolation room

"Prior to my mission at Kalaupapa, I was a student nurse at St. Francis Hospital School of Nursing (Honolulu) in 1954. St. Francis was the only one in the state to admit patients with leprosy from Kalaupapa where they were air-evacuated for treatment or surgery. When we

received word that a patient would be coming, an isolation room was prepared on the 4th floor. A wooden wheelchair was covered with a bath blanket. The patient was received in the basement of the hospital and covered from head to toe with the blanket and had to wear a mask while being transported to his room. Plastic utensils and paper plates were used for meals. The isolation was required because leprosy was considered very dangerous at that time. The ban was lifted in 1969."
- From Sister Miriam Dionise's Memoirs, written in 2010

In 1980, Sister Aileen, superior general at the time, asked Sister Miriam to fill in for Sister Gretchen Martin, who had taken ill. And so, Sister Miriam travelled to Kalaupapa where she worked as a home care nurse, in dialysis, and as a clinical nurse. Her home care duties also included housecleaning as needed. She worked there from 1980 to 1983.

My first week there

"Some of my experiences there were very rewarding. I loved the patients. When I first arrived at the settlement, they were somewhat suspicious of me, due to past experiences (of newcomers). My first week there, a number of the patients and I went to clean St. Philomina (sic) Church. After the cleaning, we spread our potluck lunch on the lawn. After grace was prayed, the residents waited for me to begin. When I selected foods that they had brought, I guess I passed inspection and (they) accepted me as one of them. "
- From Sister Miriam Dionise's Memoirs, written in 2010

Sister Miriam and Sister Dativa would take the food rations of the patients and turn them into cookies, cakes, poke (raw fish salad), fried and boiled fish and sushi.

"The patients expressed deep gratitude for the help the sisters gave them," Sister Miriam said.

Sister Miriam lived with Sisters Richard Marie, Dativa, and Wilma during her stay in Kalaupapa. Sister Miriam remembered that on free days, Sister Richard Marie would pack a lunch and go fishing for the day. Sister Wilma, the nursing supervisor, made ceramics.

"Rachel Nakoa was a resident who was very skillful in sewing, making cushions, lap blankets, trinkets, pillows, and the like. She worked along with Sister Dativa. Sister Dativa had a pottery shop with a kiln and she made Christmas crèches, figurines, paperweights, and more. She and Rachel ran our gift shop. Twice a year, we had a crafts and art fair and sold handcrafts to tourists and residents."
- From Sister Miriam Dionise's Memoirs, written in 2010

When asked about Happy, the dog, Sister Miriam said that it was a gift for Sister Francine many years earlier. While Sister Miriam lived there, they had a black dog whose name she could not recall.

Sister Miriam also spoke of the 1969 lifting of the isolation ban. Previously the sisters had to take extra precautions such as changing their clothes when they returned to the convent and having their clothes fumigated overnight when they travelled off the peninsula.

"Fumigation of mail also took place," Sister Miriam explained. "A small opening cut into the envelope made this possible."

Sister Miriam also remembered that she had climbed the pali one time.

"It took a very long time," she said.

Chapter 10: **Na Kokua - The Helpers**

Three Sisters at Kalaupapa – in 2012

Sister Frances Therese Souza
At Kalaupapa 1989 – 1994 and 1995 to present

"I like to think of the people as people"

Of the nearly 100 residential patients that Sister Frances Therese came to know in her first years at Kalaupapa, Alice who was born in 1893 was the only one who knew Mother Marianne. Alice was in her mid 20s when Mother Marianne died in 1918. All the other patients came to Kalaupapa after 1918.

When Sister Frances Therese first went to Kalaupapa in 1989, she served as a nurse and did dialysis for those who needed it.

"I like to think of the people as people, not patients," she said. I did not react to any disfigurement I saw. I simply thought it was a privilege and honor to do Mother Marianne's work."

Those 100 patients have now dwindled to 17, and only nine currently live at Kalaupapa. Over those 20 plus years, Sister Frances Therese has experienced the deaths of 88 of the patients.

"The hardest part now," she said, "is the passing of the residents. The loss is deeply felt.

"You know the end for Kalaupapa is coming," she added. "I would like to stay until the last patient is gone."

The Exhumation

"The exhumation was difficult for all of us," Sister Frances Therese said. "Change of any kind was especially difficult for the residents.

"Some of the items found were rosettes and nails from the coffin; also, Mother Marianne's crucifix and rosary."

Sister Frances Therese figured that Mother Marianne was right handed because she wore her rosary on her left side.

"The exhumation was a privilege and very uplifting," Sister Frances Therese added. "Vince, in charge of the exhumation let the sisters put their hands on the skull of Mother Marianne.

"Even though there was no rain insight, a rainbow appeared. Sister Alicia Damien took a picture of that rainbow."

Sister Frances Therese explained how she sat next to the zinc box containing the remains of Mother Marianne as the truck drove to the airport.

The Insight

While kneeling near the zinc box, an insight came to Sister Frances Therese.

"As Mother Marianne was the first to come and serve as nurse to the

Chapter 10: Na Kokua - The Helpers

patients of Kalaupapa," Sister Frances Therese realized that she "might be the last nurse from the community of sisters to serve the people there."

"Ah, the rhythm of life," she pondered.

Close to Mother Marianne

Sister Frances Therese has felt a certain closeness, a spiritual closeness, to Mother Marianne for many years. She said: "Mother Marianne has helped me through some tight spots and tough work situations.

"I didn't worry because Mother Marianne was by my side. I wasn't afraid."

"At the time of the exhumation," she said, "I realized more deeply that the life of Mother Marianne in Kalaupapa was not easy. She had to give up a lot. I appreciate her endurance and her sacrifice."

Convent Living

Over her years at Kalaupapa, Sister Frances Therese lived with several other sisters – including Sisters Eligia, Dativa, and Richard Marie.

By this time, the sisters no longer had to change out of their work clothing when returning to the convent. That practice, initiated by Mother Marianne, came to its end in 1969 when isolation of people with the disease of leprosy stopped. Medical knowledge of how the disease spread meant that contagion was no longer a threat.

The sisters liked to go fishing and Sister Frances Therese joined in this. One time she caught a four-pound enuhuna. Her best record for needle nose fish reached seven in a half hour. Sister Richard Marie holds the record for catching 50 in a half hour.

Three Sisters at Kalaupapa

Of the three sisters living at Kalaupapa, one works as a nurse in the hospital, and the other two serve as volunteers. They give talks to pilgrims who visit the sites connected with Mother Marianne – Bishop Home, St. Elizabeth Chapel, and the gravesite.

Sister Theresa Chow
Kalaupapa – 2009 to present

Sister Theresa Chow, who attended the 2005 exhumation of the remains of Mother Marianne, usually speaks on that topic.

Sister Rose Annette Ahuna usually speaks on the virtues of Mother Marianne among other aspects of the saint's life.

Having heard Sister Theresa's talk so often, Sister Rose Annette now also talks about the exhumation.

When the regular bookstore workers are off the island, Sister Rose Annette and Sister Theresa take care of business in the store. Nothing is computerized, so they need to inventory each sale by hand on a four-page list and then ring up each sale with its respective PLU (price look up) number.

Both sisters do yard work. Sister Rose Annette tidies the front of the building and uses a blower to keep the long driveway clean. She also tends to Mother Marianne's gravesite.

Sister Theresa raises vegetables in the garden some distance from the convent. She takes care of the back area of the Bishop Home and tends to the banana patch.

Sister Theresa, a trained librarian, dusts, cleans, sorts, shelves, and rearranges the library materials at Marianne Cope Library, the local library for the settlement.

Sister Rose Annette and Sister Theresa took the initiative to create lists of the sisters who served at Kalaupapa from the time of Mother Marianne to the present and made the framed display, which graces the walls of the Bishop Home.

Convents at Kalaupapa

Mother Marianne, Sister Leopoldina, and Sister Mary Vincent lived at the first convent at Kalaupapa. Named St. Elizabeth Convent, the cottage contained a room that served as a tiny chapel. In 1939, the convent underwent reconstruction and kept the name of St. Elizabeth Convent. St. Elizabeth Chapel was built as a separate structure and sits next to the convent.

The convent before and after the ban

"The settlement is divided into three areas. Bayview area overlooked the bay that housed the single men. McVeigh, further up the hill, housed the married couples. Bishop Home is where the sisters live and the house used to be surrounded by a white picket fence, which is no longer there.

"There were two cottages around our convent and Barbara Marks and Alice Kamaka lived in each one. Before the isolation was lifted, the residents could only meet with the sisters by the covered gate in front of the convent. For Mass, the residents could only enter in the front

of the convent and sit in the back (of the chapel). There was a railing separating the sisters from the residents. The sisters entered the right side door next to the convent. Now that the ban had been lifted in 1969, the residents and staff were able to enter the convent and the Sisters may visit them in their homes.
- From Sister Miriam Dionise's Memoirs, written in 2010

In 2012, Sister Theresa and Sister Rose Annette live in the St. Elizabeth Convent, which also serves as a display area for Mother Marianne memorabilia and the history of the Franciscan Sisters at the settlement.

Sister Frances Therese, the nurse, lives in another cottage, closer to the hospital and about a half mile from the Bishop Home.

In the early days, a few years after the death of Father Damien, a convent was built at Kalawao for the use of the sisters who worked there. At first, the sisters walked the three-mile distance over and back each day. The convent, named Our Lady of Mercy and built in 1894, sat in the Kalawao compound of the Baldwin Home near Father Damien's church. Later, others used the building as their home.

Shopping at – and for - Kalaupapa

The Sisters currently living at Kalaupapa like to ponder how shopping took place in the past and to compare it with present day shopping. In the past, the patients had first pick of bread on Mondays, vegetables on Wednesdays, and milk on Thursdays.

Now, the orders for bread, vegetables, and milk must be placed a week ahead of time in order for the deliveries to be made. They can pick up bread between 10 a.m. and noon on Mondays, veggies after 10 a.m. on Wednesdays, and milk after 10 a.m. on Thursdays.

A store and bar is open daily except Sundays from 4 to 8 p.m. Here, they can get ice cream, candy bars, soft drinks, beer and wine.

Chapter 10: **Na Kokua - The Helpers**

Once a Year

The barge brings large items only once a year during the summer when the seas are calm and docking is safe.

Here's how it works for the sisters. They go to Honolulu and do their shopping and purchasing. They take their items to the pier to put them into the container.

The barge leaves on a Friday night and arrives Saturday morning around 7 to 8:30 at the pier in Kalaupapa. The whole community of people turns out for this annual occasion.

As the items are unloaded, they are lined up along the street. Workers from the NPS (National Park Service) deliver the items, large and small, to the Bishop Home for the sisters and elsewhere for the others.

The items range from canned goods to televisions, kitchen appliances, cars, and anything in between. The once-a-year arrival is like Christmas in July.

In 2012, the barge left on July 10 and needed to be packed and ready to go by then. The sisters welcomed the 1700-pound, five-foot tall, marble statue of St. Marianne, commissioned by John Parreira for sculpting in China. Sister Theresa Chow wrote that the statue was placed in St. Francis Church opposite the statue of St. Damien. The sisters are "still considering exactly where to set the statue because of its weight," Sister Theresa added.

The Kalaupapa Community

The sisters attend all the community meetings for the patients and residents of Kalaupapa. The State of Hawai'i and the NPS report on general living conditions in the settlement, on the crater, which gives off sulfuric smells, the wildlife, and the clearing of brush as fire prevention and enhancement of the appearance of the area.

Sister Rose Annette Ahuna
At Kalaupapa 2009 – to present

"I wanted to continue the legacy"

At an April 2009 regional meeting in Hawai'i, Sister Patricia Burkard, general minister of the sisters, asked for volunteers to go to Kalaupapa. Both Sister Rose Annette and Sister Therese Chow volunteered and both moved to Kalaupapa on August 15, 2009. Their residence is at St. Elizabeth Convent, the same location for the sisters since 1888, though the convent now in use is a second construction, not the original cottage.

"I wanted to continue the legacy of Mother Marianne," Sister Rose Annette said.

Saint Francis High School

Sister Rose Annette, one of six children, said that in her childhood, she heard no mention of Mother Marianne or Father Damien or the leprosarium at Kalaupapa. For high school, she went to St. Francis

Chapter 10: **Na Kokua - The Helpers**

High School in Honolulu as a boarding student, and again has no recollection of any mention of Mother Marianne or Father Damien from those years.

"On our train ride from San Francisco to Syracuse to enter the convent," Sister Rose Annette explained, "an African American porter took me and the two other girls with me under his wings, so to speak. He was very fatherly to us."

Assigned to St. Francis High School, Sister Rose Annette returned to Honolulu and took charge of the boarding students. At the request of the principal, she taught the students about Mother Marianne.

In the 1950s, she spent a day at Kalaupapa, and this much to the consternation of her mother who had all kinds of questions about who did the cooking and if they would eat with the patients.

"That day, seeing that the patients ate at a separate table from the visitors," Sister Rose Annette said, "I became aware of the distinction between patients and those not afflicted with leprosy."

Some years later, Sister Rose Annette found a picture of St. Francis High School with a caption that the school was a memorial to Mother Marianne Cope.

"I became gung-ho on promoting Mother Marianne," she said.

"Mother Marianne came from Syracuse to Hawai'i and left her position, works that she had developed and established, and came to the Hawaiian Islands where it was so primitive in comparison to Syracuse.

"The girls who entered the convent went from Hawai'i to Syracuse, going from small island life to a larger, bigger setting in a much more progressive state."

At Saint Francis High School, an all-girls school at the time, a problem with pimps from the West Coast (of the mainland) coming to Hawai'i to establish prostitution caused concern. The pimps worked the side street near the school as well as near other all-girls schools.

"Sister Joan of Arc (Souza) immediately sought the aid of the police department," Sister Rose Annette recalled, "and went on an all-out effort to inform parents, teachers, and students to be aware of this problem and to curtail any further interference.

"This was a parallel experience to what Mother Marianne had to do when intruders threatened the girls at Bishop Home."

"Mother Marianne was an ever-giving person at the beck and call of patients and the sisters too. Even at night, Sister Rose Annette elaborated, " Mother Marianne never sent any of the other sisters to take care of the problem. She would immediately go herself and see that the situation was righted and settled."

Educate People

"We have to continue to educate our young people," Sister Rose Annette said, "about how royalty could send patients, the men, women, and children, to a desolate area with little support or help until Father Damien and Mother Marianne came to improve the situation.

"I admire how Mother Marianne accepted everyone, regardless of religion, status, nationality, culture, or condition.

"We are called to meet people where they are and to do what we can to give help and hope," she said.

"Mother Marianne made a commitment that she would do what was best for the patients. She knew the patients needed to be educated, so she got Sister Antonia Brown to become a Hawai'i-licensed teacher for the Bishop Home in those early days."

In the Footsteps of Marianne

"I wish you all the blessing you may stand in need of to become a perfect child of Saint Francis – that you may say with him in all sincerity – "My God and my All."
- Mother Marianne in 1903 / http://www.stmariannecope.org/

Chapter 10: Na Kokua - The Helpers

"God giveth life; He will take it away in His own good time. Meanwhile it is our duty to make life as pleasant and as comfortable as possible for those of our fellow-creatures whom He has chosen to afflict."
- Mother Marianne in 1905 / http://www.stmariannecope.org/

'Our commitment is no different from that of Mother Marianne. In the spirits of Saints Francis and Clare of Assisi, she embraced with great affection her own family and her sisters in community even under the most trying circumstances. Whether she was laboring in a factory, administering a hospital, serving in congregational leadership, dealing with royalty or bureaucracy, or gently tending to the broken lives of outcasts in Hawai'i, Mother Marianne was on fire with the God who loved her and whom she loved."
- Sister Marion Kikukawa, at the time of the 140th anniversary of the Sisters of St. Francis of Syracuse, who are now part of the Sisters of St. Francis of the Neumann Communities

In the early 20th century, two women and a child make music with St. Francis Church in the background.

Photo: Courtesy of the Congregation of the Sacred Hearts of Jesus and Mary

Chapter 11

Music and Musical Instruments
A Pleasant Place

Sister Leopoldina, for the first time in thirty years, and Sister Benedicta ventured out beyond the Bishop Home's fence into dark Kalaupapa, going in search of Charlie, the coffin maker. They found him eventually, after searching about in the night, so "gray and cheerless... everything so bleak, the wind wailing mournfully as it swept through the long graceful limbs of the ironwood trees" that Mother Marianne had planted as barriers to Kalaupapa's storms.
-P&E

"I tried to balance the physically demanding work at the hospital with quiet moments gardening. I planted, watered and watched the miracle of each bloom.

"My patients were part of the beautiful plants I cultivated. They were seeds planted in rich soil and cared for physically and spiritually. And they bloomed into beautiful flowers ready for God's heavenly altar. Of all the positions I held throughout my life, I cherished most my work as God's gardener."
-Joan Albarella, *Always in My Heart*

In this chapter

Mother Marianne brought beauty of spirit and of space to the patients at Kalaupapa. Marianne saw to it that lace and ribbons added color to their clothes, that gardens and flowers and trees brightened the outdoors around the cottages, and that music and song delighted their ears.

A Hawaiian sense of Ohana (family) and of "talking story" came down through the years.

Sisters of the 21st century have created contemporary hymns to honor St. Marianne and to sing her praises.

Contemporary musicians have created some songs specifically for Kalaupapa.

Beauty of Spirit

'After the piano arrived (Sister Antonia identified it as "a Wetermeyer made in Tyrole") "there was always music…. The girls had beautiful voices, so that the Bishop Home was a pleasant place, all were in good spirits until 'The Spring Fever' moved them."

- Hanley, O.S.F. Sister Mary Laurence; O. A. Bushnell (2009-11-01). *Pilgrimage and Exile: Mother Marianne of Moloka'i* (Kindle Locations 6561-6563). Mutual Publishing, LLC. Kindle Edition.

" … the girls would sing outside near her window, while she was resting. This they did and dear Mother enjoyed it more than I can say. They did sing sweetly, God has given them music as a gift. One piece was particularly touching: a duet sung by Teresa and Little Emma Kia. Emma is blind and has not a finger left but she accompanied the song on the Autoharp and played wonderfully by tying a little stick to her poor stumps. It was pathetic to see them. Teresa did not show the sickness much but our dear little saintly Emma was too sad a sight to describe. Though she had neither eyes nor fingers her voice was clear and sweet."

Chapter 11: **Music and Muscial Instruments**

- Hanley, O.S.F. Sister Mary Laurence; O. A. Bushnell (2009-11-01). *Pilgrimage and Exile: Mother Marianne of Molokaʻi* (Kindle Locations 7900-7904). Mutual Publishing, LLC. Kindle Edition.

Ohana - Family

The day will come when the number of Hansen's patients living at Kalaupapa will arrive at zero. But there will be no zero as those 8,000 plus patients of the 1860s onward live on in memories preserved in song and music, in arts and crafts, in oral and written histories, in literature and paintings and photographs, in museums and in the National Park of Kalaupapa.

'Common Calamity' – to Compassion

The Ohana (family) spirit that grew out of the "common calamity" (words of Robert Louis Stevenson) into compassion lives on not only at Kalaupapa – but around the global neighborhood of all those who love St. Marianne.

Those who "talk story" in preserving the culture of those hundred plus years of banishment (1866 to 1969) and another almost 50 years of history to the present continue to hand on so much of all that should not be lost.

Mother Marianne and all the sisters of all those years helped to create a little space on this earth that epitomizes the graces missionaries bring to particular places.

Kekina Band

"There were many talented residents who had beautiful singing voices. Kuulei was one of them. Ted Higa played the harpsichord, Henry played the guitar, and another person played the ukulele. I learned to play a little guitar music when I was at St. Francis (Hospital) watching PBS. Even though they had claw-like fingers, they were able to produce beautiful music. We would get together and play for parties at the settlement upon request. I suggested that we have a name for our band

and came up with Kekina Band, a name of a small tomato-like fruit that grew abundantly in Kalaupapa at that time. I also made a banner and displayed it on the music stand."
- From Sister Miriam Dionise's Memoirs, written in 2010

Charles E. King

Charles E. King (1874 – 1950) played a large role in the story of Hawai'i's music. Those who wish to learn more about Hawaiian music often look for one or more of his three books: *King's Book of Hawaiian Melodies*, *King's Songs of Hawai'i*, and *King's Songs of Honolulu*.

Having one-quarter Hawaiian ancestry, Mr. King took music lessons from Liliuokalani. Queen Emma served as his godmother.

As a composer, bandleader, and publisher, Charles held strong beliefs that the songs must hold the history and culture of Hawai'i.

Often called the "Dean of Hawaiian Music", Mr. King has his place in the Hawaiian Music Hall of Fame.

Saint Marianne Hymn
By Deborah Nailos and Sister Barbara Jean Wajda

O Saint Marianne, we rejoice in your holiness
Your love of God is more than words can say.
You spent your lifetime in service of others,
Always bringing hope and brightening up each day.

Refrain
Saint Marianne, teacher, healer, guide,
May we, like you, in God's deep love abide.

Where there was a need, you saw God's Will and responded.
You did not hold back, but answered every call.
Your spirit of peace, concern and cheerful giving
Gave hope and strength and healing to all.

Chapter 11: **Music and Muscial Instruments**

Refrain
Saint Marianne, teacher, healer, guide,
May we, like you, in God's deep love abide.

To the sick and dying you gave consolation.
Your healing presence brought confidence and peace.
You know how to reach the heart of each person,
Imparting God's own loving touch to each.

Refrain
Saint Marianne, teacher, healer, guide,
May we, like you, in God's deep love abide.

You inspire us to follow your example
Open our eyes and let our hearts stand by
As the need of others to us are revealed,
Let a cheerful, "YES" like yours, be our reply.

Refrain
Saint Marianne, teacher, healer, guide,
May we, like you, in God's deep love abide.

- Words 2012 - by Sister Barbara Jean Wajda and Deborah Nailos
- Melody – traditional Hawaiian – Makalapua
(Used with permission from Sister Barbara Jean Wajda and Deborah Nailos)

Hymn in honor of Saint Marianne
By Sister Theresa Laureta

Dear Saint Marianne, Aloha!
We greet you with rainbows in our hearts.
O, Saint Marianne, we pray you
To bless your people here below.

Saint Marianne, you journeyed o'er the sea,

Impassioned and longing to bring comfort.
Your faithful acts of mercy
        inspire us today.
We remember, O holy Marianne.

Saint Marianne, you touched the exiled heart.
You fulfilled your solemn promise to Hawai'i, -
Warm waters soother your feet.
        Quiet breezes cool your face.
We honor you, O gentle Marianne.

Saint Marianne, great pilgrim of the isles;
We name you true daughter of Moloka'i.
Your spirit spurs us onward
        as we look to Heaven's home.
We praise you, O dear Saint Marianne.

Tune, 1916 - Matthew Kane - Ka Makani Ka'ili Aloha
English Lyrics, 2012 - Sister Theresa Laureta, OSF
(Used with permission – from Sister Theresa Laureta)

The melody of Sister Theresa Laureta's hymn honoring St. Marianne and the Ka Makani melody in the film score of *The Descendants* are one and the same melody.

Aloha 'oe

Many young piano students learn the "Aloha 'oe" song of Queen Liliuokalani. She used it as her farewell to the Hawaiian monarchy and her reign when the United States annexed Hawai'i as a territory. About 50 versions of this song by various artists appear on iTunes. There are renditions by Les Paul and Mary Ford, by Andy Williams, and by David Ho, to name a few.

Queen Liliuokalani wrote more than 160 songs and chants. *The Queen's Songbook* (1999) collected many of these into one place.

Chapter 11: **Music and Muscial Instruments**

Other Hawaiian Musicians

George Kahumoku Jr. and Daniel Ho have released two albums of hymns titled *Hymns of Hawai'i 1* and *Hymns of Hawai'i 2*. Some are familiar hymns like "How Great Thou Art" and "Amazing Grace" sung in the Hawaiian language. Others are more specifically Hawaiian lyrics, like "The Queen's Prayer" and "West Maui Mountains".

Jeff Linskey recorded a single with the title of "Kalaupapa". He also has several other songs such as 'Sunset of Kalaupapa' and 'Kalaupapa, My Hometown.'

Music brought a great deal of comfort to the patients and residents at Kalawao and Kalaupapa. Their memoirs tell of wonderful happiness in the choirs of the several churches and of other musical events.

Henry Berger, a bandleader, came to Hawai'i and served as instructor for the royal family, including Liliuokalani, who named him as the father of Hawaiian music.

Mr. Berger wrote "Ode St. Anne" in honor of Mother Marianne for her feast day on July 26, 1917, a year before she died.

Kalaupapa music and podcasts on iTunes

Kalaupapa,
    Someday, Darrell Labrado, R&B / Soul
Kalaupapa,
    single, Jeff Linsky, World
Kalaupapa Daydream,
    Waimake Helelei, Dennis Kamakahi & Stephen Inglis, World
Kalaupapa My Hometown,
    Waimaka …, Dennis Kamakahi & Stephen Inglis, World
Sunset of Kalaupapa,
    Waimake Helelei, Dennis Kamakahi & Stephen Inglis, World
Na Pua O Kalaupapa,
    Waimake Helelei, Dennis Kamakahi & Stephen Inglis, World
Kalaupapa,

Kalakoa, Maui Jam, World
The Sunset of Kalaupapa,
  Ku, Brother Noland and Tony Conjugacion, World
Kalaupapa Kalico,
  Na Poe Makole, S and S

Quotes – about Music
- from *Pilgrimage and Exile*

At the time of the sisters arrival in Honolulu – At Our Lady of Peace Cathedral in Honolulu

"The exultant music, the sweet incense drew the sisters in. The brightness of many candles upon the high altar, the image of the crucified Christ raised above it, called them forward, into the great open space beneath the vaulted and painted ceiling. Through their tears the Sisters of St. Francis saw the tall paintings high upon the walls at either side of the altar, the one representing Christ the Redeemer offering the world His Sacred Heart, full of grace and mercy, the other representing the Blessed Virgin Mary offering Her Sacred Heart, full of love and compassion."
- Hanley, O.S.F. Sister Mary Laurence; O. A. Bushnell (2009-11-01). *Pilgrimage and Exile: Mother Marianne of Moloka'i* (Kindle Locations 2128-2132). Mutual Publishing, LLC. Kindle Edition.

Organ music – for all

"When, in 1884, an organ was purchased for the sisters, the console was set outside the sliding partitions, so that Protestants too might enjoy its music."
- Hanley, O.S.F. Sister Mary Laurence; O. A. Bushnell (2009-11-01). *Pilgrimage and Exile: Mother Marianne of Moloka'i* (Kindle Locations 3197-3198). Mutual Publishing, LLC. Kindle Edition.

Music Clubs

"A variety of social events, such as picnics, hikes, parties, dances, gatherings of music clubs and funeral societies, as well as promenades

to and from church, helped the better adjusted residents to pretend that they were not entirely cut off from the pleasures of this world."
- Hanley, O.S.F. Sister Mary Laurence; O. A. Bushnell (2009-11-01). *Pilgrimage and Exile: Mother Marianne of Moloka'i* (Kindle Locations 6331-6333). Mutual Publishing, LLC. Kindle Edition.

Ode St. Anne – in honor of Mother Marianne

Also in Honolulu on July 26, 1917, Captain Henry Berger, the Prussian musician who had directed the Royal Hawaiian Band ever since King Kamehameha V invited him to the islands in 1872, presented the premier performance of "Ode St. Anne," created in honor of Mother Marianne and her patroness.

"Berger composed the music for the ode, and his sister-in-law, Mrs. Therese Bowler Hughes, wrote the words. Inasmuch as Captain Berger helped Brother Dutton to organize "the Leper Band" for musical boys at Baldwin Home, and released to Kalawao whatever ancient instruments the Royal Hawaiian Band could afford to discard, Mother Marianne probably heard "An Ode to St. Anne" more than once. She must also have heard "The Mother Marianne Hymn," which Captain Berger composed several years earlier."
- Hanley, O.S.F. Sister Mary Laurence; O. A. Bushnell (2009-11-01). *Pilgrimage and Exile: Mother Marianne of Moloka'i* (Kindle Locations 7744-7750). Mutual Publishing, LLC. Kindle Edition.

(Note – While the ode is often called – "An Ode to St. Anne" – the actual title is – "Ode St. Anne")

The Mother Marianne hymn

She must also have heard "The Mother Marianne Hymn," which Captain Berger composed several years earlier. This hymn, according to Berger's son-in-law and biographer, was "very popular" among the Leprosarium's patients until about 1940. The original copy of "Ode St. Anne" is preserved in Syracuse, but the music for "The Mother Marianne Hymn" seems to have disappeared, along with the memory of its melody."

- Hanley, O.S.F. Sister Mary Laurence; O. A. Bushnell (2009-11-01). *Pilgrimage and Exile: Mother Marianne of Moloka'i* (Kindle Locations 7749-7752). Mutual Publishing, LLC. Kindle Edition.

Mother Marianne's last days

"… and the girls would sing outside near her window, while she was resting. This they did and dear Mother enjoyed it more than I can say. They did sing sweetly, God has given them music as a gift. One piece was particularly touching: a duet sung by Teresa and Little Emma Kia. Emma is blind and has not a finger left but she accompanied the song on the autoharp and played wonderfully by tying a little stick to her poor stumps. It was pathetic to see them. Teresa did not show the sickness much but our dear little saintly Emma was too sad a sight to describe. Though she had neither eyes nor fingers her voice was clear and sweet."

- Hanley, O.S.F. Sister Mary Laurence; O. A. Bushnell (2009-11-01). *Pilgrimage and Exile: Mother Marianne of Moloka'i* (Kindle Locations 7900-7904). Mutual Publishing, LLC. Kindle Edition.

The beauty of - Ferns and Flowers

In Her Own Words
Sister Fran Gangloff

When I reread *Pilgrimage and Exile* in 2012, the frequent references to flora – ferns and flowers and bushes and trees – struck me as something dear to Mother Marianne. Perhaps in her Central New York childhood, she explored the Mohawk Valley for wildflowers and the city of Utica for garden flowers.

In the dismal landscape of Kalaupapa, she created gardens and groves to bring moments of beauty for the patients, for the sisters, and also for herself. She tended parlor ferns indoors and fruit and vegetable gardens outdoors.

Marianne's spirit of beauty inspired me to study Hawaiian flowers and ferns and to collect information about the meaning and symbols of

Chapter 11: **Music and Muscial Instruments**

flowers. I linked the qualities of flowers with the qualities of Marianne's life and legacy. In times of meditation, I wrote 12 prayer poems that became the small book of – *Ferns and Flowers* - now available at the online gift shop at the Saint Marianne Museum in Syracuse.

"… with graceful designs, featuring Hawaiian fern fronds, delicate flowers, a cross, and the legend "Convent of St. Francis"
(*Pilgrimage and Exile*, kindle location - 8316)

"gathered such delicate ferns and pretty leaves and infrequent flowers as the might find along the way"
(*Pilgrimage and Exile*, kindle location - 6195)

"… yield of their fruits and flowers. And she knew how the sight of them could lift up the spirits of sickened people"
(*Pilgrimage and Exile*, kindle location - 4191)

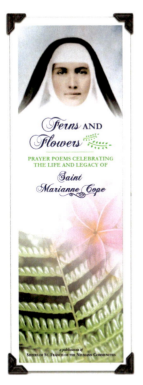

http://saintmariannecopegiftshop.ecrater.com/p/15564978/ferns-and-flowers-book-by-sister

A Family photo from the collection of Father Juliotte's from 1901-1907

Photo: Courtesy of the Congregation of the Sacred Hearts of Jesus and Mary

Chapter 12

Voices of the Patients of Kalaupapa

"Try to accept what God is pleased to give you—no matter how bitter. God wills it is the thought that will strengthen you and help you over the hard places that we all have to experience if we wish to be true children of God.... I shall offer up Holy Communion for you. I trust God will grant you the graces that you need to sanctify yourself. Time is flying. Let us make use of the fleeting moments. They will never return."
- P&E

In this chapter

Some few patients of Kalaupapa over the years have put their experiences into books and into other ways of communicating the sorrows and joys of their life in isolation and exile.

A new book with the title *Kalaupapa: A Collective Memory* by Anwei Skinsnes Law uses letters, petitions, memoirs, music, and oral histories to keep alive the memory of as many of those exiled persons as possible. With almost 600 pages, this book provides a comprehensive account of Kalaupapa in five sections of a timeline:

1866 – 1883
1884 – 1901
1902 to 1929
1930 to 1945
1946 to present

Mother Marianne and the pioneer sisters at Kalaupapa figure in sections two and three. Other sisters find their place in sections four and five.

In the Preface, Anwei Law spells out her connections with the people of Kalaupapa over several decades and praises the Archives of the Sisters of St. Francis at Syracuse where she did a great deal of research.

"…the bond that has existed between the Sisters of St. Francis and the people of Kalaupapa for well over a century was readily apparent." (p. xviii)

Other authors and photographers have written their perspectives in books and photos, all of which add to the cultural heritage of Kalaupapa.

The sisters and patients loved each other

"The sisters had become very fond of Julia, "a quiet well-behaved child… graceful in her ways and loved by everyone."
- Hanley, O.S.F. Sister Mary Laurence; O. A. Bushnell (2009-11-01). *Pilgrimage and Exile: Mother Marianne of Molokaʻi* (Kindle Locations 3958-3959). Mutual Publishing, LLC. Kindle Edition.

Kalaupapa: A Collective Memory

Anwei Law, author of books about Kalaupapa and Father Damien, also wrote the 2012 book with the title of *Kalaupapa: A Collective Memory* .

Reviewing the years of 1886 with the opening of the Molokaʻi settlement through 1969 when the government lifted the mandatory quarantine of patients with Hansen's disease, Law used music, letters, petitions, memoirs, and oral history interviews to allow many of the some 8,000 people tell their own stories.

Chapter 12: **Voices of the Patients at Kalaupapa**

Anwei and her husband Henry, of Seneca Falls, N.Y. not far from the Syracuse Sisters of St. Francis, and longtime advocates for persons dealing with leprosy, have co-authored a recent book (2012) on Father Damien - *A Bit of Taro, A Piece of Fish, and A Glass of Water.*

Both Anwei and Henry lived for many years at Kalaupapa and still travel often from their Seneca Falls home to Hawai'i. They are active in IDEA – an international association for Integration, Dignity, and Economic Advancement for persons around the globe who deal with Hansen's disease.

Yesterday at Kalaupapa

Emmett Anthony Cahill (1913 – 2004) told the 125-year history of the leprosy settlement at Kalaupapa in his book titled – *Yesterday at Kalaupapa: a Photographic History* (1990).

As a social activist, Emmett Cahill urged the creation of Kalaupapa as a national historical park until that became a reality.

In the 1970s, Cahill organized a support group in Hawai'i to parallel the grape boycott organized by Cesar Chavez in California.

A native of Kenmore, near Buffalo, N.Y. and a Catholic, Cahill served in the Pacific during World War II. He moved with his wife in 1946 to Honolulu where he continued his interest in all things Hawaiian.

In part I of the book, the author takes a serious look at Hansen's disease.

In part II, he tells of Father Damien, Mother Marianne, and Brother Dutton as the Catholic presence, as well as the Protestant and Mormon services to the patients. He includes a chapter about Marianne as written by Sister Mary Laurence Hanley.

In part III, he makes connections and links to the world at large. He writes of the visits of Jack London, and others, and of the Trapp Family Singers who hailed from the same hometown as Brother Dutton.
He shows the signs and sites of the area through 1990.

One photo shows St. Elizabeth Convent of the Franciscan Sisters. Another shows a Franciscan sister with a group of girls.

Yet another photo shows a Buddhist temple and their priests praying.

With A Saga of Pain and Joy as a subtitle, Cahill combines an abundance of photos with his text to make that period of history come alive.

The Molokaʻi Settlement – 1907

This document, now available as a reproduction of the original document at the University of California Library at Berkeley, takes the reader back a century to how things were then.

In 1907, the Board of Health of the Territory of Hawaiʻi, put out a booklet of text and illustrations titled *The Molokaʻi Settlement*.

The photos show the residence (convent) of the Sisters and Bishop Home at which the Sisters cared for the female patients with leprosy.

The booklet notes that five sisters, five brothers, three priests, one minister, and some Mormon elders reside in the settlements of Kalaupapa and Kalawao on the small northern peninsula of the Island of Molokaʻi.

The authors of the booklet noted: "It is a high honor to be accorded the friendship of the devoted Mother Superior and Sisters of the Order of St. Francis, as well as that of the Clergy and Brothers, all of whom serve the inmates of the Settlement."

The Colony

In his book titled The Colony (2006), John Tayman traces the story of a century on the Kalaupapa Peninsula of the Island of Molokaʻi.

The four-part book indicates the rise in the population of the settlement from 13 persons in 1866 to the height of the population to 1,144 around 1900 and the gradual decrease thereafter.

Chapter 12: **Voices of the Patients at Kalaupapa**

The author devotes several pages to the presence of Mother Marianne and Sister Leopoldina as well as Father Damien and the work of Walter Gibson.

The later pages of the book tell of the 2005 exhumation of the remains of Mother Marianne and the transfer to Syracuse.

Olivia, Henry, Bernard and other 21st century patients who have recently passed also make their appearance in the narrative.

This book also explains "leper squint" as the tiny windows in medieval churches, openings that allowed leper patients of those centuries to be present at Mass and to receive sacraments – from a distance that protected healthy people.

Henry Kalalahilmoku Nalaieula

Born in 1926, Henry grew up on a sugar plantation on the Big Island of Hawai'i.

At age 10, he found himself at Kalihi Hospital at Honolulu on O'ahu Island. Five years later, the authorities sent him to Kalaupapa.

When new drugs came in the mid 1940s, Henry benefitted somewhat from them. At age 23, his improved health allowed him to be "paroled" and qualified to leave the settlement.

Henry spent time at Carville, Louisiana, at one of the two mainland leprosarium hospitals, where he received ongoing treatment for the ravages of leprosy in his body.

Over the years, Henry learned to play the ukulele and bass and loved to play in music groups. He also developed a talent for drawing and painting.

When he chose to return to Kalaupapa, he found a job as a tour guide and took great pride in showing visitors the graves of Father Damien and Mother Marianne. He enjoyed working for the Kalaupapa National Historic Park founded in 1984.

Henry grew very fond of Father Damien and treasured his time in Belgium for the beatification of the saint in 1995. The group Henry traveled with had the privilege of bringing back the relic arm of Father Damien.

Late in life, Henry learned that two of his sisters had gone to Kalaupapa and died young.

Henry wrote his book with the title of *No Footprints in the Sand: A Memoir of Kalaupapa* (2006) with the help of Sally-Jo Bowman. The book gives a good sense of life at the settlement in the 1940s including the impact of the attack on Pearl Harbor. The book title refers to the reality that the deformed feet of leper patients leave no footprints.

Henry spent his last years at Baldwin House at Kalaupapa with the Sacred Hearts brothers.

Henry died in April 2009 at the age of 83.

Margaret of Moloka'i

50 years after Mother Marianne's arrival at Moloka'i, Mel White tells the story of Margaret Kaupuni in his book entitled Margaret of Moloka'i (1981).

In four parts the books tells about her childhood, her time at Kalihi Receiving station, her more than 30 years at Moloka'i, and her time at O'ahu Tower Project.

While Margaret practiced the Protestant / Congregationalist religion, she also speaks of the Catholic presence in the several Sisters of St. Francis at Bishop Home in the 1930s through the 1960s. She loved hearing the sisters singing hymns and praying psalms in the convent chapel. She mentions Mother Jolenta by name several times and wonders how the sisters could bear the heat in their wool habits and headgear.

Margaret pondered the courage of the sisters as they waded through the water to reach shore from the boat. She appreciated how the sisters

Chapter 12: **Voices of the Patients at Kalaupapa**

kept order, how they protected the girls and women, even waiting up late until every bed was occupied. She admired the love and encouragement the sisters gave to patients, many of whom had given up all hope.

In another passage, Margaret tells of the anger the patients and residents felt when the Belgium authorities in the mid-1930s came to exhume and transfer the remains of Father Damien. Though she wasn't Catholic, Margaret loved the presence of the saintly priest. She joined the crowd that wept at his gravesite and muttered angry words and feelings. She joined in the singing of – Aloha 'oe – to this beloved priest.

Mel White tells Margaret's story from her childhood through her treatment as a leper patient and on to her "cure" (no longer contagious) and leaving Moloka'i to live in a city apartment on O'ahu. He writes with sensitivity of her marriage, her stillborn child, and four other infants taken immediately away and carried up the pali for adoption.

Though "Ma" Clinton and "Mother" Alice, ministers of the Protestant church, console Margaret and encourage her, Margaret also retains fond memories of the Franciscan sisters who staffed Bishop Home residence and cared deeply for the women and girls.

"When you can't stop crying, plant some roses." one of the ministers told her. "Then one day when you feel like laughing again, you'll have rosebuds to give away."

Women's Rights / Human Rights and Dignity

Olivia, Mother Marianne, and other Franciscan women

Olivia Robello Breitha (1916 – 2006)

When the exhumation of the remains of St. Marianne Cope from her grave in Kalaupapa took place, Olivia said: "I'm glad they didn't get all of her." What had disintegrated had to remain in place.

In her memoir with the title of Olivia: *My Life of Exile on Kalaupapa*

(1988), Olivia tells of her first day at the leper settlement at age 16 and how Mother Jolenta took her to the infirmary because of a fever and chills.

Olivia, born on Kaui Island in 1918, the year that Mother Marianne died, tells of a happy childhood as a Catholic. Poverty forced her father to take several different jobs and they moved about quite often.

When she was 16, she remembers listening to – *Little Grass Shack* – a popular Hawaiian song – and learning that she needed to go for "snips of skin" for analysis. Feeling scared, she went to Kahili Hospital where she lived for three years for treatments for Hansen's disease. She lamented the way people treated her family because they had a leper patient in the family.

In June 1937, the staff at Kahili told her that "treatment is no longer of benefit to you" and that she would be sent to Kalaupapa. She met this news with fears and tears over separation from her family who lived near Kahili.

Life went on for Olivia at Kalaupapa. She tells in her book of vivid memories of the World War II blackouts and of food rationing. She met and married John and together they raised chickens to sell.

In the mid 1940s new meds gave the patients some manner of control over the disease. The "skin snips" continued as a way of testing for the absence or presence of the disease.

Her parents came to Kalaupapa and opened a bakery.

Some years later, the chicken farm had trouble meeting its quota and Olivia and John shut down the farm. John moved to Carville in Louisiana for treatment and died there.

Olivia did return to Honolulu for a time but came back to Kalaupapa. She links the treatment of AIDS patients with that of leprosy patients and pleads against unnecessary isolation and quarantine.

When Olivia died at age 90, so many paid homage to this woman who put a human face on a disease that so many misunderstood.

She wrote, spoke, and lived as an advocate of human rights for persons affected with the stigma of leprosy. She sent written testimony to the U.S. Congress on behalf of a monument at Kalaupapa to honor the 8,000 persons who lived over the years.

Olivia and other women of Kalaupapa have been entered into the life and legacy book at the National Women's Hall of Fame at Seneca Falls, N.Y.

Mother Marianne also has her place at the National Women's Hall of Fame.

Women of Spirit - Catholic Sisters in America

Also, the Catholic Sisters in America included a display honoring Mother Marianne. The display included a copy of the original poem to Mother Marianne by Robert Louis Stevenson, the scales that Marianne used to measure medicines, as well as three sets of video interviews and a series of black and white slides.

A long line of Franciscan women saints

St. Marianne Cope comes from a long line of saintly women who followed the Franciscan way of living the Gospel of Jesus.

St. Clare of Assisi – 13th century / feast Aug 11

In their younger years, St. Francis used to watch St. Clare go off into the woods. When he followed her, he saw that she went to the leper settlement to take care of the wounds of those lepers. At the time, St. Francis could not bring himself to do such a thing, but he greatly admired her. Later, St. Francis embraced a leper and the revulsion went away. St. Clare not only helped those afflicted with the disease, but also inspired St. Francis and others.

St. Elizabeth of Hungary - feast November 17 (feast – formerly on November 19 – from 1670 until 1969)

Now a patron saint of nurses, St. Elizabeth founded hospitals and made it her business to care for the sick and provide for them. One time, she came upon a cold leper close to death. She took him home and placed him in her own bed. Her husband came home and found St. Elizabeth bathing the leper's forehead. The angry husband pulled off the sheets – and there he saw a vision of the crucified Christ. Another miracle in St. Elizabeth's life turned bread to roses when her husband forbade her to feed the poor.

The convent and the chapel in Kalaupapa bear the name of St. Elizabeth of Hungary. Mother Marianne professed her vows on the feast of this saint – on November 19.

St. Agnes of Bohmeia (Prague) – 13th century / feast March 2

This princess founded hospitals and when she learned of the Poor Clares, she wrote to St. Clare of Assisi. The two corresponded for 20 years without ever meeting each other. Agnes joined the Poor Clares in her own city and took care of and cooked for the lepers and paupers in her locality.

Bl. Mary of Oignies

Bl. Mary obtained permission from her husband to take care of lepers in their home. Her husband assisted her with their care.

St. Angela of Foligno – 13th to early 14th century / feast

St. Angela found great spiritual joy in washing lepers and caring for their wounds. On a certain Holy Thursday, St. Angela and her companion went to the local hospital to bring food for the sick. Because it was Holy Thursday, they washed the feet of the women and the hands of the men in imitation of Jesus washing the feet of the apostles. Then

Chapter 12: **Voices of the Patients at Kalaupapa**

they came upon a patient with leprosy. They cleansed the festering sores of the lepers and then drank the same water and found it very sweet.

Margaret Haven – Missionary to Moloka'i

After her retirement in 1946 from 35 years of service as a telephone operator, Margaret decided she would go as a lay missionary to help the Sisters of St. Francis at Bishop Home at Kalaupapa, Moloka'i. Maggie, as she was called, felt inspired by her brother, Father Donald Haven, a Franciscan priest and missionary to China.

Born on February 21, 1894, in Chicago, Margaret later joined the Franciscan Secular (lay) Third Order as her mother had done. Over the years, she had heard about Mother Marianne and the sisters as well as about Father Damien and Brother Joseph Dutton and all they did for the people affected by the disease of leprosy.

Maggie applied to the territorial government of Hawai'i and received permission to work at Kalaupapa. She sold her family home, with an awareness of all that this sacrifice meant to her, and travelled to Moloka'i. She said that she was willing to do whatever work there might be, scrub floors or cook meals. She baked wonderful homemade bread that everyone talked about. Father Marion Habig, OFM, who wrote a book about Margaret, said that he knew from personal experience how good that bread tasted.

In Mother Marianne's time, the Bishop Home complex had a few buildings. By the time Maggie came in the mid 1940s, Bishop Home campus contained 17 buildings.

She worked at Bishop Home alongside the sisters for 24 years. She said she had no fear of getting the disease of leprosy. She returned to Chicago where the illness of cancer brought her to her death.

Maggie died on January 16, 1977, and was laid to rest in a Franciscan habit, a privilege given to Third Order Secular members.

Part Four

The Saint Marianne Photo Album

The Saint Marianne Photo Album

Mother Marianne - 1887 - elected Mother Superior

Photo: Courtesy of the St. Marianne Cope Shrine and Museum
of the Sisters of St. Francis of the Neumann Communities

The Life and Legacy of Saint Marianne Cope

Birthplace and Childhood Home

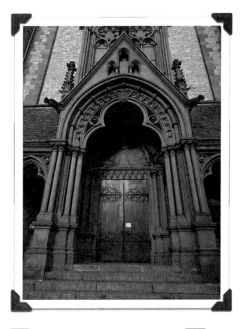

St. Peter's Heppenheim, Germany
Birth and Baptism of Barbara Koop
January 1838

Photos: Werner Franz and Kaitlyn Graves of St. Joesph's, Utica, NY. Used with permission

The Saint Marianne Photo Album

Mother Marianne, missionary   Barbara Koop, student

Windows of a Saint at St. Joespeh St. Patrick parish hall in Utica, NY

Shrine of St. Marianne Cope at same location

Photos: Tom Mayer
Courtesy of the parish and used with permission

The Life and Legacy of Saint Marianne Cope
A Sister of St. Francis

Some of the branches united/merged in the early 21st century to form the Sisters of St. Francis of the Neumann Communities
Graphics: Sisters of St. Francis

Painting of Bishop Neumann with school children and Sisters of St. Francis at St. Mary of the Angels Convent, Williamsville, NY
Photo: Sister Fran Gangloff

The Saint Marianne Photo Album

St. Elizabeth Hospital, Utica, NY, circa 1870s

St. Joseph's Hospital, Syracuse, NY, circa 1872

Photos: Courtesy of St. Marianne Cope Shrine and Museum
of the Sisters of St. Francis of the Neumann Communities

The Life and Legacy of Saint Marianne Cope

Saint Mother Marianne Hall at St. Peter's Parish, Oswego, NY

Stairway and bannister at the Hall - former convent-
stairs that Mother Marianne walked and bannisters that she touched

Photos: Courtesy of Stephanie Carmody

The Saint Marianne Photo Album

A Moment in Buffalo, NY

Photo of a vintage postcard depicting a 19th century scene of the the New York Central Exchange Street Station in downtown Buffalo, NY. Opened in 1854.

St. Marianne Cope, patron saint of those who forget things

I love the incident of the forgotten purse,
the one you left behind in Syracuse on the day of your departure.
The one with very important documents that you needed for travel
and for starting up the Mission in Hawaii.

You had to go back and get it.
And so you got off the train at Buffalo, NY, at the Exchange Street Station,
and quickly returned to Syracuse to retrieve it.
And then with great haste you boarded the westbound train
to meet up with your group in Chicago and continue on to Hawaii.

We will keep you in mind when we misplace or forget things
and trust that God will help us find them as God helped you that day.

The Exchange Street Station is the very same place
to which Franciscan Sisters came from Philadelphia to Buffalo in 1861.

This is your only time in Buffalo.
but you have many spiritual connections with
the Buffalo branch of Franciscan Sisters - now known as the
Western New York Region of -
The Sisters of St. Francis of the Neumann Communities

Photo: Public Domain

The Life and Legacy of Saint Marianne Cope
A Missionary to Hawaii

Sisters Chapel at Kapi'olani - Early 1900s
Photo: Courtesy of the Sacred Hearts of Jesus and Mary

Ecumenical Chapel at Kapi'olani - 1884
Photo: Courtesy of St. Marianne Cope Shrine and Museum of the Sisters of St. Francis of the Neumann Communities

St. Philomena Chapel at Kapi'olani
Photo: Courtesy of St. Marianne Cope Shrine and Museum of the Sisters of St. Francis of the Neumann Communities

St. Elizabeth Chapel at Kalaupapa
Still in use in early 21st century
Photo: Courtesy of St. Marianne Cope Shrine and Museum of the Sisters of St. Francis of the Neumann Communities

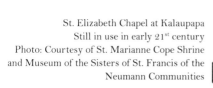

The Saint Marianne Photo Album

Mother Marianne set up Malulani Hospital on the island of Maui in 1884

Sisters Renata Nash, Antonia Brown, M. Bonaventure Caraher, Cyrilla Erhard on Maui in the 1890s

Mother Marianne in blue gingham work apron – 1899

Photo: Courtesy of St. Marianne Cope Shrine and Museum of the Sisters of St. Francis of the Neumann Communities

1843 sketch of Our Lady of Peace Cathedral at Honolulu.

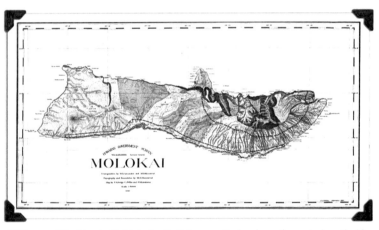
1897 map of the Island of Moloka'i with Kalaupapa Peninsula on the central north side.

Photos: Public Domain

The Saint Marianne Photo Album

Kalaupapa on Moloka'i, Hawaii

Mary and Rose Kiyoji who were raised by the Franciscan sisters

Photo: Courtesy of Congregation of the Sacred Hearts of Jesus and Mary

Saint Francis Church at Kalaupapa, Moloka'i 1901

Photos: Courtesy of Congregation of the Sacred Hearts of Jesus and Mary

The Saint Marianne Photo Album

Unidentified Girls and Women at Kalaupapa - may have been residents at Bishop Home

Photos: Courtesy of Congregation of the Sacred Hearts of Jesus and Mary

Unidentified Girls and Women at Kalaupapa - may have been residents at Bishop Home

Photo: Courtesy of Congregation of the Sacred Hearts of Jesus and Mary

The Saint Marianne Photo Album

Unidentified Girls and Women at Kalaupapa - may have been residents at Bishop Home

Photo: Courtesy of Congregation of the Sacred Hearts of Jesus and Mary

The Life and Legacy of Saint Marianne Cope

Three Franciscan Sisters and residents of the Bishop Home at Kalaupapa, Moloka'i

Sister Mary Elizabeth Gomes, OSF, with girls of the Bishop Home at Kalaupapa, Moloka'i

Photos: Courtesy of the Congregation of the Sacred Hearts of Jesus and Mary

The Saint Marianne Photo Album

Two Franciscan Sisters and a group of girls gathered
at the tomb of Mother Marianne Cope

Photo: Courtesy of the Congregation of the Sacred Hearts of Jesus and Mary

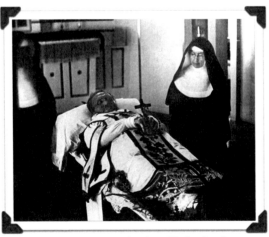

Mother Marianne at the Bier of Father Damien
Photo: Courtesy of the St. Marianne Cope Shrine and Museum of the Sisters of
St. Francis of the Neumann Communities

The Life and Legacy of Saint Marianne Cope

Legacy of Mother Marianne
those who followed

Mount Calvary Circle Cemetery

Diamond Head Cemetery near Honolulu

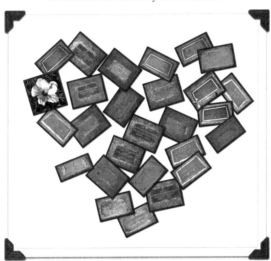

Sisters' Graves

Photos: Sister Barbara Jean Wajda

The Saint Marianne Photo Album

St. Francis of Assisi Church at Kalaupapa, Moloka'i, Hawaii (aerial view)

Photo: Sister Barbara Jean Wajda

St. Francis of Assisi Church at Kalaupapa, Moloka'i, Hawaii (ground view)

Photo: Sister Barbara Jean Wajda

St. Elizabeth Chapel at Kalaupapa, Moloka'i, Hawaii

Photo: Courtesy of St. Marianne Cope Shrine and Museum of the Sisters of St. Francis of the Neumann Communities

The Life and Legacy of Saint Marianne Cope

Rome, Italy – the Canonization 2012

St. Marianne Cope banner at the Vatican
Neck scarves worn by pilgrims

Right Page: (Top) Sister Grace Anne Dillenschneider (left) and Sister Patricia Burkard (right) take part in various ceremonies and events surrounding the canonization

(Center) Sister Barbara Jean Wajda (left) and Sister Marian Rose Mansius (right) express their joy in Italy

(Bottom) Sister Michaeleen Cabral performs a liturgical dance in the Hawaiian style

Photos: Sister Eleanore Vargas

The Saint Marianne Photo Album

The Life and Legacy of Saint Marianne Cope

*States of Grace –
New York and Hawai'i*

Artist: Edwardo Gracia
Location: Our Lady of Peace Cathedral
Honolulu, Hawai'i

Artist: Sister Marcia Klawon
Location: St. Mary of the Angels
Williamsville, New York

The Saint Marianne Photo Album

Left:
St. Marianne the Missionary window at
Co-Cathedral of St. Theres
Honolulu, Hawai'i

Bottom Left
St. Marianne window at
Cathdral of Our Lady of Peace
Honolulu, Hawai'i

Bottom Right:
St. Marianne window at
Star of the Sea Painted Church
Big Island of Hawai'i

Photos: Sister Barbara Jean Wajda

The Life and Legacy of Saint Marianne Cope

Top: Sunbeams and Rainbows on the pali at Kalaupapa
Bottom: Airport and Shore at Kalaupapa

Photos: Sister Barbara Jean Wajda

The Saint Marianne Photo Album

St. Marianne Cope Garden at Syracuse, New York,
Photo: Gerianne Dobmeier

Sunset at Kalaupapa, Moloka'i, Hawai'i
Photo: Sister Barbara Jean Wajda

Afterword

Franciscans and Lepers –
Moments of Grace, States of Grace

St. Francis and "Lepers"

In the often-told story of St. Francis of Assisi and his change of heart about meeting a person with leprosy, the moment of grace, the state of grace brought him to a new understanding. St. Clare of Assisi brought compassionate care to those afflicted with leprosy and St. Francis took notice of this. Her life inspired him to the charity of embracing the "leper" he feared.

Somewhere along the line, Mother Marianne also came to this state of grace, this moment of grace that guided her for the rest of her life. Both the Incarnation of Christ among humanity in all its pain and humility and the Resurrection of Christ in all its hope and glory gave St. Francis, St. Clare, and St. Marianne the courage to follow Christ and the Gospel in humility and charity.

St. Francis said that the Lord gave him brothers and Marianne could say that the Lord gave her sisters – the Sisters of St. Francis of the Third Order Regular – who carried on the life and ministry in New

York State and in Hawai'i as it moved toward statehood – and in time to people in need around the whole world.

Named the "beloved mother of outcasts," St. Marianne offers a model for the inclusion of all persons and all of God's creation in the spirit of St. Francis and St. Clare.

Anwei Law praises the sisters who served as missionaries to Hawaii:

"As Franciscans, they drew a different circle, a circle that included rather than excluded. The whole Franciscan mission was started because of a decision by St. Francis to redraw the structure of society - to include anyone / everyone of God's people, and St. Francis had always included those with leprosy in his circle of concern."
-Anwei Law, Kalaupapa, pages 130 - 131

Alabaster Jar

Mother Marianne had her medicine jars and vials for remedies for her patients, and she often used old bottles for flower vases and candlestick holders.

In the early 1st century when Jesus ate dinner at the home of Simon the Leper, the unnamed woman brought her alabaster jar of perfume, added her tears and kisses, and washed the feet of Jesus.

Simon asked Jesus: "Don't you know who is touching You?"

Jesus said to Simon: "Her great love has been shown to Me."

Some equate Simon, the dinner host, with Simon the Pharisee. Others say that Simon the Leper is Lazarus, the brother of Mary and Martha of Bethany, the Lazarus, the man with leprosy, healed and raised from the dead by Jesus.

At any rate, fact or fiction, this unnamed woman, like Mary of Nazareth, loved the Lord God with all her being.

The name of Lazarus has come down through the history of care for leprosy – in the terms of lazar house and lazaretto.

She kept the Great Commandment

A legend about the last days of Mary, Mother of Jesus, tells how word went out to the apostles and others that they should come as Mary would not be with them much longer.

Peter came from Rome and Paul from Asia Minor. Thomas came from India and James from Jerusalem. And the others came – from all their various places.

While gathered around Mary's bed, they reminisced with her. Remember your parents – Anna and Joachim. And your favorite cousin – Elizabeth.

Oh, remember the night that the Baby came. And Joseph – how you missed him when he left this earth. And how you lived alone when Jesus went out on his public ministry.

And oh my, that sad, sad day when they crucified him. And oh the joy – when Jesus rose from the dead. So many memories.

And one of the friends, as Mary breathed her last, said: "She was such a good Jewish woman who lived the Great Commandment. She loved the Lord God with all her heart and soul, with all her mind and spirit, with her whole being.

And … she kept the Great Commandment

Mother Marianne based her life and her decisions on the Great Commandment – love of the Lord God and love of neighbor. She sought to know and do the Will of God as a Franciscan woman of the 19th and early 20th century.

She brought her jars of ointments and used her hands to tend the sores of the suffering people of Kalaupapa. She arranged for homes and schools and hospitals for the people of central New York State and for the people of Hawai'i – the kingdom and the territory – and decades after her death, the State.

Marianne loved the Lord God by living the Great Commandment and by serving the outcasts, those most in need, of her times and her places.

Franciscan Women Saints for the 21st century

If St. Clare of the 13th century is the first Franciscan woman saint, and she is often called that, then St. Marianne is a Franciscan woman saint for the 21st century.

The Sisters of St. Francis of the Neumann Communities chose in July 2012 this mission statement:

Rooted in the Gospel,
we are sisters to all,
serving with reverence,
justice, and compassion.

"All the Sisters join me in sending your our 'Aloha' – please pray for us that this spirit that reigns may continue."
-Mother Marianne, February 1887 / Unpublished Letters of Mother Marianne

"I am not the singular woman saint of Kalaupapa at Molokai.
 "The Franciscan sisters who served with me and after me are all saints.
"A thousand years would not be enough to thank God for the gifts and blessings of my life and legacy.

"I do not expect a high place in heaven. I shall be thankful for a little corner where I may love God for all eternity."
-Joan Albarella, *Always in My Heart*

Acknowledgements

Thank you to …

While writing a book requires a lot of solitude, the production of a book also requires a lot of helpers.

My heartfelt gratitude goes out to …

Sister Alicia Damien Lau of Honolulu, Hawai'i, who offered many suggestions for accuracy and respect for the patients based on her many times of helping in Kalaupapa, and for her fine oral history on tapes of several sisters who had worked at the Kalaupapa mission. She also reviewed the text and offered sensitive suggestions and improvements.

Sister Barbara Jean, Wajda, OSF, a longtime friend. She currently lives and works in Honolulu. She supplied many photos of ferns and flowers, and of gravesites, and of Kalaupapa scenes, as well as many interviews of the sisters who have worked at Kalaupapa. She also read the text and offered encouragement.

Sister Anne Marie Saphara, OSF, a new friend. She shared her childhood scrapbooks of nuns and her longtime love of Mother Marianne. She also read the texts and made valuable suggestions. As an artist, she made suggestions for the the cover design.

Sister Grace Anne Dillenschneider, OSF, vice postulator for the cause of sainthood for Mother Marianne. She gave encouragement.

Sister Joanne Gangloff, OSF, my dear sister, a missionary in Kenya. Using email from my continent to hers, she read the texts and made meaningful suggestions for clarity.

Joan Albarella, author of – *Always in My Heart* – a drama about Mother Marianne and Jackie Albarella – who performed the play. Joan took great interest in the progress of this book as I took interest in the progress of the play. We shared a mutual collaboration on her play and my book.

Msgr. David Lee, a dear friend who planted the seed for States of Grace. When he invited me in January 2012 to give a talk on Mother Marianne during our parish Novena of Grace for early March 2012, he planted the seed for this book with its prayer poems, graced life and legacy of Marianne, and related supplemental materials.

Using many books, songs, internet researches, photos, and time for reflection and writing, that seed has also sprouted into some bookmarks, a calendar, and some other publications by our congregation's St. Marianne Commission and Office of Communications.

Darlene Yamrose at the St. Marianne Museum in Syracuse, who helped me locate photos and information, and also offered encouraging comments.

Cheryl Aughton and Deborah Allen at the Office of Communications for the Sisters of St. Francis of the Neumann Communities for help in locating photos for this book

Parishioners of the former St. Agatha Parish in South Buffalo, now part of Our Lady of Charity Parish along with St. Ambrose and Holy Family, for welcoming and encouraging me as a "writer in residence" at St. Agatha House these past five years and ongoing.

Acknowledgements

Parishioners and pastors at St. Peter in Oswego and at St. Joseph – St. Patrick's in Utica for permission to use photos related to their sites.

Stuart Ching, archivist in Honolulu for the Congregation of the Sacred Hearts of Jesus and Mary (SS. CC.) – for his assistance with the recently discovered photos of residents of Kalaupapa in the years 1901 to 1907.

Sister Michael Marie O'Brien, archivist at St. Anthony Convent in Syracuse - for supplying historical information about the sisters who worked in Kalaupapa.

Those who read and reviewed and proofed the manuscript – Sydney Schmidt, Cheryl Aughton, Sister Lorraine Wesolowski, and others already mentioned.

Sister Mediatrice Hutchinson and Sister Mary Farrell for help with obtaining permissions from elderly sisters and all the sisters who agreed to be interviewed about Kalaupapa and Mother Marianne and who gave permission for their memories and photos to be used in the book.

In contact with many of our Sisters in Hawai'i and elsewhere, I have gained an understanding of Mother Marianne's courage and wisdom, her holiness and grace.

And writing a book also relies on the resources of one's lifetime to date – and so -

Thank you too – to my Mom and Dad who read to us when we were little and took us frequently to both the Depew and Lancaster libraries for books.

When I cherish flowers and ferns, I think of Mom and Dad too, for they taught me much about houseplants, garden flowers, and wild flowers.

Thank you to my sister and brothers – Joanne, John, and George, and Roey and Judy, and their children and grandchildren - my wonderful family of several generations for all their interest and encouragement of my writing projects.

And to my first grade teacher – Sister Mary Ora, OSF – who had me fascinated as a five year old with her boxes of word cards and who taught me as an adult a course in writing for children.

And to my eighth grade teacher – Sister Mary Evelyn, OSF - who sent my Americanism essay on Amelia Earhart and her solo flight - on to the national competition.

And to my 9th grade English and homeroom teacher – Agnes Walsh – then Sister Marguerite – who still remembers exactly the seat I had in her classroom. She has provided much encouragement over these many years including several recent phone conversations.

And to many of the sisters who are my friends and who give so much encouragement to my writing pursuits – Sister Margaret Therese Toohill and Sister Margaret Toohill, Sister Bea Leising, Sister Barbara Eirich, Sister Kathleen Osbelt, and others who offered encouraging words along the way.

And to Jeff Campbell and Lorien Sheppard of Tau Publishing for their design and production work in bringing this book to fruition.

Appendix

Permissions

Permission to use materials came from the following:

Quotes from the book entitled *Pilgrimage and Exile*
    From the Sisters of St. Francis of the Neumann Communities
    Via Sister Grace Anne Dillenschneider, vice postulator

All copyright privileges belong to the Sisters of St. Francis of the Neumann Communities and cannot be used or reproduced without obtaining permission from them. All rights are reserved by the Sisters.

Photos from the St. Marianne Museum and the Office of Communications
    From the Sisters of St. Francis of the Neumann Communities
    Via Sister Grace Anne Dillenschneider, vice postulator

All copyright privileges belong to the Sisters of St. Francis of the Neumann Communities and cannot be used or reproduced without obtaining permission from them. All rights are reserved by the Sisters.

Quotes from the play – *Always in My Heart* – copyrighted, 2012
    From Joan Albarella, author

Quotes from the book – *Kalaupapa: A Collective Memory*
    Anwei Skinsnes Law, 2012, author

Quotes from the book entitled *The Missionary Movement in American Catholic History* by Sister Angelyn Dries,
    From Doris Goodnough at Orbis Books, Maryknoll

Photos of St. Peter Church and Baptismal Font of Heppenheim, Germany
From Werner Franz and Kaitlyn Graves
Via Bonnie Fazio of St. Joseph St. Patrick Parish, Utica, N.Y.

Photos by Stephanie Carmody - of "Saint Mother Marianne Hall" and the interior stairway and bannister in Oswego, N.Y., with permission from Father George Wurz, pastor of St. Peter Church in Oswego, via Stephanie Carmody

Photos by Tom Mayer - of Mother Marianne Windows in the Parish Center and of the St. Marianne Shrine at the Parish of St. Joseph St. Patrick in Utica, N.Y, via Irene at the parish.

Permission from each sister – for photos used of each of them
    Sister Alicia Damien Lau
    Sister Barbara Jean Wajda
    Sister Anne Marie Saphara
    Sister Mary Francis Gangloff
    Sister Cheryl Wint
    Sister Blanche Marie Messier
    Sister Mary Christopher Dixon, via Sister Mary Farrell
    Sister Rose Annette Ahuna
    Sisters Agatha, Laurenza, William Marie, Richard Marie, and Mary Andrew, all of Honolulu, via Sister Barbara Jean Wajda
    Sister Theresa Chow
    Sister Frances Therese Souza, via Sister Theresa Chow
    Sisters Ruth Esther Sherman, Blanche Marie Messier, Patricia Clark, Roseanne LaManche, Gwendolyn Larkins, and

Appendix

Norma Mihalko, all of Syracuse, via Sister Mediatrice Hutchinson
Photos of Sister Mary Laurence Hanley, Sister Wilma Halmasy, Sister Dativa, all deceased,
From the Sisters of St. Francis of the Neumann Communities

Permission for St. Marianne hymns
    Sister Teresa Laureta
    Sister Barbara Jean Wajda

Sources and Resources
Mother Marianne Cope – and related topics books and sources - in chronological order

Unpublished

Letters of St. Marianne in Chronological Order, 1872 – 1911, St. Marianne Museum, Syracuse, N.Y.

Resources - Interviews

Series of eight taped interviews of Sisters who worked at Kalaupapa – Interviews done in 2010 by Sister Alicia Damien Lau of Honolulu

Sister Roseanne LaManche   1949 to 1952 and 1955 to 1961
Sister Norma Mihalko   1955 – 1960
Sister Christopher Dixon   1959 to 1966
Sister Richard Marie Toal   1960 to 1971 and 1973 to 2000
Sister Mary Andrew Bomba   1966 to 1975 and 1992 to 1995
Sister Patricia Clark   1969 to 1975
Sister Miriam Dionisi Cabacungan   1980 to 1983
Sister Mary Agatha Perreira   1988 to 1989

Series of interviews with typed notes of Sisters who worked at Kalaupapa – Interviews done in 2012 by Sister Barbara Jean Wajda

Notes on her mother and on her own life, Sister Ruth Esther Sherman

In their own words

Sister Cheryl Wint
About her 2012 time at Damien and Marianne Heritage Museum

Sister Anne Marie Saphara
About her childhood and teen scrapbooks and years leading up to her entering the convent

Sister Alicia Damien
About the exhumation of the remains of Mother Marianne

Sister Barbara Jean
About the exhumation as observed by other sisters

Sister Blanche Marie Messier
About her many years working with Sister Mary Laurence Hanley – for the Cause of Mother Marianne

Sister Ruth Esther Sherman
About her creation of statues of Mother Marianne and Damien

Published

1935 – first biography
Jacks, L. V. *Mother Marianne of Moloka'i.* N.Y. The Macmillan Company, 1935.

1963
Betz, Eva K. *The Quiet Flame. Mother Marianne of Moloka'i.* Milwaukee, The Bruce Publishing Company. 1963. (Children's book)

1981 – official biography
Hanley, Sister Mary Laurence, OSF. *A Song of Pilgrimage and Exile. The Life and Spirit of Mother Marianne of Moloka'i.* Chicago, Franciscan Press, 1981.

Appendix

1992 - updated
Hanley, Sister Mary Laurence, OSF. *Pilgrimage and Exile. Mother Marianne of Moloka'i.* University of Hawai'i Press. 1992.

1999
Durkin, Mary Cabrini, OSU, and Sister Mary Laurence Hanley, collaborator. *Mother Marianne of Moloka'i – Heroic Women of Hawai'i.* Strasbourg, Editiones du Signe. 1999. (Children's book)

1999
Durkin, Mary Cabrini, OSU, and Sister Mary Laurence Hanley, collaborator. *Mother Marianne of Moloka'i: Valiant Woman of Hawai'i.* Strasbourg, Editiones due Signe. 1999. (Adult book)

2002
Osbelt, Kathleen, OSF. Presenting the Life of a Saint in a Postmodern World – Mother Marianne Cope, 1838 – 1918. Milwaukee, Wisconsin. American Franciscan History Symposium Papers. 2002.

2009
Raphael, Maryanne. *Saints of Moloka'i.* Waveryly, Ohio. Writers World International Press. 2009.

c. 2010
Hanley, Sister Mary Laurence, OSF. *Pilgrimage and Exile.* Amazon Kindle.

2010
deVolder, Jan. *The Spirit of Father Damien: The Leper Priest – a Saint for our Time.* San Francisco, Ignatius Press. 2010

2012
Albarella, Joan. *Always in My Heart – the Life of Saint Marianne Cope.* Buffalo, N.Y.. 2012

2012
Gangloff, Sister Mary Francis, OSF. *Ferns and Flowers – Prayer Poems*

on the Life of Mother Marianne Cope. Syracuse, N.Y.. 2012.

Other sources

Syracuse diocesan newspaper
http://www.thecatholicsun.com/

Honolulu diocesan newspaper
http://www.Hawai'icatholicherald.com/

Mother Marianne website
http://www.stmariannecope.org/

Personal Accounts of Kalaupapa Residents

Breitha, Olivia Robello. *Olivia – My Life of Exile in Kalaupapa.* Arizona Memorial Museum Association. 1988.

Nalaieulaa, Henry, with Sally Jo Bowman. *No Footprints in the Sand – A Memoir of Kalaupapa.* Honolulu. Watermark Publishing. 2006.

White, Mel. *Margaret of Moloka'i.* Waco, Texas. Word Books, 1981.

Related Topics – Books – Non-Fiction

Armstrong, Regis J. and Peterson, Ingrid J. *The Franciscan Tradition.* Collegeville, MN, Liturgical Press. 2012. Pages 128 – 134 – Marianne Cope of Moloka'i.

Barnes, Dr. Phil. *A Concise History of the Hawaiian Island.* Hilo, Hawai'i, Petroglyph Press. 1996.

Bunson, Maggie. *Faith in Paradise – A Century and a Half of the Roman Catholic Church in Hawai'i.* St. Paul Editions. 1977.

Cahill, Emmett. *Yesterday at Kalaupapa. A Saga of Pain and Joy.* Honolulu, Hawai'i, Editions Limited. 1991.

Appendix

Dries, Angelyn, OSF. *The Missionary Movement in American Catholic History.* Maryknoll, N.Y. Orbis Books. 1998.

Halmasy, Sister Wilma, OSF. *Letters from the Land of Long Farewells.* Kalaupapa, Molokaʻi. Syracuse, N.Y.. Sisters of St. Francis. Date – c. 2010.

Harada, Takayuki. *Kalaupapa in Poetry.* Honolulu, Scripta. 2010.

Hawaiʻi. Board of Health. *The Molokaʻi Settlement* (Illustrated) Territory of Hawaiʻi: Villages Kalaupapa and Kalawao. 1907. Reprint.

Kalakaua, King David, His Majesty. *The Legends and Myths of Hawaiʻi – The Fables and Folklore of a Strange People.* Honolulu, Mutual Publishing. First printing – 1888. 6th printing – 2007.

Law, Anwei Skinsnes, and Law, Henry G. *Father Damien ... "A Bit of Taro, A Piece of Fish, and A Glass of Water".* Seneca Falls, N.Y. IDEA Center for the Voices of Humanity. 2009

Law, Anwei Skinsnes. *Kalaupapa – A Collective Memory.* University of Hawaiʻi Press. May 2012.

Levin, Wayne, photographer, and Law, Anwei Skinsnes Law, writer. *Kalaupapa – A Portrait.* Arizona Memorial Museum Association and Bishop Museum Press. 1989.

Linnéa, Sharon. *Princess Kaiulani – Hope of a Nation, Heart of a People.* Grand Rapids, Michigan, Eerdman Books for Young Readers. 1999.

Noyes, Martha H. *Then there were none.* Honolulu, Bess Press. 2003. (see related film)

O'Malley, Vincent J. CM. *Saints of Asia. 1500 to the Present.* Huntington, Indiana. Our Sunday Visitor. 2007.

Stevenson, Robert Louis. *Father Damien – an Open Letter to the Reverend Doctor Hyde of Honolulu from Robert Louise Stevenson.* London. Chatto

& Windus. 1914.

Stoddard, Charles Warren. *The Lepers of Moloka'i*. Notre Dame, Indiana, Ave Maria Press. 1885.

Tayman, John. *The Colony – The Harrowing True Story of the Exiles of Moloka'i*. N.Y. Scribner. 2006.

Wood, Paul, and Dahlquist, Ron, photographer. *Flowers and Plants of Hawai'i*. Waipahu, Hawai'i, Island Heritage Publishing, 13th printing. 2011.

Gerould, Katherine Fullerton. *Hawai'i: Scenes and Impressions*. 1916

London, Jack. *The Lepers of Moloka'i*. 1908

100th anniversary book of the Sisters of Syracuse

Gugelyk, Ted, and Bloombaum, Milton. *The Separating Sickness. Interviews with Exiled Leprosy Patients at Kalaupapa, Hawai'i*. University of Hawai'i, First Edition 1979. Fourth Edition, Separating Sickness Foundation, 2005.

Bunson, Margaret, and Bunson, Matthew. *St. Damien of Moloka'i – Apostle of the Exiled*. Huntington, IN, Our Sunday Visitor, Inc. 2009.

Malo, Makia with Young, Pamela. *My Name is Makia: A Memoir of Kalaupapa*. Honolulu, Hawaii, Watermark Publishing, 2012.

Brocker, James H. *The Lands of Father Damien - Kalaupapa*, Moloka'i, Hawai'i, 1998

Related Books – fiction

Brennert, Alan. *Moloka'i, a Novel*. N.Y. St. Martin's Griffin. 2003.

Cindrich, Lisa. *In the Shadow of the Pali. A Story of the Hawaiian Leper Colony*. Putnam Juvenile. 2002.

Appendix

Hemmings, Kaui Hart. *The Descendants.* N.Y. Random House, 2007. (see related film)

Michener, James. Hawai'i

Quinn, Gaellen. *The Last Aloha, a Novel.* Fort Bragg, CA, Lost Coast Press. 2009.

Journals

Manoa, *Almost Heaven: On the Human and Divine*, Winter 2011. University of Hawai'i.
(includes 15 photos of Kalaupapa of 1901 to 1907, made from glass plate negatives recently found in an old box, taken by Father Paul-Marie Juliotte, resident in Kalaupapa, 1901 to 1907, and assisted by Brother Aloysius (Louis) Leissen. The photos belong to the Congregations of the Sacred Hearts.)

Films

1966. *Hawai'i*– based on James Michener's book

1996. *Moloka'i: The Story of Father Damien.* A film by Paul Cox.

No Date Given. *Song Exile: True Life Story of Mother Marianne*

No Date Given. *Moloka'i, Kalaupapa: The People, the Place, the Legacy.* VHS. Panorama International Productions.

2008. *Father Damien: Simple Courage, An Historical Portrait for the Age of AIDS.* Olenea Media. 2008.
2009. *The Soul of Kalaupapa: Voices of Exiles.* Dr. Fred Woods and Available at Brigham Young University TV –
http://byutv.org/watch/5f63953e-de11-457b-99b7-c07b73eb084b/iris-the-soul-of-kalaupapa-voices-in-exile

2010. *Princess Kaiulani.* Roadside Assistance Studio

2011. *The Descendants.* Fox Searchlight Studio.

Then there were none. Documentary film by Elizabeth Kapuʻuwaillani Lindsey Buyers, Ph.D. (see related book)

Drama

Albarella, Joan. *Always in My Heart – The Life of Saint Marianne Cope.* Buffalo, N.Y.. 2012.

Morris, Aldyth. *Damien.* 1976. 1977.
    (in Manoa, Winter 2011, pages 48 – 77)

Music

The Descendants – film score

Photos

Public Domain
SSCC - Photos Courtesy of the Congragation of the Sacred Hearts of Jesus and Mary
Mother Marianne Museum (now known as St. Marianne Museum) - Photos courtesy of the St. Marianne Cope Shrine of the Sisters of St. Francis of the Neumann communities
Office of Communications of the Sisters of St. Francis of the Neumann Communities
Sister Barbara Jean Wajda
Gerianne Dobermeir
Sister Mary Francis Gangloff
Sister Eleanore Vargas

Appendix

About the Collaborators

Sister Anne Marie Saphara, OSF, an artist and designer, works in the congregation's Communication Office. She contributed to the cover design and made other suggestions for this book project. Formerly, she worked as a graphic artist for the United States Defense Department.

Sister Barbara Jean Wajda, OSF, a teacher at St. Francis School, Honolulu, has visited Kalaupapa several times. She enjoys photography of flowers and places and people. For this book, she interviewed several sisters who worked at Kalaupapa on assignment or as na kokua (volunteers) over the years.

Sister Alicia Damien Lau, OSF, director of Health Care and consultant for Damien Health Care, both in Honolulu, and inspired by Father Damien since her youth, has volunteered as a kokua at Kalaupapa for more than 25 years. She holds a wealth of information about St. Marianne.

Index

A
Absolute Faith, 45, 46
Alice A. Ball, 77
Aloha, 106, 180, 233, 234, 247, 284, 297
Always in My Heart, 18, 21, 59, 91, 229, 284, 286, 290, 293, 298
Anglican, 140, 141, 145
Anwei Skinsnes Lay, 74, 75. 76, 241, 242, 243, 282, 290, 295
Arlene LaRue, 48
Assisi, Italy, 19
Assumption Church, 94

B
Baldwin Home, 125, 135, 222, 237
"Ball method", 77
ban, 29, 30, 78, 198, 215, 216, 221, 222
Barbara Cope, 62, 88
beatification, 17, 19, 20, 21, 22, 23, 24, 25, 28, 40, 146, 246
Beloved mother of outcasts, 20, 282

Bishop Home, 10, 24, 28, 52, 63, 64, 120, 125, 127, 129, 131, 132, 134, 137, 145, 156, 157, 164, 165, 167, 168, 169, 170, 171, 172, 173, 174, 175, 197, 220, 221, 222, 223, 226, 229, 230, 244, 246, 247, 251, 267, 268, 269, 270
Bishop Neumann, 92, 98, 99, 258
blessed, 18, 20, 22, 23, 26, 29, 40, 94, 107, 129, 133, 139, 168, 202, 236
Buffalo, 18, 61, 62, 86, 92, 93, 99, 106, 174, 243, 261, 286, 293, 298
Barbara Koop, 51, 61, 83, 84, 256, 257

C
Calvinist, 65, 112, 126, 143
canonization, 11, 17, 18, 19, 20, 21, 22, 23, 27, 34, 48, 50, 54, 61, 63, 76, 139, 146, 183, 274
Catholic, 17, 18, 20, 30, 43, 48, 55, 61, 62, 65, 85, 86, 95, 97, 103, 104, 105, 108, 110, 112, 113, 118, 120, 126, 138, 139, 140, 141, 143, 145, 147, 172, 173, 174, 194, 196, 197, 198, 201, 202, 243, 246, 247, 248, 249, 290, 294, 295
chapel, 24, 25, 51, 52, 92, 94, 98, 109, 110, 112, 113, 129, 130, 131, 132, 137, 144, 145, 163, 220, 221, 222, 246, 250, 262, 273
Charles E. King, 232
Christmas, 40, 50, 131, 141, 200, 201, 216, 223
Charles Reed Bishop, 63, 164
Congregation of the Sacred Hearts of Jesus and Mary, 65, 125, 148, 287; Photos from, 10, 32, 70, 160, 228, 240, 265, 266, 267, 268, 269, 270, 271
convivencia, 138, 139
correspondence, 48, 73, 76, 114, 127, 130

D
Damien and Marianne Heritage Center, 33, 42
death, 20, 30, 48, 50, 60, 64, 65, 72, 84, 91, 102, 103, 132, 135, 140, 142, 144, 146, 147, 152, 154, 156, 157, 163, 165, 166, 167, 173, 218, 222, 250, 251, 284
Deborah Nailos, 232, 233
"devil winds", 132, 153

E
ecumenical, 113, 141, 262

Index

Edward Clifford, 126, 128, 140
Edwardo Gracia, 276
Episcopalian, 65, 112
Ernie Pyle, 179, 180
exhumation, 17, 18, 19, 20, 21, 23, 24, 26, 27, 28, 168, 218, 219, 220, 245, 247, 292

F

Father Damien de Veuster, 12, 29, 35, 37, 38, 40, 66, 73, 74, 76, 103, 111, 112, 121, 122, 125, 126, 127, 128, 130, 131, 132, 133, 137, 138, 139, 140, 141, 146, 147, 150, 156, 157, 179, 180, 181, 189, 195, 198, 199, 200, 222, 224, 225, 226, 242, 243, 245, 246, 247, 251, 271, 293, 295, 296, 297
Father Pamphile de Veuster, 103, 126, 146, 147
Father Paul Juliotte, 12, 45, 126, 146, 147, 148, 160, 240, 297
feast day, 20, 72, 84, 163, 235
feast of St. Elizabeth, 30, 250
ferns, 83, 131, 238, 239, 285, 287, 294
flowers, 156, 179, 229, 230, 238, 239, 285, 287, 294, 296, 299

G

Grace, 3, 4, 11, 12, 18, 33, 71, 87, 91, 101, 110, 112, 118, 125, 161, 183, 21, 235, 236, 241, 281, 286, 287, 276

H

Hansen's disease, 12, 17, 29, 30, 48, 52, 53, 71, 73, 75, 77, 78, 104, 111, 141, 162, 169, 172, 187, 194, 201, 203, 205, 208, 214, 231, 242, 243, 248
Hawai'i, 4, 11, 12, 15, 17, 18, 19, 20, 23, 24, 26, 27, 29, 35, 36, 38, 40, 41, 42, 46, 48, 52, 53, 54, 55, 59, 60, 62, 63, 64, 65, 66, 67, 68, 69, 76, 77, 98, 101, 102, 103, 104, 105, 106, 107, 108, 113, 116, 117, 118, 119, 121, 125, 127, 131, 137, 140, 141, 147, 148, 150, 151, 154, 155, 162, 163, 165, 166, 168, 169, 170, 171, 172, 173, 175, 185, 189, 193, 194, 196, 198, 203, 207, 208, 210, 223, 224, 225, 226, 227, 232, 234, 235, 243, 244, 245, 251, 277, 279, 282, 284, 285, 287, 293, 294, 295, 296, 297
Henry (Kalalahilmoku Nalaieula), 231, 245, 246, 294
Heppenheim, 20, 39, 83, 84, 85, 256, 290

Heritage communities, 98
Honolulu, 11, 19, 24, 26, 27, 33, 41, 42, 43, 53, 55, 62, 63, 64, 66, 76, 83, 101, 102, 103, 104, 106, 107, 109, 112, 113, 114, 117, 118, 119, 125, 127, 128, 134, 136, 141, 142, 143, 145, 147, 151, 153, 164, 165, 167, 168, 169, 172, 173, 174, 175, 185, 186, 190, 193, 195, 197, 201, 204, 205, 208, 212, 214, 223, 225, 232, 236, 237, 243, 245, 248, 264, 272, 276, 277, 285, 287, 290, 291, 294, 295, 296, 299
hymn, 106, 144, 230, 232, 233, 234, 235, 237, 246, 291

I
interfaith, 141, 143, 163
ironwood trees, 229
isolation, 12, 29, 30, 66, 68, 78, 173, 192, 193, 194, 203, 211, 214, 215, 216, 219, 221, 241, 248

J
Jack London, 149, 243
Joan Albarella, 18, 59, 91, 229, 284, 286, 290
Jonathan Napela, 139, 140
journal, 46, 130, 137, 153, 297

K
Kaka'ako, 83, 101, 108, 110, 111, 112, 114, 116, 122, 128, 129, 143, 144, 145, 157, 165, 173
Kalaupapa, 10, 11, 12, 17, 19, 20, 21, 24, 26, 27, 29, 30, 32, 34, 35, 36, 37, 38, 39, 40, 42, 43, 44, 45, 46, 52, 53, 63, 64, 66, 68, 70, 74, 75, 77, 78, 103, 106, 111, 121, 124, 125, 126, 127, 128, 129, 130, 131, 133, 134, 136, 137, 138, 139, 140, 141, 142, 147, 148, 151, 152, 153, 154, 155, 157, 159, 161, 162, 163, 164, 165, 166, 167, 168, 169, 170, 171, 172, 173, 174, 175, 176, 179, 180, 181, 182, 183, 184, 185, 186, 187, 188, 189, 191, 192, 193, 194, 195, 196, 197, 198, 199, 200, 201, 202, 203, 204, 205, 206, 207, 208, 209, 210, 211, 212, 213, 214, 215, 217, 218, 219, 220, 221, 222, 223, 224, 225, 229, 230, 231, 232, 235, 236, 238, 241, 242, 243, 244, 245, 246, 247, 248, 249, 250, 251, 262, 264, 265, 266, 267, 268, 269, 270, 273, 278, 279, 282, 283, 284, 285, 287, 290, 291, 294, 295, 296, 297, 298, 299
Kalaupapa National Historic Park (NPS), 27, 28, 185, 223, 231, 243, 245

Index

Kalawao, 29, 66, 77, 78, 125, 126, 127, 130, 133, 135, 136, 138, 139, 140, 147, 181, 189, 200, 222, 235, 237, 244, 295
Kalihi, 136, 245, 246
Kapiʻolani, 52, 54, 67, 68, 101, 107, 108, 118, 119, 134, 136, 138, 164, 165, 167, 168, 169, 170, 171, 172, 174, 180
Kateri Tekakwitha, 20, 21, 48, 61
Katherine Gerould, 126, 149, 150, 151, 152, 155, 297
kokua, 12, 19, 30, 74, 78, 140, 146, 161, 164, 183, 184, 185, 193, 201, 203, 205, 206, 213, 299

L

leprosy, 12, 19, 29, 35, 44, 52, 66, 67, 68, 71, 72, 73, 74, 75, 76, 77, 78, 79, 101, 102, 103, 104, 107, 108, 109, 110, 113, 120, 121, 122, 126, 127, 130, 140, 147, 148, 149, 150, 151, 157, 170, 171, 172, 179, 180, 206, 214, 215, 219, 225, 243, 244, 245, 248, 249, 251, 281, 282, 283, 296
"leper", 48, 73, 75, 76, 101, 104, 105, 118, 129, 130, 143, 149, 150, 162, 179, 183, 237, 245, 246, 247, 248, 249, 250, 251, 281, 282, 293, 296, 297
letter, 28, 34, 36, 37, 38, 39, 40, 74, 75, 87, 92, 97, 98, 102, 104, 105, 106, 109, 113, 128, 129, 131, 133, 136, 137, 147, 152, 154, 179, 209, 241, 242, 284, 291, 295, 296
Letters from the Land of Long Farewells, 34, 39, 40, 295

M

Makanula, 121
Malulani, 54, 55, 113, 114, 116, 263
Manoa, 46, 55, 167, 195, 196, 207, 297, 298
Margaret (Kaupuni), 246, 247
Mary and Rose (Kiyoji), 138, 265
Masanao Goto, 76
Maui, 11, 52, 54, 55, 101, 112, 113, 116, 127, 143, 152, 162, 164, 166, 167, 169, 170, 173, 204, 208, 235, 236, 263
missionary, 11, 12, 75, 98, 101, 102, 110, 113, 146, 147, 148, 161, 163, 180, 194, 196, 251, 257, 262, 277, 286, 290, 295
Mohandas Gandhi, 72, 73, 74, 79

Moloka'i, 11, 17, 18, 20, 24, 34, 35, 36, 42, 48, 52, 53, 55, 66, 72, 75, 76, 78, 84, 88, 102, 103, 106, 112, 114, 115, 117, 118, 120, 121, 122, 125, 127, 134, 135, 138, 139, 141, 143, 144, 145, 146, 147, 148, 149, 150, 151, 153, 155, 157, 162, 169, 171, 172, 174, 175, 186, 203, 210, 230, 231, 234, 236, 237, 238, 242, 244, 246, 247, 251, 264, 265, 266, 270, 273, 279, 292, 293, 294, 295, 296, 297

monarchy, 60, 67, 78, 107, 136, 234

Mormon, 65, 103, 126, 132, 138, 139, 140, 141, 142, 145, 146, 201, 202, 243, 244

Mother Jolenta Wilson, 40, 53, 168, 176, 246, 248

Mother Marianne, 11, 12, 18, 19, 20, 21, 22, 23, 24, 25, 26, 28, 29, 30, 33, 34, 35, 36, 38, 39, 40, 42, 44, 45, 46, 47, 48, 49, 50, 51, 52, 53, 54, 55, 56, 57, 59, 60, 61, 62, 63, 64, 67, 68, 72, 73, 74, 75, 79, 81, 84, 87, 88, 90, 91, 92, 95, 96, 97, 98, 99 101, 102, 103, 104, 105, 106, 107, 108, 109, 110, 111, 112, 113, 114, 115, 116, 117, 118, 119, 120, 121, 122, 125, 126, 127, 128, 129, 130, 131, 132, 133, 134, 136, 137, 138, 139, 140, 141, 143, 144, 145, 146, 147, 148, 149, 150, 152, 153, 154, 155, 156, 157, 159, 161, 162, 163, 164, 165, 166, 167, 168, 170, 173, 176, 181, 185, 186, 187, 188, 189, 190, 195, 199, 203, 205, 208, 209, 210, 211, 213, 214, 217, 218, 219, 220, 221, 222, 224, 225, 226, 227, 229, 230, 231, 235, 236, 237, 238, 242, 243, 245, 246, 247, 248, 249, 250, 251, 255, 257, 260, 263, 271, 272, 281, 282, 283, 284, 285, 286, 287, 290, 292, 293, 294, 297, 298

N

na kokua, (see kokua)

Neumann Communities, Sisters of St. Francis, 17, 19, 22, 33, 55, 94, 99, 227, 284, 286, 289, 291, 298; Photos from, 90, 255, 258, 259, 261, 262, 263, 271, 273

New York, 11, 12, 15, 17, 18, 20, 21, 23, 46, 47, 52, 56, 58(map), 59, 60, 61, 62, 63, 64, 67, 85, 86, 87, 92, 96, 97, 111, 144, 171, 175, 185, 195, 214, 238, 282, 283 (see also Oswego, Syracuse, and Utica)

O

Ode St. Anne, 154, 235, 237

ohana (family), 54, 230, 231

Olinda Gomes, 117, 121, 135 (see also Sister Elizabeth Gomes)

Olivia Breitha, 202, 245, 247, 248, 249, 294

Index

orange grove, 156
Oswego, 92, 95, 96, 166, 260, 287, 290
Our Lady of Peace Cathedral, Honolulu, 53, 66, 106, 147, 236, 264, 276

P

***P&E* (See also** *Pilgrimage and Exile*), 17, 33, 59, 71, 83, 91, 101, 125, 161, 183, 241
paintings, 231, 236, 276
pali (cliffs), 124, 131, 156, 180, 200, 204, 211, 212, 216, 247, 278, 296
philosophy, 55, 96, 113, 155, 203
Picpus Fathers, 146, 148
Pilgrimage and Exile, 18, 33, 34, 35, 48, 50, 84, 88, 112, 115, 118, 143, 144, 145, 146, 162, 196, 210, 230, 231, 236, 237, 238, 239, 242, 289, 292, 293
poem, 134, 140, 239, 249, 286, 293
Pope Benedict XVI, 17, 19, 20, 22, 53
Pope John Paul II, 20
profession, 51, 94, 95, 129, 137, 148, 173, 211
Protestant, 103, 104, 112, 126, 138, 139, 141, 143, 144, 145, 201, 236, 243, 246, 247

R

Robert Louis Stevenson, 126, 134, 135, 140, 231, 249
Rome, Italy, 19, 20, 21, 36, 38, 169, 274, 275

S

saint, 4, 11, 15, 17, 18, 19, 20, 23, 25, 29, 30, 33, 34, 45, 47, 48, 53, 54, 55, 61, 62, 63, 71, 72, 76, 85, 95, 99, 102, 129, 130, 138, 140, 154, 184, 201, 220, 224, 225, 226, 227, 232, 233, 234, 239, 246, 249, 250, 253, 257, 260, 261, 266, 284, 290, 293, 295, 298
Sandwich Islands, 65, 67, 103, 118, 154
Schuyler Street (Utica), 39, 86
scrapbook, 46, 47, 49, 285, 292
Shrine and Museum of St. Marianne, 255, 259, 262, 263, 271, 273
Sister Agatha Perriera, 177, 185, 207, 208, 209, 290, 291
Sister Albina Sluder, 137, 156, 165, 176
Sister Alicia Damien Lau, 13, 27, 60, 185, 191, 218, 285, 290, 291, 292, 299

Sister Anne Marie Saphara, 13, 33, 46, 46, 47, 48, 49, 285, 290, 292, 299
Sister Anonymous, 185, 205
Sister Antonia Brown, 94, 170, 176, 226, 230, 263
Sister Anysia Adler, 175, 176
Sister Barbara Jean Wajda, 13, 26, 184, 185, 190, 203, 205, 207, 232, 233, 274, 285, 288, 290, 291, 292, 298, 299; Photos from, 100, 124, 182, 272, 273, 277, 278, 279
Sister Blanche Marie Messier, 22, 23, 33, 36, 290, 292
Sister Carmela Chmeilewska, 169, 170, 176
Sister Cheryl Wint, 33, 41, 42, 290, 292
Sister Columba O'Keefe, 174, 176
Sister Cordis Marie Burns, 174, 177
Sister Crescentia Eilers, 116, 134, 155, 161, 164, 165, 166, 176
Sister Cyrilla Erhart, 173, 176, 183, 263
Sister Dativa Padilla, 164, 172, 173, 177, 184, 195, 197, 198, 208, 209 215, 216, 219, 291
Sister Elizabeth Gomes, 10, 117, 121, 135, 161, 164, 166, 176, 270 (see also Olinda Gomes)
Sister Fran Gangloff, 13, 60, 76, 238, 290, 294, 298; Photos from, 16, 258
Sister Frances Cabrini Morishige, 28, 62, 177, 185, 185, 192, 193, 199, 210
Sister Frances Therese Souza, 163, 177, 185, 217, 218, 219, 222, 290
Sister Francine Greis, 172, 177, 211, 213 216
Sister Grace Anne Dillenschneider, 23, 274, 286, 289
Sister Gwendolyn Larkins, 185, 206, 207, 290
Sister Hermina Wameling (Sister Mary Magdaline), 171, 176
Sister John Vianney Murdy, 170, 177, 211
Sister Joseph Marie Brager, 171, 176
Sister Julia Albicker, 170, 176
Sister Laurenza Fernandez, 184, 203, 204, 205, 210, 290
Sister Leopoldina Burns, 37, 50, 75, 104, 108, 115, 117, 125, 127, 128, 130, 131, 145, 153, 155, 156, 160, 161, 162, 164, 165, 176, 221, 229, 245
Sister Lucy Wessner, 169, 176
Sister Marcia Klawon, 276
Sister Margaret Mary Bennis, 169, 176
Sister Marian Rose Mansius, 274

Index

Sister Marianne, 52, 56, 94, 96, 97, 98
Sister Marianne Carvalho, 162, 166, 167
Sister Marie Celine Wagner, 164, 171, 176
Sister Martina Feichtner, 174, 177, 211
Sister Mary Andrew Bomba, 177, 184, 190, 191, 198, 199, 200, 201, 202, 204, 290, 291
Sister Mary Anna, 52, 62, 91, 92, 94
Sister Mary Benedicta Rodenmacher, 117, 136, 144, 146, 168, 176, 229
Sister Mary Berchmans Schack, 169, 176
Sister Mary Bernardina, 51, 56, 92, 93, 96, 97, 98, 99, 133
Sister Mary Christopher Dixon, 177, 184, 188, 189, 211, 290, 291
Sister Mary Claudia Cabral, 173, 177, 204, 211
Sister Mary Francis Kostka, 172, 177, 211
Sister Mary Laurence Hanley, 18, 19, 22, 23, 28, 33, 34, 35, 36, 37, 38, 39, 50, 51, 84, 87, 88, 112, 115, 118, 143, 144, 145, 146, 153, 162, 175, 196, 210, 230, 231, 236, 237, 238, 242, 243, 291, 292, 293
Sister Mary Louis Warth, 174, 176
Sister Mary Teresa Talbott, 171, 176
Sister Michaeleen Cabral, 274
Sister Miriam Dionise Cabacungan, 142, 185, 214, 215, 216, 222, 232, 291
Sister Norma Mihalko, 177, 184, 186, 187, 211, 291
Sister Patricia Burkard, 24, 26, 224, 274
Sister Patricia Clark, 184, 202, 203, 290, 291
Sister Richard Marie Toal, 164, 177, 184, 190, 191, 199, 201, 204, 205, 206, 209, 211, 215, 219, 290, 291
Sister Rose Annette Ahuna, 163, 178, 182, 185, 220, 221, 222, 224, 225, 226, 290
Sister Roseanne LaManche, 185, 209, 210, 211, 212, 213, 290, 291
Sister Ruth Esther Sherman, 184, 194, 195, 196, 197, 290, 291, 292
Sister Theresa Chow, 163, 178, 185, 220, 221, 223, 290
Sister Theresa Laureta, 233, 234, 290
Sister Vera O'Brien, 167, 177, 211
Sister Vincentia McCormick, 166, 176
Sister William Marie Eleniki, 185, 213, 290
Sister Wilma Halmasy, 34, 39, 40, 164, 175, 177, 199, 209, 211, 215, 291, 295
"sisters of mercy", 67, 111, 113

Sisters of St. Francis, 11, 28, 33, 40, 41, 47, 48, 51, 53, 55, 56, 57, 62, 78, 79, 91, 92, 93, 95, 97, 98, 105, 111, 135, 143, 163, 164, 166, 167, 168, 169, 172, 174, 183, 184, 185, 194, 196, 197, 203, 227, 236, 242, 243, 246, 251, 281, 295
spirituality, 110, 115, 150, 155
St. Anthony Convent, 20, 23, 24, 25, 52, 94, 98, 287
St. Clare of Assisi, 44, 72, 227, 249, 250, 281, 282, 284
St. Elizabeth Chapel, 52, 163, 220, 221, 262, 273
St. Elizabeth Convent, 24, 129, 163, 164, 170, 209, 221, 222, 224, 244
St. Elizabeth Hospital, 56, 92, 98, 173, 188, 209, 210, 214, 259
St. Elizabeth of Hungary, 30, 72, 129, 250
St. Francis of Assisi Church, 24, 201, 223, 228, 266, 273
St. Francis Wooden Church, 266
St. John Neumann, 18, 61, 91, 92
St. Joseph Hospital, 56, 57, 92, 96, 113, 139, 144, 196, 214, 259
St. Joseph St. Patrick Parish, 96, 257, 287, 290
St. Joseph Parish, 56, 85, 86, 91, 93, 96
St. Marianne, 4, 11, 12, 17, 18, 19, 20, 21, 27, 33, 46, 55, 63, 75, 90, 94, 95, 119, 167, 182, 183, 223, 230, 231, 234, 247, 249, 255, 257, 259, 261, 262, 263, 271, 273, 274, 277, 279, 281, 282, 284, 286, 289, 290, 291, 298, 299
St. Marianne Museum, 75, 119, 286, 289, 291, 298
St. Marianne Shrine, 290
St. Peter Church, Heppenheim, 20, 39, 83, 85, 95, 256, 290
St. Peter Parish, Oswego, 95, 287, 290
St. Philomena Chapel, 130, 262
stained glass windows, 257, 277
state, 4, 12, 17, 18, 52, 59, 60, 61, 62, 63, 68, 69, 73, 85, 86, 92, 96, 97, 109, 110, 114, 117, 143, 175, 194, 208, 209, 214, 223, 225, 281, 282, 283, 284
Steam Woolen Mill, 86, 87, 88, 96
Syracuse, 19, 20, 21, 22, 23, 24, 25, 27, 34, 37, 40, 47, 49, 50, 51, 53, 56, 59, 62, 67, 74, 75, 83, 92, 93, 94, 95, 96, 97, 98, 99, 104, 105, 106, 111, 113, 114, 116, 117, 118, 119, 120, 127, 129, 139, 144, 153, 154, 162, 163, 164, 167, 168, 171, 174, 175, 185, 188, 196, 197, 199, 206, 212, 214, 225, 227, 237, 239, 242, 243, 245, 259, 261, 279, 286, 287, 291, 294, 295, 296

Index

T
talk story, 42, 43, 138, 139, 231
talking story, 42, 202, 230
territory, 11, 63, 64, 67, 107, 137, 234, 244, 284, 295

U
Utica, 18, 25, 38, 39, 47, 48, 51, 56, 61, 62, 82, 83, 85, 86, 87, 91, 92, 93, 96, 173, 188, 209, 210, 214, 238, 256, 257, 259, 287, 290

V
venerable, 18, 20, 23, 24, 28, 157

W
Wailuku, 54, 101, 112, 113, 127, 128, 135, 145, 153, 170, 173, 183
Walter Murray Gibson, Walter Gibson, 83, 103, 104, 107, 108, 109, 110, 112, 114, 115, 120, 141, 143, 245
World Leprosy Day, 72, 73

Numbers
1969, 12, 29, 30, 39, 68, 77, 78, 129, 154, 162, 164, 165, 169, 171, 173, 177, 181, 184, 185, 186, 193, 194, 198, 201, 203, 211, 215, 216, 219, 222, 231, 242, 250, 291